CROCHET
MASTER CLASS

CROCHET
MASTER CLASS

LESSONS AND PROJECTS FROM TODAY'S TOP CROCHETERS

JEAN LEINHAUSER

and

RITA WEISS

POTTER
CRAFT

NEW YORK

Published in the United States by Potter Craft, an imprint of the Crown Publishing
Group, a division of Random House, Inc., New York.
www.crownpublishing.com
www.pottercraft.com

POTTER CRAFT and colophon is a registered trademark of Random House, Inc.

Library of Congress Cataloging-in-Publication Data

Leinhauser, Jean.
    Crochet master class : lessons and projects from today's top
crocheters / Jean Leinhauser and Rita Weiss.
        p. cm.
    ISBN 978-0-307-58653-7
1. Crocheting. I. Weiss, Rita. II. Title.
    TT820.L439 2010
    746.43'4--dc22   2010022301

Printed in China

Design by Susi Oberhelman
Photography by Alexandra Grablewski,
Carol Wilson Mansfield, and Marshall Williams

10 9 8 7 6 5 4 3 2 1

FIRST EDITION

Senior Technical Editor: Ellen W. Liberles
Editors: Mary Ann Frits, Susan Lowman, Kathy Wesley
Photo of Cat Afghan on page 35 from *Afghans for All Reasons & All Seasons* by
Jean Leinhauser and Rita Weiss, published by Leisure Arts,
is used here by special permission of the publisher.

CONTENTS

INTRODUCTION

What if you could take a class with a master crocheter? Or finally learn how to do tapestry crochet, Irish crochet, or free-form crochet from the very best needleworkers around? What if you could stay in the comfort of your home and learn these wonderful techniques from crocheters around the world? We've made that possible in this collection featuring masters of crochet.

Between the two of us we have almost one hundred years of involvement in crochet. And during that time we have always been fascinated by crocheters who could find new uses for their hooks and yarn or thread, or who have resurrected an old skill and added new twists to it.

We like to think of those innovative crocheters as real masters, and we've always wanted to thank them for keeping crochet a vital, living craft. And because writing books has been our livelihood for so many years, we decided to write a book that would honor each of the masters and would make more people aware of these wonderful skills.

With so many talented crocheters we've known and read about, this was not to be an easy job! First we drew up a list of the skills and the crocheters we wanted to honor. There were old favorite techniques like filet crochet, for example, and the filet master who immediately came to mind was a young man from East Germany who escaped and made his home in California: Harmut Hass. Through his website and his many articles and books, he has brought new interest in and developed new techniques that expand the scope of filet crochet.

Some other techniques presented more of a challenge in finding a present-day practitioner. For example, we loved the look of Bruges crochet, an imitation of the famed Bruges tape laces, which we discovered in vintage pieces of crocheted table linens in photos from years ago. We were afraid, however, that we would not be able to find someone who was working in this craft today. So imagine our surprise when, a few years ago at the Crochet Guild

of America's annual Chain Link conference fashion show, we saw a model coming down the runway wearing a spectacular contemporary outfit made of Bruges crochet! And, sitting in the audience quietly smiling was the creator of that outfit, Tatyana Mirer. We had found our master!

Then there were all the other crocheters who breathed new life into techniques such as Irish crochet, overlay crochet, hairpin lace, and bullion stitch. Some of these crocheters had discovered old, nearly forgotten techniques almost by accident and then became fascinated by them. Their constant experimentation has resulted in fresh, innovative pieces that keep the craft alive, well, and constantly moving forward.

Our purpose in this book is to showcase the work of these talented designers and then let you try your hand at each skill with a project designed just for this book.

Our masters have indicated the skill level needed for each project, following the skill level definitions developed by the Craft Yarn Council of America. A definition of these skill levels appears on page 189. In addition, each project specifies which yarn the master used and also gives you relevant information about the yarn so that you can substitute a yarn of your choice if you wish. The weight of the yarn is indicated by a yarn symbol, which is explained on page 189.

And, just in case you want to brush up some of your crochet skills, we've given you a simple refresher course, which begins on page 183.

We invite you now to join us as we introduce you to some the world's most talented and interesting crocheters, who tell you how they got started and eventually focused on refining a special skill, who explain their craft, enchant you with a mini-gallery of photographs of their other crochet work, and who then provide you with a project that will enable you to expand your own crochet experience.

Jean Leinhauser and Rita Weiss

We like to think of these innovative crocheters as real masters, and we've always wanted to thank them for keeping crochet a vital, living craft.

WOVEN CROCHET

with
Jenny King

"A gift of a Tartan rug for one's family or clan is among the most personal of gifts. I was fascinated with woven Tartan/plaid afghans that seemed to transform stripes into checks, and I was determined to master a crochet version of the technique. My mother, who didn't know how to crochet, demanded that I learn the technique so I could teach her. Today it's my mum's favorite."

—JENNY KING

Until recently Jenny King's major crochet achievement was the designing and making of her own crocheted wedding dress and veil, which she created more than thirty years ago. Today her major achievement is teaching Australians to crochet for the first time and reigniting a spark of interest in lapsed crocheters all over Australia and New Zealand.

Several years ago the largest craft show held in Australia and New Zealand made Jenny the featured artist. This gave her the opportunity to promote crochet as a modern and exciting craft. She was interviewed on TV and in the press, which allowed her not only to promote crochet but to teach hundreds of people to crochet. Her quote was that she was taking over the world one crocheter at a time.

Self-taught from the age of eight, Jenny has been crocheting for more than forty years, designing and marketing clothes, including bikinis, since the age of fourteen. Today, Jenny self-publishes her pattern books, covering a diverse cross section of crochet, from woven afghans, such as the one featured here, to bead crochet. Her aim is to write easy-to-understand and contemporary patterns to encourage people to crochet. Her designs appear in magazines all over the world as well as in exhibitions where many of them have won awards.

Jenny, her three children, and her husband reside on the "Sunshine Coast" in Queensland, Australia. Jenny is busy, however, traveling all over lecturing and teaching—especially teaching classes in her specialty, woven crochet. She also teaches through her website www.jennykingdesigns.com.

Jenny King may be best known for her woven crochet afghans, but she is also an accomplished crochet fashion designer. Her garments run the gamut from a trendy bathing suit, to a cap, to a warm poncho done in one of her beloved plaids.

HOW TO DO **WOVEN** CROCHET

Woven crochet has the look of hand-woven fabric. It is easy and fun to do and is at its best when several colors are used to create bright checked and plaid designs.

In this technique, which uses only the double crochet and chain stitches, an open mesh base is worked first in horizontal rows, usually with alternating colors following a specific order. Then, crocheted chain lengths are threaded into a tapestry or yarn needle and woven vertically, from top to bottom, under and over the mesh chain stitches, again usually following a specific color sequence.

WORKING THE MESH BASE

Chain an even number. For a practice swatch, ch 20.

ROW 1: Dc in 6th ch from hook; *ch 1, sk next ch, dc in next ch; repeat from * across; ch 4 (counts as first dc and ch-1 sp of following row), turn.

ROW 2: Dc in next dc; *ch 1, sk next ch-1 sp, dc in next dc; repeat from * across to beginning ch-6; ch 1, sk next ch, dc in next ch; ch 4, turn.

ROW 3: Sk first ch-1 sp, dc in next dc; *ch 1, sk next ch-1 sp, dc in next dc; repeat from * across to turning ch-4; ch 1, sk next ch, dc in next ch; ch 4, turn.

Repeat Row 3 for desired length. Fasten off; weave in yarn ends. **[FIG 1]**

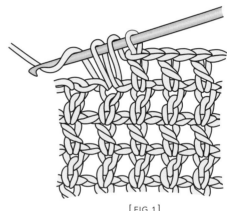

[FIG 1]

WEAVING INTO THE BASE

Weaving is done in vertical rows one row at a time, again usually following a specified color sequence. For the practice swatch, cut individual yarn lengths a few inches (cm) longer than the length of the mesh foundation. Thread the yarn into a tapestry needle and weave it under and over the ch-1 sts of horizontal rows, working in and out of the mesh sps, starting at the top left corner and working down to the bottom edge. On the next row of weaving, alternate unders and overs as shown in diagram. [FIG 2]

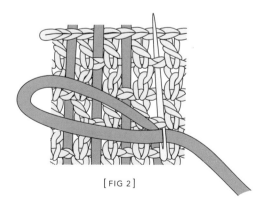

[FIG 2]

Continue alternating weaving rows across the entire mesh foundation. On the actual afghan, instead of plain yarn, crochet chains for weaving into the base, making each chain a few inches (several cm) longer than the mesh foundation.

> ····· · · · TIP FROM THE MASTER · · · · ·····
>
> The beauty of making the Tartan/woven project is that it is simple enough to do in front of TV and not have to think about it, but the excitement of waiting to see what the next color looks like makes it so much fun. No reading a wordy pattern line by line in this technique! I usually crochet up a whole ball of one color and then cut it off into lengths as I need it. This means that I can crochet chains in the dark at the movies and roll up the chains as the final credits are on, or in the car (while I am the passenger), or while standing on the sideline at a kid's game with the ball of yarn under one arm and the crochet chains shoved in the pocket of my jacket.

PRINCESS OF WALES **MEMORIAL TARTAN**

Designed by Jenny King

SKILL LEVEL
■□□□ Beginner

SIZE
Approximately 54" x 60" inches
(137cm x 152.5cm)

MATERIALS
- Red Heart ® *Super Saver*®
  (100% acrylic, each approximately
  7 oz [198g] and 364 yd [333m],
  (4) medium/worsted weight)
  - 728 yd (666m) / 2 skeins in
    color 312 Black
  - 1092 yd (999m) / 3 skeins in
    color 381 Light Blue
  - 1092 yd (999m) / 3 skeins in
    color 9594 Aqua
  - 728 yd (666m) / 2 skeins in
    color 3820 Denim Blue
  - 364 yd (333m) / 1 skein in
    color 319 Cherry Red
  - 1092 yd (999m) / 3 skeins in
    color 311 White
- One size H-8 (5mm) crochet
  hook, or size needed to
  obtain gauge
- Long, large-eyed yarn or
  weaving needle

GAUGE
18 sts and 9 rows = 4" (10cm) in
mesh pattern

NOTES
- When completing a color,
  fasten off yarn, leaving a 4"
  (10cm) yarn end.
- When adding next color, make
  a slip knot on hook and join with
  a dc in last dc of previous row.

To honor the memory of the late Diana, Princess of Wales, an official tartan was designed to be used as an aid in raising money for her favorite charities. The blues, red, white, and black form a pattern that is based on a variation of the Royal Stewart plaid design, one of the most popular and recognizable tartans in the world. My afghan is a crocheted adaptation of the memorial tartan.

MESH BASE

With first color in color sequence chart, ch 236.

ROW 1: Dc in 6th ch from hook (counts as a ch–1 sp, a dc, and a ch–1 sp on following row); *ch 1, sk next ch, dc in next ch; repeat from * across; ch 4 (counts as first dc and ch–1 sp on following rows), turn—116 ch–1 sps.

NOTE: Be sure to count the spaces carefully, since the number must be correct for the color sequence to work correctly.

ROW 2: Sk first ch–1 sp, dc in next dc; *ch 1, sk next ch–1 sp, dc in next dc; repeat from * across to beg ch–6, ch 1, sk next ch, dc in next ch; ch 4, turn.

ROW 3: Sk first ch–1 sp, dc in next dc; *ch 1, sk next ch–1 sp, dc in next dc; repeat from * across to turning ch–4, ch 1, sk next ch, dc in next ch; ch 4, turn.

Repeat Row 3 for pattern, following color sequence below for number of rows for each color.

Tartan Plaid Pattern Color Sequence Chart

4 rows black	1 row aqua	6 rows aqua
1 row white	1 row white	3 rows white
1 row aqua	4 rows black	1 row black
1 row white	8 rows denim	1 row white
6 rows aqua	10 rows light blue	1 row red
3 rows white	1 row white	1 row white
1 row black	4 rows light blue	1 row black
1 row white	1 row white	3 rows white
1 row red	10 rows light blue	6 rows aqua
1 row white	8 rows denim	1 row white
1 row black	4 rows black	1 row aqua
3 rows white	1 row white	1 row white
6 rows aqua	1 row aqua	4 rows black
1 row white	1 row white	

At the end of the last row, weave in all yarn ends.

PREPARING CHAINS FOR WEAVING

Place the mesh base on a flat surface and measure its exact length. The weaving chains should each measure at least 4" (10cm) longer than the mesh base. Leave a 4" (10cm) yarn end loose at both beginning and end of each chain.

Make the following number of chains:

20 black
26 white
28 aqua
2 red
24 light blue
16 denim

Weaving

Thread the first chain into the yarn or weaving needle; start at the top left corner of afghan, and weave over and under the mesh down to the bottom left corner. Continue weaving with the next chain, following the exact Tartan Plaid Pattern Color Sequence in the left-hand column, and be sure to alternate the under and over movements for each subsequent chain to achieve the woven fabric effect. Keep the chains from twisting as you work, and leave ends loose until all weaving is completed.

When weaving is completed, place afghan on a flat surface and adjust chains as needed. Thread loose yarn ends at top and bottom of each chain into needle and weave back into the chain and mesh dc to secure. Cut off any excess yarn.

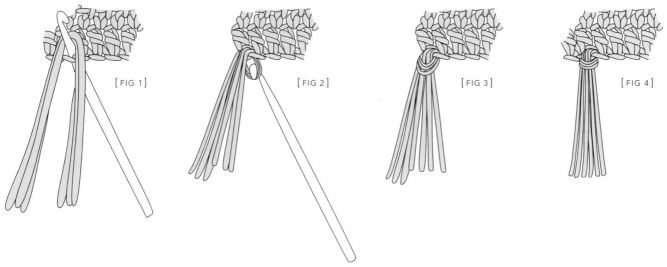

[FIG 1]   [FIG 2]   [FIG 3]   [FIG 4]

Fringe

For each knot, use three strands approximately 20"
(51cm) long, matching the color in the woven chain
length.

Fold the strands for one knot together and fold in half.
[FIG 1]

With right side facing and using a crochet hook, draw
the folded ends through the stitch from right to wrong
side. [FIG 2]

Pull the loose ends through the folded section. [FIG 3]

Draw the knot up firmly. [FIG 4]

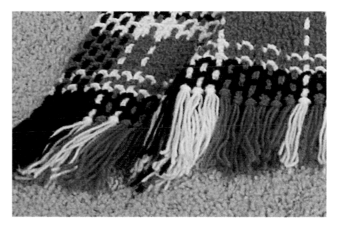

HAIRPIN LACE

with
Jennifer Hansen

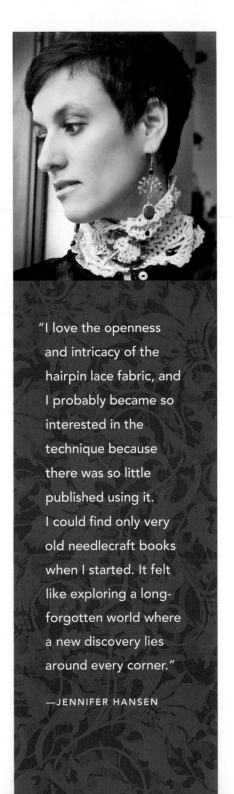

According to *Yarn Market News*, the bible of the yarn industry, Jennifer Hansen is "one of the names that immediately comes to mind when thinking of the creative forces that have helped transport crochet from the realm of acrylic afghans to the sexy world of figure-flattering fashions."

Only a few years ago, no one who crochets had ever heard of Jennifer Hansen. In fact, Jennifer Hansen couldn't even crochet. Today she is the founder and chief creative force behind Stitch Diva Studios, a company that provides innovative knit and crochet patterns for the retail and wholesale markets. In addition, she has single-handedly rescued hairpin lace from its position as a minor crochet technique suitable only for edgings and trims and turned it into fashion fit for the runway.

Jennifer never planned a career in crochet. She planned a career in architecture and spent her college years in the architectural lab building models. After graduation, Jennifer worked for about ten years in the Information Technology industry as an application architect.

Several years ago Jennifer became pregnant and was determined to make something for the new baby. A friend offered to teach her to crochet so that Jennifer could make a baby afghan, and in one afternoon at her friend's home, Jennifer had learned enough to enable her to fill an entire chest with baby clothes by the time her son was born. Her first project was a big and completely uneven blanket, but when she completed the blanket, she felt she now understood crochet. She covered her mistakes with fringe.

Once she knew the basics of crocheting, Jennifer began expanding her knowledge by reading everything she could find on crochet and by scouring the web. It was during this period of researching crochet that Jennifer discovered hairpin lace, a craft that had all but disappeared from the scene. She began to experiment with hairpin lace as a technique for fashion.

After the birth of her son, Jennifer, not wanting to return to a traditional workday, sought a way to channel her interests and talents into a profession that would give her the flexibility to spend more time with her baby. She was knitting and crocheting all the time, and she thought she'd like to start a business based on the craft, but she had no idea how to begin.

On an Internet crochet chat group, she read that several crocheters were interested in learning how to make the shawl that Jessica Simpson wore on the TV show *Newlyweds*. Jennifer felt confident that she could write the pattern without too much difficulty (her professional and educational background building acrchitectural models gave her an advantage in understanding garment design).

She wrote the pattern and posted it on eBay, listing it for $2.50. The next morning she awoke to discover that the bidding was up to $45. Her business had begun!

Today Stitch Diva Studios provides innovative, easy-to-follow knit and crochet patterns that are available by mail, by immediate download, and at yarn stores. In addition, her website, www.stitchdiva.com, offers a unique selection of knit and crochet tutorials, classes, tools, and accessories that complement her unique crochet and knit patterns.

Crochet goes high fashion in these two garments by Jennifer Hansen. At left, a long tunic top buttons to below the waist, where a wide lacy ruffle completes the look. The ruffle is echoed in the shoulder straps. At right, an open-back evening top showcases a traditional crochet lace design at the shoulders and at the fitted waist.

At left, the graceful curves of hairpin lace add motion and interest to a sleek dress. At right, the center braid holds the open lace in shape, while a gathered flounce contrasts with the straight lines of the hairpin strips.

HOW TO DO HAIRPIN LACE

In the early nineteenth century, young women spent hours creating miles and miles of laces to decorate the large quantities of household linens and delicate personal undergarments that would fill their hope chests.

Early hairpin lace actually was made on hairpins—hairstyles of the day required a great number of them, from small pins of gold or silver to larger ones of ivory or tortoiseshell. These would have made perfect fixed-width forms on which to create hairpin lace, which requires two fixed wires a set distance apart to serve as a loom. These forms were later made of metal bent into a "U" shape, or similar shapes in wood. These were also called forks, staples, or frames.

These early forms were each of one set width; the crocheter needed a separate one for each width of lace she wished to make. In the 1920s, commercial forks were made that could be adjusted to several widths.

THE BASIC STRIP

Although there are many ways to create a hairpin lace strip (also referred to as braid), most hairpin lace patterns call for the basic strip. Where projects usually differ is in the methods used to join the strips. The basic strip is made on the loom by working single crochet stitches through the front thread of the uppermost loop on the loom.

Set up the loom by setting the prongs to the width for which the pattern calls. The width settings of hairpin lace looms vary from one manufacturer to another. Before working, make sure to orient the loom so that the frame side that can be slid off the most easily (for slipping off the work) is held toward the bottom. [FIG 1]

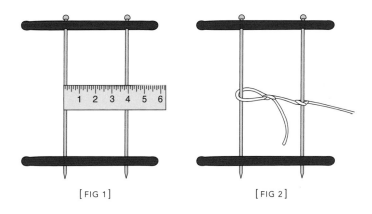

[FIG 1]　　　　[FIG 2]

Remove the bottom bar or crosspiece from loom. Secure the yarn with a slip knot to one prong of the hairpin lace loom. Wrap the yarn from front to back over the opposite

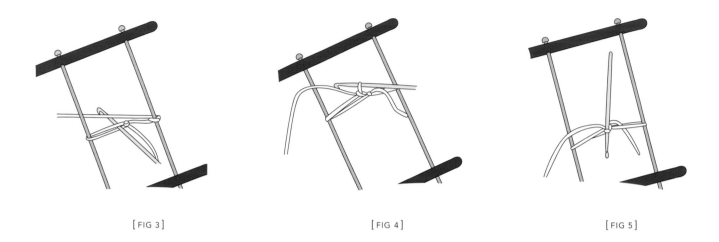

[FIG 3] [FIG 4] [FIG 5]

prong and bring the yarn to the back of the loom. Replace the bottom bar or crosspiece. The side of the loom to which you attach the loop is the side that you will work with the crochet hook for the entire strip. Most right-handers find it easier to attach the loop to the left-side prong, while left-handers prefer the right. [FIG 2]

At this point, mark the starting loop so that you will later be able to identify the starting edge of your strip. Insert the hook from bottom to top through the front thread of the loop on the loom. [FIG 3]

Pull through a loop, and then chain 1. This completes the first stitch of the strip—the first "setup" stitch of the strip is different from all the rest of the stitches of the braid. [FIG 4]

Prepare to turn the loom by twisting the hook so that the handle side faces up, and insert the handle end of the hook through the loom above the work. Keep the loop on the hook. [FIG 5]

Grab the hook from the opposite side of the loom, still keeping the loop on the hook. [FIG 6]

Flip the loom, allowing the yarn to wrap around the loom as you turn. (Note: Side B and Side A have been reversed.) Hold the hook in the front with one hand, keeping tension on the yarn in the back with the other. [FIGS 7, 8]

· · · · MASTER'S GOLDEN RULE #2 · · · ·

When working the strip, consistently flip the loom so that your "non-home prong" flips toward your home prong, passing toward you while your home prong passes behind.

Insert the hook under the thread of the topmost loop on the "home prong," pull through a loop, and then pull through another loop—single crochet. [FIG 9]

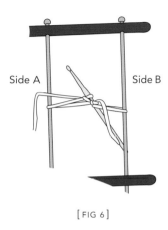

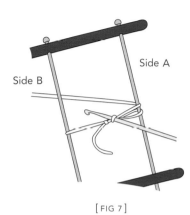

[FIG 6]   [FIG 7]   [FIG 8]

Flip the loom. Continue doing a single crochet in the uppermost loop of the "home prong" then flipping the loom. Most projects will require you to create a strip with more loops than can fit on the loom, so you will need to move loops off the loom as you work. When you feel you no longer have enough room to work comfortably, you will need to remove most of the loops from the frame.

Keep the work as low as possible on the loom in order to allow as much room as possible to pass the crochet hook from front to back. Maintain tension on the yarn with your non-hook hand to control placement of the loops on the loom. **[FIG 10]**

Continue working until desired strip length is attained. To finish your last loops, insert your hook from top to bottom through the back thread of the loop on the prong opposite to the one just worked. **[FIG 11]** Yarn over and pull loop through the loop on the hook. Fasten off.

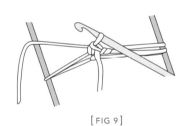

[FIG 9]

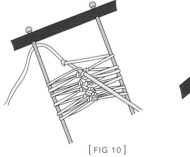

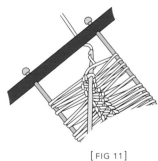

[FIG 10]   [FIG 11]

FEATHER AND FAN **CARDI WRAP**

Designed by Jennifer Hansen, Stitch Diva Studios

SKILL LEVEL

■■■□ Intermediate

SIZES

- S/M (L/XL)
- Instructions are written for size S/M. Changes for size L/XL are in parentheses. If only one number appears, it applies to all sizes.
- Finished width across back 16 (19)" (40.5 [48]cm)
- Upper arm circumference 11¾ (14)" (30 [35.5]cm)

MATERIALS

- Berroco *Bonsai* (97% bamboo, 3% nylon, each approximately 1¾ oz [50g] and 77 yd [71m], (4) medium/worsted weight)
  - 924 yd (852m) / 12 hanks in color 4103 Bamboo (A)
- Berroco *Touché* (50% cotton, 50% rayon, each approximately 1¾ oz [50g] and 89 yd [82m], (4) medium/worsted weight)
  - 890 yd (820m) / 10 hanks in color 7900 Bleach (B)
- One size D-3 (3.25mm) crochet hook, or size needed to obtain gauge
- Size 16 tapestry needle
- 10 locking-type stitch markers
- Adjustable hairpin lace loom that adjusts to within ⅛" (3mm) of the settings specified in the instructions

GAUGE

38 loops = 4" (10cm)

I love unconstructed cardi wraps. They look good on any body shape and size, and because the design of this garment type is so simple—since there's not a lot of shaping required—the focus is given to the construction of the hairpin fabric. The lacy garment is half shawl, half cardigan and is designed as a rectangle composed of nine hairpin lace strips, which are joined to form the shawl body. Sleeves are made with four tapered hairpin lace strips created by gradually narrowing the loom width.

STITCH PATTERN

PUFF STITCH (PS): Yo, insert hook in specified st or sp and draw up a lp; (yo, insert hook into same st and draw up a lp) 2 times more; yo and draw through all 7 lps on hook.

PUFF STITCH BOBBLE (PB): Work puff stitch in indicated st, ch 1, sl st in same st.

MAKE FLOUNCE: (Sl st into next untwisted lp) 22 times; join with a sl st in first sl st made.

WRAP BODY

NOTE: Mark right side of all strips; right side is side facing you as you work.

With Color A, make the following hairpin lace strips:

STRIP A (Make 1): Set loom width to 2½" (6.5cm); make 620 (676) loops measuring about 65¼ (71¼)" (165.5 [181]cm) long.

NOTE: For all strips, the number of loops specified is the total number of loops along both edges of the strip; thus Strip A should have 310 loops on both right and left edges for a total of 620 loops for S/M size.

STRIP B (Make 4): Set loom width to 3 (3¼)" (7.5 [8]cm); make 228 loops measuring about 24" (61cm) long

STRIP C (Make 2): Set loom width to 3 (3¼)" (7.5 [8]cm); make 172 (228) loops measuring about 18 (24)" [45.5 [61]cm] long.

STRIP D (Make 2): Set loom width to 3½" (9cm); make 620 (676) loops measuring about 65¼ (71¼)" (165 [181] cm) long.

NOTE: Be sure to leave at least 6" (15cm) for starting and ending yarn tails on Strip E to be used later during assembly.

STRIP E (MAKE 1): Set loom width to 3½" (9cm); make 1,888 (2,000) loops measuring about 198¾ (210½)" (505 [534.5]cm) long.

EDGINGS FOR STRIPS A, B, C, AND D

The fan motif is created by joining large groups of loops on one side of the strip to form a fan-shaped flounce. Work all loops twisted except groups of 8 or 14 loops, which should be worked untwisted.

RIGHT EDGING

Hold any A, B, C, or D strip with right side of work facing you, ready to work across long edge of strip and starting from the beginning edge. Join Color B with a sl st in the first 2-lp group, (ch 2, sc in next 2-lp group) 3 times; *ch 2, sc in next 14-lp group, (ch 2, sc in next 2-lp group) 7 times; repeat from * across until 22 lps remain; ch 2, sc in next 14-lp group, (ch 2, sc in next 2-lp group) 4 times—11 (12) fans on Strips A and D, 4 (4) fans on Strip B, and 3 (4) fans on Strip C. Fasten off; weave in ends.

LEFT EDGING

When right edging is complete, rotate strip to finish opposite long edge, keeping the right side of work facing you. Join Color B with sl st in first 8-lp group; *(ch 2, sc in next 2-lp group) 7 times, ch 2, sc in next 14-lp group; repeat from * across until 22 lps remain; (ch 2, sc in next 2-lp group) 7 times, ch 2, sc in next 8-lp group—10 (11) fans and 2 half fans on Strips A and D, 3 (3) fans and 2 half fans on Strip B, and 2 (3) fans and 2 half fans on Strip C. Fasten off; weave in ends.

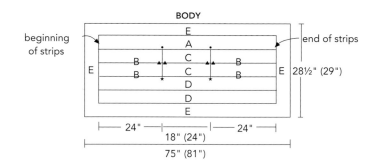

[FIG 1]

Joining Strips A, B, C, and D

Refer to the diagram for placement of Strips A, B, C, and D for joining long edges. [FIG 1] Strips are joined by working into chain spaces between loops on edging. With wrong sides together, place one strip on top of another with loops of back strip a little higher than front strip and hold in normal crochet position. Strips will be joined so that the flare on the fan of one strip will join to the point of the fan on the adjacent strip as pictured. [FIG 2]

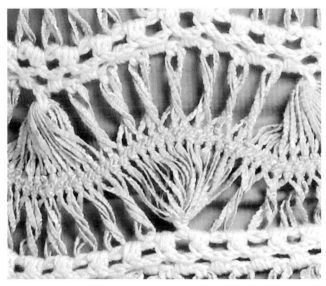

[FIG 2]

Work Join Pattern to join long edges of both D strips.

JOIN PATTERN

Join Color B with sl st in beg sl st on front strip, ch 2, work PS in same st as joining, ch 1, PS in last sc on back strip, ch 1, sk first ch-sp on front strip, PS in next ch-sp on front strip, ch 1, sk first ch-sp on back strip, PS in next ch-sp on back strip, ch 1; *PS in next ch-sp on front strip, ch 1, PS in next ch-sp on back strip, ch 1; repeat from * across to last ch-sp on front strip; sk last ch-sp on front, PS in last sc on front strip, ch 1, sk last ch-sp on back strip, PS in beg sl st on back strip. Fasten off; weave in ends.

ARMHOLE OPENINGS

When joining Strips B and C to Strips A and D, there is a slight variation to join pattern at armholes. To join Strips B and C to Strip A with Strip B in front and Strip A in back, work join pattern until one ch-sp remains on front strip; *sk last ch-sp on front strip, work PS in last sc on front strip; ch 1, hdc in next sc on back strip (mark this hdc)*.

Holding Strip C in front and Strip A in back, work across Strips C and A as follows: **ch 1, PS in beg sl st on front strip, ch 1, PS in next ch-sp on back strip**; continue in join pattern across until one ch-sp remains on front strip; repeat from * to * once; holding another Strip B in front and Strip A in back, work across Strips B and A as follows: repeat from ** to ** once; continue in join pattern across. Fasten off; weave in ends.

Join Strips B and C to Strip D in same manner with Strip D as back strip, starting at left edge and working toward beginning of strip at right edge. To finish forming armhole openings, join each Strip B together and each Strip C together (see Fig 1) in Join Pattern, working PS in first and last sts of strips, skipping first and last ch-sps on each join. Mark first or last ch-1 sp created on these joins at armhole openings.

EDGING INNER SIDE OF STRIP E

Edge only one long side of Strip E. This edge will be joined to the edge of the previously joined body section, forming fan motifs on top and bottom as well as flounces on the sides of the garment. With right side of Strip E facing you, join Color B with sl st in first 2-lp group, (ch 2, sc in next 2-lp group) 3 times, ch 2, sc in next 14-lp group; (ch 2, sc in next 2-lp group) 7 times, ch 2, sc in next 24-lp group (bottom left-hand corner made; mark this corner); working along left side, [(ch 2, sc in next 2-lp group) 5 times, ch 2, make flounce] 2 times; [(ch 2, sc in next 2-lp group) 4 times, ch 2, make flounce] 2 times; (ch 2, sc in next 2-lp group) 3 times; ch 2, sc in next 18-lp group (top left-hand corner made); working along top edge, (ch 2, sc in next 2-lp group) 3 times; [ch 2, sc in next 14-lp group, (ch 2, sc in next 2-lp group) 7 times] 10 times; ch 2, sc in next 14-lp group, (ch 2, sc in next 2-lp group) 3 times; ch 2, sc in next 18-lp group (top right-hand corner made); working along right side, (ch 2, sc in next 2-lp group) 3 times, [ch 2, make flounce, (ch 2, sc in next 2-lp group) 4 times] 2 times, [(ch 2, make flounce, (ch 2, sc in next 2-lp group) 5 times] 2 times; ch 2, sc in next 24-lp group (bottom right-hand corner made); working along bottom edge, [(ch 2, sc in next 2-lp group) 7 times, ch 2, sc in next 14-lp group] 9 times, (ch 2, sc in next 2-lp group) 3 times, ch 2; join with sl st in beg sl st, making sure not to twist strip. Fasten off; weave in ends.

JOIN STRIP E TO BODY

Mark the lower left corner of the joined center body section. Lay this body section right side down on a flat working surface with D sections nearest you. Position Strip E, right side down, around body section, matching marked corners.

With wrong sides of Strips D and E facing you, with Strip E in front and Strip D in back, join Color B with sl st in first ch-sp on Strip E, ch 2, PS in same ch-sp as joining, ch 1, then on Strip D in 11th ch-sp from marked corner work PS, ch 1, continue in Join Pattern until ch-sp before corner fan on Strip E; PS in next ch-sp on Strip E, ch 1, PS in edge of last 2-lp group on Strip D, ch 1, PS in corner sc on Strip E, ch 1, hdc in edge of same 2-lp group on Strip D, ch 1, puff st in next ch-sp on Strip E, ch 1; working along left-hand edge, work evenly along side edge in Join Pattern, working puff st around last 2 lps at edge of each strip and also in last ch-sp of strip joins, work puff st in center of each flounce (counts as ch-sp), making sure that each flounce is centered with strip joins of inner cardi; continue along left-hand edge until ch-sp before next corner of Strip E; work corner in same manner as first corner; work in Join Pattern along top edge, joining Strip E to Strip A until ch-sp before next corner of Strip E; work corner in same manner as first corner; work in Join Pattern along side edge in same manner as previous side edge until ch-sp before next corner of Strip E; work corner in same manner as first corner; work in Join Pattern along bottom edge to end of Strip E; join with sl st in beg sl st. Fasten off; weave in ends.

EDGING

Maintain fan motif along upper and lower sides of cardi while working edging.

With right side of work facing you, starting at bottom near left-hand corner and working across bottom edge toward bottom right-hand corner (counterclockwise around cardi), join Color B with sl st in 14-lp group opposite first seven 2-lp groups of strip (four 2-lp groups from beg of Strip E and three 2-lp groups from end of Strip E); *(ch 2, work PB in next 2-lp group) 7 times, ch 2, sc in next 14-lp group; repeat from * across bottom edge to corner 24-lp group at bottom right-hand corner; (ch 2, PB in next 2-lp group) 12 times around corner; working along side edge, **ch 3, sc in next 6-lp, 8-lp, or 10-lp group (when other edge of Strip E has 3 (4, 5) 2-lp groups between flounces, work 6 (8, 10)-lp group, (ch 3, PB in next 2-lp group) 11 times (around flounce); repeat from ** across side to corner 18-lp group at top right-hand corner; ch 3, (PB in next 2-lp group, ch 2) 9 times around corner; working along top edge, work top edging of cardi similar to bottom edge, maintaining fan pattern by working (sc, ch 2) in each 14-lp group opposite each seven 2-lp groups on other edge of Strip E and (puff bobble, ch 2) in each 2-lp group opposite 14-lp groups on other edge of Strip E across top edge to corner 18-lp group at top left-hand corner; work corner same as top right-hand corner; work side edge same as other side edge across to corner 24-lp group at bottom left-hand corner; work corner same as bottom right-hand corner; work along bottom edge same as top edge across to beg; join with sl st in joining sl st. Fasten off; weave in ends.

SLEEVES

Each sleeve is composed of 4 strips as shown in the following diagram. As each strip for the sleeve is worked, the width of the loom is adjusted downward. Make sure to leave a minimum 6" (15cm) starting yarn tail for each strip; these tails will be used later during assembly. **[FIG 3]**

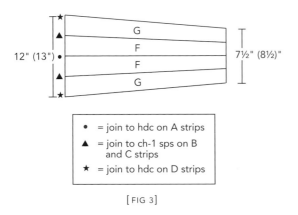

12" (13")   7½" (8½)"

- • = join to hdc on A strips
- ▲ = join to ch-1 sps on B and C strips
- ★ = join to hdc on D strips

[FIG 3]

With Color A, make the following strips:

STRIP F (MAKE 4): Set loom width at 3 (3¼)" (7.5 [8]cm) for the first 80 loops, 2¾ (3)" (7 [7.5]cm) for next 20 loops, 2½ (2¾)" (6.5 [7]cm) for next 20 loops, 2¼ (2½)" (5.5 [6.5]cm) for next 20 loops, and 2 (2¼)" (5 [5.5]cm) for the last 16 loops—156 lps total measuring about 16½" (42cm) long.

STRIP G (MAKE 4): Set loom width at 3 (3¼)" (7.5 [8]cm) for first the 20 loops, 2½ (2¾)" (6.5 [7]cm) for the next 20 loops, 2¼ (2½)" (5.5 [6.5]cm) for the next 20 loops, 2 (2¼)" (5 [5.5]cm) for the next 20 loops, 1¾ (2)" (4.5 [5]cm) for the last 76 lps—156 lps total, measuring about 16½" (42cm) long.

JOINING STRIPS

You will join strips together as indicated in Figure 3, following directions below. These joins not only serve to join sleeve strips, but to attach sleeves to the body. Joins will start with sl st in marked hdc or ch-1 sps on body as indicated by attachment points in diagrams. Be sure to join strips beginning from starting end of strip (wide end) and working toward fastened-off end of strip (narrow end). Join strips as follows, working in untwisted lps.

JOIN STRIP F TO STRIP G

Place a Strip F and a Strip G together with wrong sides facing. Then join Color B with sl st in marked ch-1 space on Strip B or C armhole edge; then continue to crochet along long shaped edges of Strips F and G, working as follows: ch 3, sc in first 2-lp group on front strip; *ch 3, sc in next 2-lp group on opposite strip; repeat from * across until 24 lps remain on joining edge of each strip; start sleeve flare as follows: (ch 4, sc in next 2-lp group on opposite strip) 4 times, (ch 5, sc in next 2-lp group on opposite strip) 4 times, (ch 6, sc in next 2-lp group on opposite strip) 4 times, (ch 7, sc in next 2-lp group on opposite strip) 4 times, (ch 8, sc in next 2-lp group on opposite strip) 4 times, (ch 9, sc in next 2-lp group on opposite strip) 4 times. Fasten off; weave in ends.

JOIN STRIP F TO STRIP F

With wrong sides of two F Strips together, hold one strip in front of the other; join Color B with sl st in marked hdc on Strip A. Working along both F Strips, ch 3, sc in first 2-lp group on front strip, (ch 6, sc in next 2-lp group on opposite strip) 9 times, (ch 5, sc in next 2-lp group on opposite strip) 10 times; (ch 4, sc in next 2-lp group on opposite strip) 10 times; *ch 3, sc in next 2-lp group on opposite strip; repeat from * across. Fasten off; weave in ends.

JOIN STRIP G TO STRIP G

With wrong sides of 2 Strips G together, hold one strip in front of the other; join Color B with sl st in marked hdc on Strip D. Working along both Strips G, ch 9, sc in next 2-lp group on first strip, (ch 9, sc in next 2-lp group on opposite strip) 9 times, (ch 8, sc in next 2-lp group on opposite strip) 10 times, (ch 7, sc in next 2-lp group on opposite strip) 10 times, (ch 6, sc in next 2-lp group on opposite strip) 10 times, (ch 5, sc in next 2-lp group on opposite strip) 10 times, (ch 4, sc in next 2-lp group on opposite strip) 10 times; *ch 3, sc in next 2-lp group on opposite strip; repeat from * across. Fasten off; weave in ends.

FINISHING

Use start and end tails of Strip E to join start and end of Strip E together through spine of strip. Use starting tails of Strips F and G to join spines of sleeve strips to spines of Strips B and C. Weave in all remaining ends.

TAPESTRY CROCHET

with
Carol Ventura

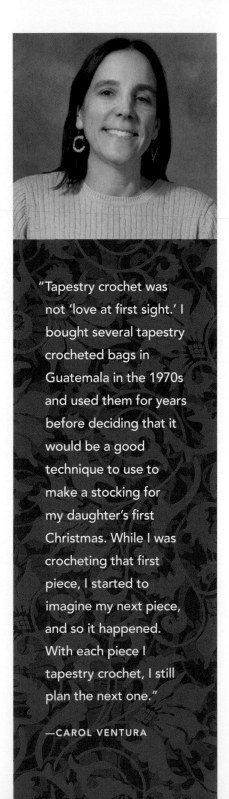

Carol Ventura's early upbringing may have provided the impetus for a life that is filled with travel and education. Because her father was in the Navy, her family lived in many different places. They enjoyed traveling together, where in addition to viewing famous monuments, they visited museums and factories where they watched people at work. Carol's father also loved photography, and he passed this hobby on to his daughter.

She was introduced to tapestry crochet in Guatemala while working with a weaving cooperative as a Peace Corps volunteer in the 1970s. Here the men made tapestry crochet purses, and Carol bought several to take home. Finally in 1980 when she wanted to make a Christmas stocking, she pulled apart one of the purses to see how tapestry crochet was done; she became completely fascinated with the technique.

Carol now travels to exotic corners of the world, spreading her enthusiasm for tapestry crochet. Wherever she goes, she carries her tapestry crochet with her. During the summer of 2004, she traveled to China as part of a Fulbright program, the purpose of which was to encourage the understanding of non-Western cultures among teachers. Although she spoke no Chinese, Carol managed to meet crocheters and show them the basics of tapestry crochet.

In addition to designing projects in tapestry crochet, Carol, an art history professor, began to study the background of tapestry crochet and soon discovered that it was employed not only in Guatemala, where she first saw the purses worn as part of traditional Mayan garb, but throughout the world. In Africa, she found that on special occasions people wore hats made of tapestry crochet. In Europe, she found examples of tapestry crochet that had been used as decorative borders around tablecloths and linens as early as the thirteenth century CE.

To spread her love of tapestry crochet to others, Carol has written three books on the subject, developed a website (www.tapestrycrochet.com), and started a Yahoo! group. She feels that her biggest challenge has not been in designing the projects, writing the instructions, or taking the pictures, but marketing: spreading the love of tapestry crochet around the world. Her strategy is to get people to try tapestry crochet, hoping they will find it as fulfilling as she has, and then go on to teach others, who will in turn teach others. Carol regularly teaches at conferences and provides tapestry crochet projects for books and magazines. No wonder Carol Ventura is often called the "Ambassador of Tapestry Crochet."

At left, working the tapestry crochet technique in single crochet permits the subtle shading that creates this dramatic portrait of Martin Luther King. At right, the reversed black-on-white and white-on-black color combinations add charm to the whimsical cats parading around this striking afghan.

HOW TO WORK **TAPESTRY** CROCHET

In tapestry crochet, two or more thread colors are switched back and forth while creating a patterned cloth. It is a technique that uses single crochet stitches that are worked over the thread color currently not in use. Depending upon the tension and the number of yarns used, the finished fabric can be stiff or supple. Tapestry crochet has the flexibility and portability of crochet, but it often does not look crocheted. In fact, the surface looks so much like woven fabric that many people think that pieces worked with tapestry crochet were made on a loom.

Most tapestry crochet is done with single crochet stitches, with the colors not in use carried within the work. When beads are used in the project, a bead is added to the front or back of the stitch. The designs are often worked from charts.

In working the tapestry crochet stitch, insert the hook from front to back under the 2 top loops of the stitch. The carried thread is placed over the top of the stitches and is encased almost invisibly in the newly created stitches.

WORKING TECHNIQUES AND STITCHES

Carrying thread: Place the thread to be carried over the top of the stitches being worked into, then sc across as usual, encasing the carried thread between sts. [**FIG 1**]

Changing colors: Work a stitch until 2 loops remain on the hook; drop the working thread and pick up the non-working (carried) thread and draw through both loops on hook. The previous non-working thread now becomes the working thread. [**FIG 2, 3**]

The previous working thread now becomes the non-working thread and is carried over the top of stitches in the row below.

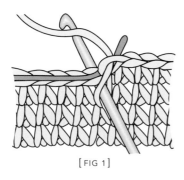

[FIG 1]

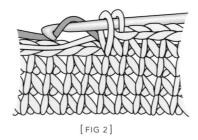

[FIG 2]

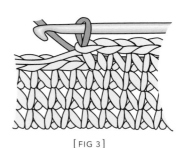

[FIG 3]

Tapestry crochet stitch: While carrying the non-working thread over stitches on the row below, insert the hook in the next st and draw up a loop with working thread, yo and draw through 2 loops on hook, encasing carried (non-working) thread between sts: tapestry crochet st made. [**FIG 4**]

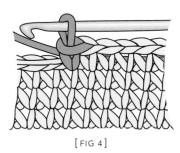

[FIG 4]

Stringing beads: Before starting the pattern, use a beading needle to thread 400 transparent dark blue beads onto navy crochet thread and 400 light blue beads on light blue thread. As you work, when only about 10 light blue beads remain, cut light blue thread, leaving a 36" (91.5cm) end. String light blue beads on light blue thread and begin to carry the new beaded thread. Switch to the new thread when the last few beads run out; carry old thread for 10 stitches, then cut it.

Bead tapestry crochet stitch: While carrying the non-working thread, insert the hook in the next st, push a bead down and draw up a loop with working thread; yo and draw through 2 loops on hook, allowing the bead to fall to the back of the stitch: bead tapestry crochet stitch made.

Decreasing in beaded stitches: The crochet 2 sts together decrease is worked as follows: While carrying non-working thread, insert the hook in the next stitch, push a bead down, draw up a loop with working thread, insert hook in next stitch (no bead this time), draw up a loop with working thread, yo and draw through 2 loops on hook—decrease made.

Adding or discontinuing a color: Carry new color for about 10 sts, encasing it, before using it in pattern. To end a color, complete last st of color to be discontinued and cut, leaving a short end to be carried and covered for about 10 sts.

BEADED **TAPESTRY CROCHET BAG**

Designed by Carol Ventura

SKILL LEVEL
⬛⬛⬛⬜ Intermediate

SIZE
Approximately 8⅛" x 7" (20.5cm x 18cm) (excluding handles)

MATERIALS
- DMC® *Senso Size 3 Crochet Thread* [100% cotton, each approximately 1¾ oz [50g] and 150 yd [137m], **(2)** fine weight)
  - 300 yd (274m) / 2 balls in color 1010 Light Blue
  - 150 yd (137m) / 1 ball in color 1011 Navy
  - 150 yd (137m) / 1 ball in color 1002 Ecru
- One size C-2 (2.75mm) steel crochet hook, or size needed to obtain gauge
- Stitch marker
- 3,200 (165g) size 8/0 translucent dark blue seed beads
- 2,488 (165g) size 6/0 light blue seed beads
- 2 heavy beading needles
  Note: Photographed model was made using Fire Mountains Gems and Beads seed beads.

GAUGE
35 sts and 32 rows = 4" (10cm)

NOTES
- See Working Techniques and Stitches on page 36–37.
- As the bag is crocheted, note that you are working around from the inside of the piece. The beaded side, behind the surface facing you, is the outside as shown in the photograph.

This could well be the most complicated pattern I've ever designed for publication, but I wanted to challenge the crocheter to go to the next level. Tapestry crochet fabric looks woven, but this time the motif has a woven look, too! I chose 2 different-sized beads to reinforce the illusion.

Working with beads may seem a bit intimidating at first, but after a few rows it becomes easy. Interestingly, the beads appear on the opposite of the working side.

BAG

Beg at bottom of bag, ch 70 with light blue and ecru threads held together. Leave 12" (30.5cm) long thread ends.

RND 1: With ecru thread, work tapestry crochet st in 2nd ch from hook, changing to light blue to complete st; (with light blue, bead tapestry crochet st in each of next 4 chs, with ecru, tapestry crochet st in each of next 3 chs) 9 times; with light blue, bead tapestry crochet st in each of next 4 chs, with ecru, work 3 tapestry crochet sts in last ch; now working on opposite of beg ch, carrying thread tails, as follows: (with light blue, bead tapestry crochet st in each of next 4 lps, with ecru, tapestry crochet in each of next 3 lps) 9 times; with light blue, bead tapestry crochet st in each of next 4 lps, with ecru, tapestry crochet st in next lp, 2 tapestry crochet sts in last lp—141 sts. Do not join. Insert stitch marker in this last st. On following rnds, move this marker up to last st of rnd just completed as you go. You will be working around and around, working up from the bottom.

NOTE: As you near end of Rnd 2, begin to carry navy thread, leaving a thread tail and carrying it about 10 sts before it is needed in the work.

RND 2: Sk first st, (bead tapestry crochet 4 light blue, tapestry crochet 3 ecru) 20 times. On the following round, continue to carry ecru until you have completed about 10 sts beyond last ecru st worked; cut off ecru thread close to work. As you continue to work, add needed colors and eliminate no longer needed colors in this manner.

NOTE: If you are already comfortable working tapestry crochet sts and bead tapestry crochet sts, you may find it easier to follow the chart on page 41. If not, simply follow the written directions below.

RNDS 3–5: (Bead tapestry crochet 17 navy, 4 light blue, 3 navy, 4 light blue) 5 times.

RND 6: (Bead tapestry crochet 17 navy, 4 light blue, 3 navy, 4 light blue) 4 times; bead tapestry crochet 17 navy, 4 light blue; begin to carry ecru; bead tapestry crochet 3 navy, 4 light blue; cut carried navy close to work, about 10 sts after last used.

RND 7: (Tapestry crochet 3 ecru, bead tapestry crochet 4 light blue) 20 times.

RND 8: (Tapestry crochet 3 ecru, bead tapestry crochet 4 light blue) 19 times; thread 400 dark blue beads onto navy thread; begin to carry navy, tapestry crochet 3 ecru, bead tapestry crochet 4 light blue, cut carried ecru close to work.

RNDS 9–11: (Bead tapestry crochet 3 navy, 4 light blue, 17 navy, 4 light blue) 5 times.

RND 12: (Bead tapestry crochet 3 navy, 4 light blue, 17 navy, 4 light blue) 4 times; bead tapestry crochet 3 navy, 4 light blue, 17 navy; begin to carry ecru; bead tapestry crochet 4 light blue; cut carried navy.

RND 13: (Tapestry crochet 3 ecru, bead tapestry crochet 4 light blue) 20 times.

RND 14: (Tapestry crochet 3 ecru, bead tapestry crochet 4 light blue) 19 times; thread 400 transparent dark blue beads onto navy, beg to carry navy; tapestry crochet 3 ecru, bead tapestry crochet 4 light blue; cut carried ecru close to work.

RNDS 15–17: (Bead tapestry crochet 3 navy, 4 light blue, 3 navy, 4 light blue, 14 navy) 5 times.

RND 18: (Bead tapestry crochet 3 navy, 4 light blue, 3 navy, 4 light blue, 14 navy) 4 times; bead tapestry crochet 3 navy, 4 light blue, 3 navy, 4 light blue; begin to carry ecru; bead tapestry crochet 17 navy.

RND 19: Tapestry crochet 3 ecru, bead tapestry crochet 4 light blue; cut carried navy; (tapestry crochet 3 ecru, bead tapestry crochet 4 light blue) 19 times.

RND 20: (Tapestry crochet 3 ecru, bead tapestry crochet 4 light blue) 19 times; thread 400 transparent dark blue beads onto navy; begin to carry navy; tapestry crochet 3 ecru, bead tapestry crochet 4 light blue; cut carried ecru close to work.

RNDS 21–23: (Bead tapestry crochet 10 navy, 4 light blue, 3 navy, 4 light blue, 7 navy) 5 times.

RND 24: (Bead tapestry crochet 10 navy, 4 light blue, 3 navy, 4 light blue, 7 navy) 4 times; bead tapestry crochet 10 navy, 4 light blue, 3 navy, 4 light blue; begin to carry ecru, bead tapestry crochet 7 navy.

RND 25: Tapestry crochet 3 ecru, bead tapestry crochet 4 light blue; cut carried navy; (tapestry crochet 3 ecru, bead tapestry crochet 4 light blue) 19 times.

RND 26: (Tapestry crochet 3 ecru, bead tapestry crochet 4 light blue) 19 times; begin to carry navy, tapestry crochet 3 ecru, bead tapestry 4 light blue; cut carried ecru close to work.

RNDS 27–49: Repeat Rnds 3–25.

RND 50: (Tapestry crochet 3 ecru, bead tapestry crochet 4 light blue) 20 times. Do not fasten off.

HANDLES AND RIM

RND 1: Tapestry crochet 3 ecru, bead tapestry crochet 11 light blue, tapestry crochet 3 ecru, bead tapestry crochet 11 light blue, tapestry crochet 3 ecru, bead tapestry crochet 9 light blue; with light blue and ecru held together, ch 78 for first handle; insert hook in 36th st away from base of ch, bead tapestry crochet 9 light blue, tapestry crochet 3 ecru, bead tapestry crochet 11 light blue, tapestry crochet 3 ecru, bead tapestry crochet 9 light blue; with light blue and ecru held together, ch 78 for second handle; insert hook in 36th st away from base of ch, bead tapestry crochet 2 light blue.

NOTE: Move marker to last st of round.

RND 2: Bead tapestry crochet 7 light blue, tapestry crochet 3 ecru, bead tapestry crochet 11 light blue, tapestry crochet 3 ecru, bead tapestry crochet 9 light blue, bead tapestry crochet 77 light blue in handle ch; bead tapestry crochet 2 light blue sts together, bead tapestry 8 light blue, tapestry crochet 3 ecru, bead tapestry crochet 11 light blue, tapestry crochet 3 ecru, bead tapestry crochet 9 light blue, bead tapestry crochet 77 light blue on handle ch; bead tapestry crochet 2 light blue sts together; bead tapestry crochet 1 light blue.

RND 3: (Bead tapestry crochet 7 light blue, tapestry crochet 3 ecru, bead tapestry crochet 11 light blue, tapestry crochet 3 ecru, bead tapestry crochet 8 light blue, bead tapestry crochet 2 light blue sts together; bead tapestry crochet 76 light blue, bead tapestry crochet 2 light blue sts together) twice. Remove stitch marker.

RND 4: With light blue and ecru threads held together, sc in each of next 32 sts, sc next 2 sts together, sc in each of next 75 sts, sc next 2 sts together, sc in each of next 31 sts, sc next 2 sts together, sc in each of next 75 sts, sc next 2 sts together, sl st in first sc. Fasten off; weave in ends.

RND 5: Insert hook under upper 2 lps of st in upper right inside corner of rim and handle (next to st where ch started), draw through lp of light blue thread, leaving a 2" (5cm) tail; with light blue, ch 1; carry light blue tail and begin to carry ecru thread (leaving a 2" [5cm] tail), bead tapestry crochet 1 light blue in same st as joining, bead tapestry crochet 1 light blue, tapestry crochet 3 ecru, bead tapestry crochet 11 light blue, tapestry crochet 3 ecru, bead tapestry crochet 11 light blue, tapestry crochet 3 ecru, bead tapestry crochet 2 light blue, bead tapestry crochet 77 light blue on handle (inserting hook in bottom of original ch).

RND 6: Carrying ecru tail, bead tapestry crochet 2 light blue, tapestry crochet 3 ecru, bead tapestry crochet 11 light blue, tapestry crochet 3 ecru, bead tapestry crochet 11 light blue, tapestry crochet 3 ecru, bead tapestry crochet 2 light blue together, bead tapestry crochet 76 light blue, bead tapestry crochet 2 light blue together, bead tapestry crochet 1 light blue, tapestry crochet 3 ecru, bead tapestry crochet 11 light blue, tapestry crochet 3 ecru, bead tapestry crochet 11 light blue, tapestry crochet 3 ecru.

RND 7: With light blue and ecru threads held together, sc next 2 sts together, sc in each of next 74 sts, sc next 2 sts together, sl st in first sc. Fasten off; weave in ends.

Working on opposite side of bag, repeat Rnds 5–7.

FINISHING

Pull on carried tails at bottom of bag to cinch in width (if necessary). Tie overhand knot, then cut them.

Place bag on a flat surface and cover with a towel to protect beads. With steam iron held just above towel, gently steam bag into shape.

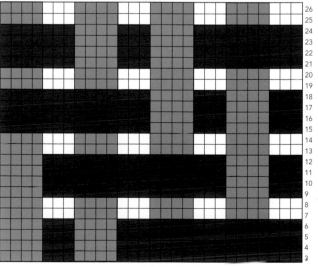

Read from right to left and bottom to top.

ARAN CROCHET

with
Jane Snedden Peever

"I love Celtic work and am fascinated by the beauty of intricately woven Celtic knot work. To reproduce this in crochet was a challenge I undertook with passion. I love to inspire the creative spark in others and to show them what can be accomplished when you open your heart to it. Creativity in any form brings joy into the lives of all those it touches."

—JANE SNEDDEN PEEVER

From as early as Jane can remember she has always loved to be creative. Never one to "color within the lines," Jane always loved to follow her own path when it came to artistic adventures. As she says, "I love to prove that anything is possible when you follow your creative heart."

As a child she loved doing crafts, and at the age of 10, her mother taught her to crochet. From that moment, it became her favorite craft. Learning to knit soon followed, and the passion for color and texture was well on its way. She found herself putting her own twist on patterns and soon found it more fun to utilize her own ideas from scratch. This led to a lot of trial and error, ripping and redoing.

By the time Jane graduated with a business degree from Queen's University in Kingston, Ontario, Canada, she decided to break from the pack and follow her heart. She moved back to her hometown of Pembroke, Ontario, married, managed a local craft shop, and eventually fulfilled her dream by opening her own yarn shop. This offered Jane a great palette of yarn to pick from for her designs, and she started to design kits to sell in her store and on the Internet.

A few years into designing the kits, Jane noticed that an editor was searching for sweater designs for a forthcoming book. The required designs were for crocheted sweaters, and Jane had never made a crocheted sweater, but she was up to the challenge. She submitted a few designs, and they were accepted. Having enjoyed the speed with which crocheted sweaters could be made, she began to venture further into designing different styles and eventually one that involved cables.

She had seen a cable-styled crocheted sweater in an old book she found at the library and was quite intrigued with how this could be done. The completed

sweater, which no one believed could possibly have been crocheted, inspired many compliments.

This spurred Jane on to try other cabling ideas and to eventually take the leap and do her own book. Jane produced two books on cable sweaters, *Crocheted Aran Sweaters* and *More Crocheted Aran Sweaters*. She decided at this point to focus more on designing, and after five years of operating her shop, she closed the store. Her time is now spent raising her two children, designing for yarn companies and publishers, as well as finding time for her newly acquired creative challenge of designing silver jewelry.

Cables, cables and more cables! As seen here, the variety of crocheted cables is nearly endless. A typical Aran ribbed sweater (second from left, lower) is a style worn for centuries by the fishermen of the Aran Isles, off the coast of Ireland.

HOW TO DO ARAN CROCHET

Cables are the focal point of Aran crochet, adding texture and dimension to the work. There are various methods of producing the look of cables in crochet. The most commonly used method is with post stitches. The cables in the sample sweater were created by working front post stitches. This is simply a double or triple crochet worked around the post of a stitch in a row below instead of into the stitch top, as is usual in crochet. The post refers to the "vertical bar" of the stitch. The hook is inserted on one side of the stem, around the back, and out the other side. Cablework is then about combining the post stitch with other forms of crochet stitches to create beautiful effects.

POST STITCHES

To work a post stitch, insert the hook from front to back to front around the post of the specified stitch. The post is the main vertical portion of a stitch. The post stitches are worked around stitches two rows below the working row.

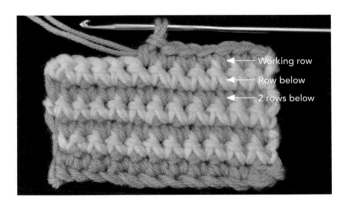

Front post double crochet (FPdc): Yo, insert hook from front to back to front around post of specified st 2 rows below and draw up a lp; (yo and draw through 2 lps on hook) twice—FPdc made. Skip the stitch on the previous row behind the FPdc just made.

Front post triple crochet (FPtr): Yo twice, insert hook from front to back to front around post of specified st 2 rows below and draw up a lp; (yo and draw through 2 lps on hook) 3 times—FPtr made. Skip the stitch on the previous row behind the FPtr just made.

· · · · · TIP FROM THE MASTER · · · · ·

Working with the cables and the textural designs creates a form of meditation. Just like following a labyrinth creates a stillness of the mind and an inner peace, following a pattern rich with cable work is a path to that peaceful place within. Now, some may feel that working with cables is anything but peaceful. My response would be to let go of the limits you set on yourself, give it a chance, and follow the flow of the pattern and it can be fun. Mistakes are made in order to learn and grow in our skills and abilities. You may surprise yourself. Remember that it is important to use row markers in your first and last stitch. If you lose track of where your row starts and ends, it will throw off the angle of the cables.

CABLES

Small cable: Skip next FPdc 2 rows below, FPdc around next 2 FP sts 2 rows below; working in front of FPdc just made, FPtr around skipped FPdc 2 rows below, skip 3 sc on previous row behind cable—small cable made (counts as 3 sts).

Large cable: Skip next 3 FP sts 2 rows below, FPtr around next 2 FP sts 2 rows below, skip 2 sc on previous row above first 2 skipped FP sts, sc in next sc on previous row above 3rd skipped FP st; working in front of 2 FPtr just made, FPtr around first 2 skipped FP sts 2 rows below, skip next 2 sc on previous row behind 2 FPtr just made—large cable made (counts as 5 sts).

COUNTING STITCHES

To ensure an accurate stitch count, unless the pattern says otherwise, every FP stitch (FPdc, FPtr and FPdc dec) represents 1 stitch; thus the sc that lies behind it in the previous row is left unworked. When instructions say to work into the next sc, after working FP stitches, it means the next sc following the required number of skipped sc.

When working FPdc sts around sc posts 2 rows below, work directly under your current stitch position. When the pattern says to work a single crochet in the previous row and then is followed by an FPdc around the sc 2 rows below, be sure to skip the sc 2 rows below that corresponds to the sc worked in the previous row. The FPdc is worked around the next 2 sc 2 rows below after the skipped sc 2 rows below.

DECREASING

Post stitch decreases are worked around the post stitches of the previous row.

Front post double crochet decrease (FPdc dec): *Yo, insert hook from front to back to front around post of the next FP st 2 rows below and draw up a lp, yo and draw through 2 lps on hook; repeat from * twice more; yo and draw through all 4 lps on hook—FPdc dec made. Skip the next sc on previous row behind FPdc.

Single crochet decrease (sc dec): (Insert hook in next st and draw up a lp) twice; yo and draw through all 3 lps on hook—sc dec made.

Three single crochet decrease (3 sc dec): (Insert hook in net st and draw up a lp) 3 times; yo and draw through all 4 lps on hook—3 sc dec made.

GAUGE

Try to work as loosely as possible while maintaining the specified gauge for the garment.

Post stitches should not "pull" on the fabric, but should lie comfortably in front of the work. If worked too tightly, post stitches can cause the fabric to pucker.

KEEPING TRACK OF STITCHES

Use stitch markers to keep track of where a pattern unit starts and stops, placing markers on each side of a pattern repeat. This is especially important with cables that are meant to "wander" across the fabric, such as the large diamond cables in this garment. Remember that every post stitch made requires skipping a stitch in the previous row. The only exception to this rule is when an increase or decrease is being incorporated into the pattern, and this is clearly stated in the pattern. When increasing and decreasing, be sure to move the stitch markers accordingly. In the case of the garment's armhole, you can work a partial pattern as you decrease stitches or move the marker over to the next full repeat and work the remaining stitches in sc only.

SHAPING THE GARMENT

The crossover fronts are both shaped by decreasing on every row only at the front edge. The cable follows the front neck shaping, slanting the cables toward the side seams. The number of stitches for the front neck edge selvedge remains the same throughout, which creates a bias fabric. Because of the bias, gently block each garment piece before sewing them together so that any distortion created by the cable work can be remedied.

CABLE **CROSSOVER** SWEATER

Designed by Jane Snedden Peever

SKILL LEVEL

■■■■▶ Experienced

SIZES

- S (M, L)
- Instructions are written for size S. Changes for sizes M and L are in parentheses. If only one number appears, it applies to all sizes.
- Finished bust 34 (38, 42)" (86 [96.5, 106.5]cm)
- Finished back length 27 (28, 29½)" (68.5 [71, 75]cm)
- Finished sleeve length 22 (22½, 23)" (56 [57, 58.5]cm)

MATERIALS

- Patons *Classic Wool* (100% wool, each approximately 3½ oz [100g] and 223 yd [205m], 🄸4🄸 medium/worsted weight) 3345 (3791, 4237) yd (3075 [3485, 3895]m) / 15 (17, 19) balls in color 229 Natural Mix
- One size H-8 (5mm) crochet hook, or size needed to obtain gauge
- 8 stitch markers
- 2 buttons, 1" (25mm) wide

GAUGE

14 sts and 16 rows = 4" (10cm) in small cable pattern

NOTES

- This garment has a fitting crossover bodice with a deep waistband. The fit will be a close fit, and the finished bust size will be close to actual bust size. The placement of the buttons for the waistband flaps will allow for some adjustment in this fit.

I wanted something classic and timeless. When you are working with lines, they need to work with the flow of the body. It was fun to shape the cables so they worked with the crossover effect of the sweater. I love to wrap myself in sweaters on a cold evening, even when I'm dressing up to go out. Thus, a wraparound seemed to be the best choice. The process of making a sweater, with all its trials and tribulations, every dropped stitch and missed crossing, makes the sweater unique. In the end, the wisdom gained and the beautiful sweater made, with your own loving hands, is well worth the walk through the labyrinth of crocheted cablework.

WAISTBAND

Ch 20.

ROW 1 (RIGHT SIDE): Sc in 2nd ch from hook and in each remaining ch across—19 sc; ch 1, turn. Place markers in each end of this row.

ROW 2: Sc in first st and in each st across; ch 1, turn.

ROW 3: Sc in first sc; *FPdc around each of next 3 sc, sc in next sc, FPdc around each of next 2 sc, sc in next sc; repeat from * once more; FPdc around each of next 3 sc, sc in last sc—13 FPdc and 6 sc; ch 1, turn.

ROW 4: Repeat Row 2.

ROW 5: Sc in first sc, work small cable in next 3 FPdc, sc in next 2 sc, FPdc around each of next 2 FPdc, work small cable around next 3 FPdc, FPdc around each of next 2 FPdc, sc in next 2 sc, work small cable around next 3 FPdc, sc in last sc—3 small cables, 4 FPdc, and 6 sc; ch 1, turn.

ROW 6: Repeat Row 2.

ROW 7: Sc in first sc, work small cable in next small cable, sc in next 3 sc, FPdc around each of next 2 FPdc, FPdc dec around next small cable, FPdc around next 2 FPdc, sc in next 3 sc, small cable around next small cable, sc in last sc—2 small cables, 4 FPdc, 1 FPdc dec, and 8 sc; ch 1, turn.

ROW 8: Repeat Row 2.

ROW 9: Sc in first sc, small cable in next small cable, sc in next 3 sc, large cable around next 5 FP sts, sc in next 3 sc, small cable around next small cable, sc in last sc—1 large cable, 2 small cables, and 8 sc; ch 1, turn.

ROW 10: Repeat Row 2.

ROW 11: Sc in first sc, small cable in next small cable, sc in next 2 sc, FPdc around each of next 2 FPtr, 3 FPdc around next sc, FPdc around each of next 2 FPtr, sc in next 2 sc, small cable around next small cable, sc in last sc—2 small cables, 7 FPdc, and 6 sc; ch 1, turn.

ROW 12: Repeat Row 2.

ROW 13: Sc in first sc, small cable in next small cable, sc in next sc, FPdc around each of next 2 FPdc, sc in next sc, small cable in next 3 FPdc, sc in next sc, FPdc around each

of next 2 FPdc, sc in next sc, small cable in next small cable, sc in last sc—3 small cables, 4 FPdc, and 6 sc; ch 1, turn.

ROW 14: Repeat Row 2.

ROW 15: Sc in first sc, small cable in next small cable, sc in next sc, FPdc around each of next 2 FPdc, sc in next sc, FPdc around each of 3 FPdc in next small cable, sc in next sc, FPdc around each of next 2 FPdc, sc in next sc, small cable in next small cable, sc in last sc—2 small cables, 7 FPdc, and 6 sc; ch 1, turn.

Repeat Rows 4–15 for waistband. When the waistband measures approximately 12 (13, 14)" (30.5 [33, 35.5] cm) from first markers, place 2nd markers at each end of next row. Continue in pattern until waistband measures approximately 17 (19, 21)" (43 [48, 53.5]cm) from 2nd markers, place 3rd markers at each end of next row. Continue in pattern until waistband measures approximately 12 (13, 14)" (30.5 [33, 35.5]cm) from 3rd markers, ending by working a right side row, place 4th markers at each end of next row. Do not fasten off.

OUTSIDE BUTTONHOLE FLAP

NOTE: This flap can be made with all single crochet in the center section (between first and last small cables) or by continuing center pattern until center section is too small for pattern to fit. See page 192 for a better view of the buttonhole flap.

ROW 1 (WRONG SIDE): Sc dec in first 2 sts, sc in next st and in each st across to last 2 sts, sc dec in last 2 sts—17 sts; ch 1, turn.

ROW 2 (RIGHT SIDE): Sc in first st, small cable in next small cable, sc in next st and in each st across to last 4 sts, small cable in next small cable, sc in last st; ch 1, turn.

ROWS 3–9: Repeat Rows 1 and 2 three times more, then repeat Row 1 once more. At end of last row—9 sts.

ROW 10: Sc in first st, small cable in next small cable, ch 3 for buttonhole, sk next sc, small cable in next small cable, sc in last st—8 sts and 1 ch–3 sp; ch 1, turn.

ROW 11: Sc dec in first 2 sts, sc in next 2 sts, sc in ch–3 sp, sc in each of next 2 sts, sc dec in last 2 sts—7 sts; ch 1, turn.

ROW 12: Sc dec in first 2 sts, FPdc dec in next small cable, sc in next sc, FPdc dec in next small cable, sc dec in last 2 sts—5 sts; ch 1, turn.

ROW 13: Sc dec in first 2 sts, sc in next st, sc dec in last 2 sts—3 sts; ch 1, turn.

ROW 14: Work 3-sc dec over next 3 sts—1 st remains. Fasten off; weave in ends.

INSIDE BUTTONHOLE FLAP

ROW 1: With right side of waistband facing, working around sc on Row 1, join with sc in first st, sc in each st across—19 sc; ch 1, turn.

ROWS 2–6: Sc dec in first 2 sts, sc in next st and in each st across to last 2 sts, sc dec in last 2 sts—9 sc at end of last row; ch 1, turn.

ROW 7: Sc dec in first 2 sts, sc in next 2 sts, ch 3 for buttonhole, sk next st, sc in next 2 sts, sc dec in last 2 sts—6 sc; ch 1, turn.

ROW 8: Sc dec in first 2 sts, sc in next st, sc in ch-3 sp, sc in next st, sc dec in last 2 sts—5 sc; ch 1, turn.

ROW 9: Sc dec in first 2 sts, sc in next st, sc dec in last 2 sts—3 sc; ch 1, turn.

ROW 10: Work 3 sc dec—1 sc. Fasten off; weave in ends.

Upper Edge of Waistband

NOTE: When working Rows 1 and 2, move markers up to corresponding stitches on current row worked as you pass them.

ROW 1: With right side of waistband facing you and outside buttonhole flap on your right, join yarn with sc in 4th marked stitch on upper edge. Working in row ends, work 40 (44, 48) more sc evenly spaced across to 3rd marker, work 59 (67, 75) sc evenly spaced across to 2nd marker, work 41 (45, 49) sc evenly spaced across to first marker—141 (157, 173) sts; ch 1, turn.

ROW 2: Sc in first st; *hdc in next st, sl st in next st; repeat from * across to last 2 sts; hdc in next st, sc in last st; ch 1, turn. Do not fasten off.

RIGHT FRONT

ROW 1 (RIGHT SIDE): Sc dec in first 2 sts, sc in next st and in each st across to first marker—40 (44, 48) sts; ch 1, turn.

ROW 2: Sc in first st and in each st across to last 2 sts, sc dec in last 2 sts—39 (43, 47) sts; ch 1, turn.

ROW 3: Sc dec in first 2 sc, FPdc in each of next 3 sc; *sc in next sc, FPdc in each of next 3 sc; repeat from * across to last 2 sc; sc in next sc, 2 sc in last sc—9 (10, 11) groups of 3 FPdc and 12 (13, 14) sc; ch 1, turn.

ROW 4: Repeat Row 2—38 (42, 46) sts.

ROW 5: Sc dec in first 2 sts, small cable in next 3 FPdc; *sc in next st, small cable in next 3 FPdc; repeat from * across to last st; 2 sc in last st—9 (10, 11) small cables and 11 (12, 13) sc; ch 1, turn.

ROW 6: Repeat Row 2—37 (41, 45) sts.

ROW 7: Sc dec in first 2 sts, small cable in next small cable; *sc in next st, small cable in next small cable; repeat from * across to last 4 sts; sc in next 3 sts, 2 sc in last st—8 (9, 10) small cables and 13 (14, 15) sc; ch 1, turn.

ROW 8: Repeat Row 2—36 (40, 44) sts.

ROW 9: Sc dec in first 2 sts, small cable in next small cable; *sc in next st, small cable in next small cable; repeat from * across to last 3 sts; sc in next 2 sts, 2 sc in last st—8 (9, 10) small cables and 12 (13, 14) sc; ch 1, turn.

ROW 10: Repeat Row 2—35 (39, 43) sts.

ROW 11: Sc dec in first 2 sts, small cable in next small cable; *sc in next st, small cable in next small cable; repeat from * across to last 2 sts; sc in next st, 2 sc in last st—8 (9, 10) small cables and 11 (12, 13) sc; ch 1, turn.

ROW 12: Repeat Row 2—34 (38, 42) sts. Do not fasten off.

SHAPE ARMHOLE

ROW 1 (RIGHT SIDE): Sc dec in first 2 sts, small cable in next small cable; *sc in next st, small cable in next small cable; repeat from * across to last 9 sts; sc in next 2 sts, 2 sc in next st, leaving remaining 6 sts unworked—6 (7, 8) small cables and 10 (11, 12) sc; ch 1, turn.

ROW 2: Sc in first st and in each st across to last 2 sts, sc dec in last 2 sts—27 (31, 35) sts; ch 1, turn.

ROW 3: Sc dec in first 2 sts, small cable in next small cable; *sc in next st, small cable in next small cable; repeat from * across to last 2 sts, sc in next st, 2 sc in last st—6 (7, 8) small cables and 9 (10, 11) sc; ch 1, turn.

ROW 4: Repeat Row 2—26 (30, 34) sts.

ROW 5: Sc dec in first 2 sts, small cable in next small cable; *sc in next sc, small cable in next small cable; repeat from * across to last st; 2 sc in last st; ch 1, turn.

ROW 6: Repeat Row 2—25 (29, 33) sts.

ROW 7: Sc dec in first 2 sts, small cable in next small cable; *sc in next st, small cable in next small cable; repeat from * across to last 4 sts; sc in next 3 sts, 2 sc in last st—5 (6, 7) small cables and 10 (11, 12) sc; ch 1, turn.

ROW 8: Repeat Row 2—24 (28, 32) sts.

ROW 9: Sc dec in first 2 sts, small cable in next small cable; *sc in next st, small cable in next small cable; repeat from * across to last 3 sts; sc in next 2 sts, 2 sc in last st—5 (6, 7) small cables and 8 (9, 11) sc; ch 1, turn.

Repeat Rows 2–9 until piece measures about 8½ (9, 9½)" (21.5 [23, 24]cm) from Row 1 of armhole shaping, ending by working a right-side row. At end of last row, do not ch 1. Fasten off; weave in ends.

BACK

ROW 1: With right side of waistband facing you and outside buttonhole flap on your right, join yarn with sc in 3rd marked st, sc in next st and in each st across to 2nd marker—59 (67, 75) sc; ch 1, turn.

ROW 2: Sc in first st and in each st across; ch 1, turn.

ROW 3: Sc in first 2 sc, FPdc around each of next 3 sc; *sc in next sc, FPdc around each of next 3 sc; repeat from * across to last 2 sts; sc in last 2 sts—14 (16, 18) groups of 3 FPdc and 17 (19, 21) sc; ch 1, turn.

ROW 4: Repeat Row 2.

ROW 5: Sc in first 2 sc, small cable in next 3 FPdc; *sc in next sc, small cable in next 3 FPdc; repeat from * across to last 2 sts; sc in last 2 sts—14 (16, 18) small cables and 17 (19, 21) sc; ch 1, turn.

ROW 6: Repeat Row 2.

ROW 7: Sc in first 2 sc, small cable in next small cable; *sc in next sc, small cable in next small cable; repeat from * across to last 2 sts; sc in last 2 sts; ch 1, turn.

ROWS 8–11 (11, 13): Repeat Rows 6 and 7, 2 (2, 3) times more. Do not fasten off.

SHAPE ARMHOLES

ROW 1 (WRONG SIDE): Sc in first st and in each st across to last 7 sts—52 (60, 68) sts; ch 1, turn, leaving remaining 7 sts unworked.

ROW 2 (RIGHT SIDE): Sc in first 3 sc, small cable in next small cable; *sc in next sc, small cable in next small cable; repeat from * across to last 10 sts; sc in next 3 sts—10 (12, 14) small cables and 15 (17, 19) sc; ch 1, turn, leaving remaining 7 sts unworked.

ROW 3: Sc in first st and in each st across—45 (53, 61) sts; ch 1, turn.

ROW 4: Sc in first 3 sc, small cable in next small cable; *sc in next sc, small cable in next small cable; repeat from * across to last 3 sts; sc in last 3 sts; ch 1, turn.

Repeat Rows 3 and 4 until Back Armhole Shaping measures approximately 8½ (9, 9½)" (21.5 [23, 24]cm), ending by working a right-side row. At end of last row, do not ch 1. Fasten off; weave in ends.

LEFT FRONT

ROW 1: With right side of waistband facing you and outside buttonhole flap on your right, join yarn with sc in 2nd marked st, sc in next st and in each st across to 2 sts before first marker; sc dec in last 2 sts—40 (44, 48) sc; ch 1, turn.

ROW 2 (WRONG SIDE): Sc dec in first 2 sts, sc in next st and in each st across—39 (43, 47) sts; ch 1, turn.

ROW 3: Work 2 sc in first sc, sc in next sc, FPdc around each of next 3 sc; *sc in next sc, FPdc around each of next 3 sc; repeat from * across to last 2 sc; sc dec in last 2 sc—9 (10, 11) groups of 3 FPdc and 12 (13, 14) sc; ch 1, turn.

ROW 4: Repeat Row 2—38 (42, 46) sts.

ROW 5: Work 2 sc in first st, small cable in next 3 FPdc; *sc in next st, small cable in next 3 FPdc; repeat from * across to last 2 sts; sc dec in last 2 sts—9 (10, 11) small cables and 11 (12, 13) sc; ch 1, turn.

ROW 6: Repeat Row 2—37 (41, 45) sts.

ROW 7: Note: Be sure to skip 3 and only 3 sts behind each small cable to maintain the proper stitch count as the cables begin to slant toward the straight arm edge at beg of row. Work 2 sc in first st, sc in next 3 sts, sk first small cable, small cable in next small cable; *sc in next st, small cable in next small cable; repeat from * across to last 2 sts; sc dec in last 2 sts—8 (9, 10) small cables and 13 (14, 15) sc; ch 1, turn.

ROW 8: Repeat Row 2—36 (40, 44) sts.

ROW 9: Work 2 sc in first st, sc in next 2 sts, small cable in next small cable; *sc in next st, small cable in next small cable; repeat from * across to last 2 sts; sc dec in last 2 sts—8 (9, 10) small cables and 12 (13, 14) sc; ch 1, turn.

ROW 10: Repeat Row 2—35 (39, 43) sts.

ROW 11: Work 2 sc in first st, sc in next st, small cable in next small cable; *sc in next st, small cable in next small cable; repeat from * across to last 2 sts; sc dec in last 2 sts—8 (9, 10) small cables and 11 (12, 13) sc; ch 1, turn. Do not fasten off.

SHAPE ARMHOLE

ROW 1 (WRONG SIDE): Sc dec in first 2 sts, sc in next st and in each st across to last 6 sts—28 (32, 36) sts; ch 1, turn, leaving remaining 6 sts unworked.

ROW 2 (RIGHT SIDE): Work 2 sc in first st, sc in next 2 sts, (skip any small cables that were cut off by armhole shaping), small cable in next small cable; *sc in next st, small cable in next small cable; repeat from * across to last 2 sts; sc dec in last 2 sts—6 (7, 8) small cables and 10 (11, 12) sc; ch 1, turn.

ROW 3: Sc dec in first 2 sts, sc in next st and in each st across—27 (31, 35) sts; ch 1, turn.

ROW 4: Work same as Row 11 on Left Front, ending with 6 (7, 8) small cables and 9 (10, 11) sc; ch 1, turn.

ROW 5: Repeat Row 3—26 (30, 34) sts.

ROW 6: Work 2 sc in first st, small cable in next small cable; *sc in next st, small cable in next small cable; repeat from * across to last 2 sts; sc dec in last 2 sts; ch 1, turn.

ROW 7: Repeat Row 3—25 (29, 33) sts.

ROW 8: Work same as Row 7 on Left Front, ending with 5 (6, 7) small cables and 10 (11, 12) sc; ch 1, turn.

ROW 9: Repeat Row 3—24 (28, 32) sts.

ROW 10: Work same as Row 9 on Left Front, ending with 5 (6, 7) small cables and 9 (10, 11) sc; ch 1, turn.

Repeat Rows 3–10 until piece measures about 8½ (9, 9½)" (21.5 [23, 24]cm) from Row 1 of armhole shaping, ending by working a right-side row. At end of last row, do not ch 1. Fasten off; weave in ends.

Lower Edging of Waistband

NOTE: Lower edging and skirt section are worked down from lower edge of waistband in one piece.

ROW 1: With right side of waistband facing you and inner buttonhole flap on your right, join yarn with sc in first marked st, work 40 (44, 48) more sc evenly spaced across to 2nd marker, work 59 (67, 75) sc evenly spaced across to 3rd marker, work 41 (45, 49) sc evenly spaced across to 4th marker—141 (157, 173) sts; ch 1, turn. Remove markers from lower edge of waistband.

ROW 2: Sc in first st; *hdc in next st, sl st in next st; repeat from * across to last 2 sts; hdc in next st, sc in last st; ch 1, turn. Do not fasten off.

SKIRT

ROW 1 (RIGHT SIDE): Sc in first st and in each st across; ch 1, turn.

ROW 2: Work 2 sc in first st, sc in next st and in each st across to last st, 2 sc in last st—143 (159, 175) sc; ch 1, turn.

ROW 3: Sc in first 2 sts, FPdc around each of next 3 sts; *sc in next st, FPdc around each of next 3 sts; repeat from * across to last 2 sts; sc in last 2 sts—35 (39, 43) groups of 3 FPdc and 38 (42, 46) sc; ch 1, turn.

ROW 4: Sc in first st; *ch 3, sk next st**; sc in next 3 FP sts; repeat from * across, ending last repeat at **; sc in last st—36 (40, 44) ch-3 sps and 107 (119, 131) sc; ch 1, turn.

ROW 5: Sc in first st; * work (dc, ch 2, dc) into sc one row below encasing ch-3 in dc sts**; work small cable in next 3 FPdc; repeat from * across, ending last repeat at **; sc in last st—35 (39, 43) small cables, 36 (40, 44) groups of (dc, ch 2, dc), and 2 sc; ch 1, turn.

ROW 6: Sc in first st; *ch 3, sk next dc, sk next ch-2 sp, sk next dc**; sc in next 3 FP sts; repeat from * across, ending last repeat at **; sc in last st—36 (40, 44) ch-3 sps and 107 (119, 131) sc; ch 1, turn.

ROW 7: Sc in first st; work (dc, ch 2, dc) into next ch-2 sp one row below encasing ch-3 in dc sts** work small cable in next small cable; repeat from * across, ending last repeat at **; sc in last st—35 (39, 43) small cables, 36 (40, 44) groups of (dc, ch 2, dc), and 2 sc; ch 1, turn.

Repeat Rows 6 and 7 until Skirt measures approximately 9 (9½, 10)" (23 [24, 25.5]cm) from beginning of skirt, ending by working a wrong-side row. Do not fasten off.

Fan Edging
NEXT ROW (RIGHT SIDE): Sc in first st; *[(dc, ch 2) 3 times, dc] in next ch-3 sp**; small cable in next small cable; repeat from * across, ending last repeat at **; sc in last st. Fasten off; weave in ends.

SLEEVES

Starting at top, ch 60 (64, 68).

ROW 1 (RIGHT SIDE): Sc in 2nd ch from hook and in each remaining ch across—59 (63, 67) sc; ch 1, turn.

ROW 2: Sc in first st and in each st across; ch 1, turn.

ROW 3: Sc in first 2 sc, FPdc around each of next 3 sc; *sc in next sc, FPdc around each of next 3 sc; repeat from * across to last 2 sc; sc in last 2 sc—14 (15, 16) groups of 3 FPdc and 17 (18, 19) sc; ch 1, turn.

ROW 4: Repeat Row 2.

ROW 5: Sc in first 2 sc, small cable in next 3 FPdc; *sc in next sc, small cable in next 3 FPdc; repeat from * across to last 2 sc; sc in last 2 sc—14 (15, 16) small cables and 17 (18, 19) sc; ch 1, turn.

ROW 6: Repeat Row 2.

ROW 7: Sc in first 2 sc, small cable in next small cable; *sc in next sc, small cable in next small cable; repeat from * across to last 2 sc; sc in last 2 sc; ch 1, turn.

Repeat Rows 6 and 7 until sleeve measures approximately 4" (10cm) from beginning, ending by working a right-side row. Do not fasten off.

SHAPE SLEEVE
ROW 1 (WRONG SIDE): Sc in first st and in each st across; ch 1, turn.

ROW 2 (RIGHT SIDE): Work same as Row 7 of Sleeve.

ROW 3: Repeat Row 1.

ROW 4: Sc dec in first 2 sts, small cable in next small cable; *sc in next sc, small cable in next small cable; repeat from * across to last 2 sts; sc dec in last 2 sts—14 (15, 16) small cables and 15 (16, 17) sc; ch 1, turn.

ROW 5: Repeat Row 1—57 (61, 65) sts.

ROW 6: Sc in first st, small cable in next small cable; *sc in next sc, small cable in next small cable; repeat from * across to last st; sc in last st; ch 1, turn.

ROW 7: Repeat Row 1.

ROW 8: Sc dec in first 2 sts, sc in next 3 sts, small cable in next small cable; *sc in next sc, small cable in next small cable; repeat from * across to last 5 sts; sc in next 3 sts, sc dec in last 2 sts—12 (13, 14) small cables and 19 (20, 21) sc; ch 1, turn.

ROW 9: Repeat Row 1—55 (59, 63) sts.

ROW 10: Sc in first 4 sts, small cable in next small cable; *sc in next sc, small cable in next small cable; repeat from * across to last 4 sts; sc in last 4 sts; ch 1, turn.

ROW 11: Repeat Row 1.

ROW 12: Sc dec in first 2 sts, sc in next 2 sts, small cable in next small cable; *sc in next sc, small cable in next small cable; repeat from * across to last 4 sts; sc in next 2 sts, sc dec in last 2 sts—12 (13, 14) small cables and 17 (18, 19) sc; ch 1, turn.

ROW 13: Repeat Row 1—53 (57, 61) sts.

ROW 14: Sc in first 3 sts, small cable in next small cable; *sc in next sc, small cable in next small cable; repeat from * across to last 3 sts; sc in last 3 sts; ch 1, turn.

ROW 15: Repeat Row 1.

ROW 16: Sc dec in first 2 sts, sc in next st, small cable in next small cable; *sc in next sc, small cable in next small cable; repeat from * across to last 3 sts; sc in next st, sc dec in last 2 sts—12 (13, 14) small cables and 15 (16, 17) sc; ch 1, turn.

ROW 17: Repeat Row 1—51 (55, 59) sts.

ROW 18: Sc in first 2 sts, small cable in next small cable; *sc in next sc, small cable in next small cable; repeat from * across to last 2 sts; sc in last 2 sts; ch 1, turn.

ROWS 19–34: Repeat Rows 3–18—12 (13, 14) small cables and 13 (14, 15) sc at end of Row 20; 10 (11, 12) small cables and 17 (18, 19) sc at end of Row 24; 10 (11, 12) small cables and 15 (16, 17) sc at end of Row 28; 10 (11, 12) small cables and 13 (14, 15) sc at end of Row 32.

Repeat Rows 17 and 18 until pieces measures approximately 12 (12, 13)" (30.5 [30.5, 33]cm) from beginning, ending by working a right-side row. Do not fasten off.

Lace Cuff

ROW 1 (WRONG SIDE): Sc in first st; *ch 3, sk next st**; sc in next 3 FP sts; repeat from * across, ending last repeat at **; sc in last st—11 (12, 13) ch-3 sps and 32 (35, 38) sc; ch 1, turn.

ROW 2 (RIGHT SIDE): Sc in first st; (dc, ch 2, dc) into sc one row below encasing ch-3 in dc sts**; small cable in next 3 FPdc; repeat from * across, ending last repeat at **; sc in last st—10 (11, 12) small cables, 11 (12, 13) groups of (dc, ch 2, dc), and 2 sc; ch 1, turn.

ROW 3: Sc in first st; *ch 3, sk next dc, sk next ch-2 sp, sk next dc**; sc in next 3 FP sts; repeat from * across, ending last repeat at **; sc in last st—11 (12, 13) ch-3 sps and 32 (35, 38) sc; ch 1, turn.

ROW 4: Sc in first st; (dc, ch 2, dc) into next ch-2 sp one row below encasing ch-3 in dc sts**; small cable in next small cable; repeat from * across, ending last repeat at **; sc in last st—10 (11, 12) small cables, 11 (12, 13) groups of (dc, ch 2, dc), and 2 sc; ch 1, turn

Repeat Rows 3 and 4 until sleeve measures approximately 21½ (22, 22½)" (54.5 [56, 57]cm) from beginning, ending by working a wrong-side row. Do not fasten off.

Fan Edging

NEXT ROW (RIGHT SIDE): Sc in first st; *[(dc, ch 2) 3 times, dc] in next ch-2 sp**; small cable in next small cable; repeat from * across, ending last repeat at **; sc in last st. Fasten off; weave in ends.

FINISHING

BODY EDGING

ROW 1: With right side of work facing you, join yarn with sc in lower right front corner of skirt, work 41 (43, 45) more sc evenly spaced up lower right front edge to point of outside buttonhole flap, work 3 sc in point, work 58 (60, 64) sc evenly spaced up upper right front edge to shoulder seam, work 23 (25, 27) sc evenly spaced across back neck, work 58 (60, 64) sc evenly spaced down lower left front edge to point of inside buttonhole flap, work 3 sc in point, work 42 (44, 46) sc evenly spaced down lower left front edge—229 (239, 253) sc; ch 1, turn.

ROW 2: Sc in first st; *hdc in next st, sl st in next st; repeat from * around sweater edge to last 2 sts; hdc in next st, sc in last st; ch 1, turn.

ROW 3: Sc in first 43 (45, 47) sts, 3 sc in next st (point of Outside Buttonhole Flap), sc in next 141 (147, 157) sts, 3 sc in next st (point of inside buttonhole flap), sc in last 43 (45, 47) sts—233 (243, 257) sc; ch 1, turn.

ROW 4: Repeat Row 2. At end of row, do not ch 1. Fasten off; weave in ends.

Because cables may tend to distort the fabric, lightly block each piece before assembling the garment.

Sew shoulder seams first, then sew sleeves into armholes. Sew sleeve seams and side seams above waistband. Try on garment and mark button placement; adjusting to suit individual fit at waist. Sew first button centered on waistband on inside of sweater at right side seam. Sew second button centered on waistband on outside of sweater at left side seam.

ENTRELAC CROCHET

with

Joyce Wyatt

Joyce Wyatt was nine years old when her mother taught her to crochet and knit, but Joyce preferred sewing, so her crochet hook was put away until she married and had children. Then one of her daughters wanted a Christmas sweater, and after looking for the ideal sweater in the store, Joyce decided to design and make it herself. She's been working with yarn ever since.

Today she is inspired to design because of all of the wonderful yarns available, from acrylics to wool, including fur, ribbon, and eyelash. She likes to see how a yarn feels or how it drapes when using a smaller or larger hook. She especially enjoys converting knit designs into crochet. She will study a knit technique, schematic drawing, and/or instruction and say to herself, "Can I crochet that?" One of her most challenging designs was a top-down-set-in sleeve knitted sweater converted to crochet.

She has designed for yarn companies, and many of her most exciting designs have appeared in crochet magazines and in published compilations of designs by many designers. A certified Craft Yarn Council of America knitting/crochet instructor, Joyce has taught for the Crochet Guild of America, the Knitting Guild Association, the National Needlearts Association, Stitches Expos, and West Coast knitting/crochet guilds. Joyce has also taught for JoAnn's Fabric Stores and The L.A. Stitchers in Southern California. The classes she enjoys the most are on entrelac crochet and entrelac knitting.

Joyce's striking designs bring out the best in the yarns she chooses. Clockwise from left: a sleek crocheted dress, an entrelac hat, a monochromatic entrelac cardigan.

HOW TO WORK **ENTRELAC** CROCHET

Entrelac is a fool-the-eye technique whose name is derived from the French word *entrelacer,* meaning "interlaced" or "interwoven." The technique produces a fabric with the look of basket weave or interwoven strips. Entrelac crochet really does look as though individual strips had been created and then woven into a pattern. But actually entrelac is created in one piece.

The technique is a great stash buster because you can use one color or as many colors as you like. Self-striping yarns also work very well for this technique. No matter which yarns you use, the results are amazing.

Usually thought of as a knitting technique, crocheters can achieve the entrelac look by using single crochet stitches. You can start out by making a sampler using some worsted-weight yarn, a size L-11 (8mm) crochet hook, and two stitch markers, or you can make our Entrelac Scarf. By the time you have finished making the scarf, you have mastered the technique.

Entrelac crochet is made with triangles and squares that are repeated across the width of the project to make rows. Row 1 is formed only with triangles in Step 1; Row 2 is formed with triangles and squares in Steps 2, 3, and 4; Row 3 is made up of squares in Step 5, Row 4 is triangles and squares again, and Row 5 is triangles in Step 6. These five rows create the pattern.

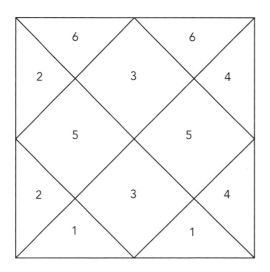

To create the interlaced effect, stitches are worked both in stitches and in sides of rows.

To practice entrelac crochet, work the pattern for the crochet scarf on page 58. Once you have made the scarf, you will be able to work entrelac crochet.

SINGLE CROCHET **ENTRELAC SCARF**

Designed by Joyce Wyatt

Scarves are the perfect projects for trying out new and/or unusual stitch patterns, shaping techniques, and color combinations. I designed this pattern so that anyone can learn to do entrelac crochet.

When taken in easy steps—as in the instructions for this dramatic scarf—learning to create entrelac's woven texture becomes easy and fun to do. Once learned, the basic concepts can be used to create many more elaborate pieces.

SKILL LEVEL

■■■▢ Intermediate

SIZE
Approximately 8½" x 60" (21.5cm x 152.5cm) (excluding corkscrew edging)

MATERIALS
- Red Heart® *Eco-Ways™ Bamboo Wool™* (55% viscose from bamboo, 45% wool, each approximately 1¾ oz [50g] and 87 yd [80m],  medium/worsted weight)
- 522 yd (480m) / 6 skeins in color 3775 Lipstick
- One size L-11 (8mm) crochet hook, or size needed to obtain gauge
- Stitch markers

GAUGE
9 sc = 3¼" (8.5cm)
9 sc rows = 3" (7.5cm)
2 base triangles = 8" (20.5cm) wide

STITCH GUIDE

SC DEC: Insert hook in first specified st and draw up a lp, insert hook in 2nd specified st, yo and draw through st and 2 lps on hook—sc dec made.

SC-HDC DEC: Insert hook in first specified st and draw up a lp, yo, insert hook in 2nd specified st and draw up a lp, yo and draw through all 4 lps on hook—sc-hdc dec made.

STEP 1

FIRST BASE TRIANGLE
Ch 2.

ROW 1 (RIGHT SIDE): Sc in 2nd ch from hook—1 st; ch 2, turn.

ROW 2: Work hdc and sc in sc—2 sts; ch 1, turn.

ROW 3: Sc in first 2 sts, sc in 2nd ch of turning ch-2—3 sts; ch 2, turn.

ROW 4: Work hdc and sc in first st, sc in next 2 sts—4 sts; ch 1, turn.

ROW 5: Sc in first 4 sts, sc in 2nd ch of turning ch-2—5 sts; ch 2, turn.

ROW 6: Work hdc and sc in first st, sc in next 4 sts—6 sts; ch 1, turn.

ROW 7: Sc in first 6 sts, sc in 2nd ch of turning ch-2—7 sts; ch 2, turn.

ROW 8: Work hdc and sc in first st, sc in next 6 sts—8 sts; ch 1, turn.

ROW 9: Sc in first 8 sts, sc in 2nd ch of turning ch-2—9 sts; ch 1 loosely. Do not turn. Place stitch marker on right side of first base triangle to indicate right side of work.

SECOND BASE TRIANGLE
ROW 1 (RIGHT SIDE): Sc loosely in left edge of last sc worked on Row 9 of first base triangle—1 st; ch 2, turn.

ROWS 2–8: Work same as Rows 2–8 on first base triangle.

ROW 9: Work as for Row 9 on first base triangle until there are 9 sts, do not turn, but rotate work to work ch 1, sc in left edge of last sc (10 sc). Place marker on right side of 2nd base triangle to indicate right side of work. Ch 1, turn to wrong side.

STEP 2

FIRST EDGE TRIANGLE
ROW 1 (WRONG SIDE): Work sc dec in next sc and sl st on 2nd base triangle—1 st, not counting sl st; turn.

ROW 2: [To yield 2 sts] Sk sl st, work sc and hdc in st—2 sts; ch 1, turn.

ROW 3: [To yield 3 sts] Work 2 sc in first st, work sc dec in next sc and next sc on 2nd base triangle, sl st in next st on same triangle—3 sts; turn.

ROW 4: Sk sl st, sc in next 2 sts, sc and hdc in last st—4 sts; ch 1, turn.

ROW 5: Work 2 sc in first st, sc in next 2 sts, sc, dec in next st and in next st on 2nd base triangle, sl st in next st on same triangle—5 sc; turn.

ROW 6: Sk sl st, sc in next 4 sts, sc and hdc in last st—6 sts; ch 1, turn.

ROW 7: Work 2 sc in first st, sc in next 4 sts, sc dec in next st and in next sc on 2nd base triangle, sl st in next st on same triangle—7 sts; turn.

ROW 8: Sk sl st, sc in next 6 sts, sc and hdc in last st—8 sts; ch 1, turn.

ROW 9: Work 2 sc in first st, sc in next 6 sts, sc dec in next st and in last st on 2nd base triangle—9 sts; ch 1, loosely. Do not turn.

STEP 3

SQUARE
ROW 1 (WRONG SIDE): Sc in edge of first 8 rows on 2nd base triangle, sc dec in edge of last row on 2nd base triangle and in first st on first base triangle, sl st loosely in next st on first base triangle—9 sc; turn.

ROW 2: Sk sl st, sc in next 9 sts; ch 1, turn.

ROW 3: Sc in first 8 sts, sc dec in next st and in next sc on first base triangle, sl st in next st on same triangle—9 sc; turn.

ROWS 4–8: Repeat Rows 2 and 3 twice more, then repeat Row 2 once more.

ROW 9: Sc in first 8 sts, sc dec in next st and in last sc on first base triangle, ch 1 loosely. Do not turn.

STEP 4

SECOND EDGE TRIANGLE

ROW 1 (WRONG SIDE): Sc in edge of each row on first base triangle—9 sc; ch 1, turn.

ROW 2: Sk first st, sc in next 8 sts—8 sc; ch 1, turn.

ROW 3: Sc in first 6 sts, sk next st, hdc in last st—7 sts; ch 1, turn.

ROW 4: Sk first st, sc in next 6 sts—6 sc; ch 1, turn.

ROW 5: Sc in first 4 sts, sk next st, hdc in last st—5 sts; ch 1, turn.

ROW 6: Sk first st, sc in next 4 sts—4 sc; ch 1, turn.

ROW 7: Sc in first 2 sts, sk next st, hdc in last st—3 sts; ch 1, turn.

ROW 8: Sk first st, sc in next 2 sts—2 sc; ch 1, turn.

ROW 9: Sk first st, hdc in rem st—1 st; ch 1, turn.

STEP 5 (Squares)

FIRST SQUARE

ROW 1 (RIGHT SIDE): Sc in edge of first 8 rows on 2nd edge triangle, sc dec in edge of last row and in first sc on square in Step 3, sl st in next st on same square—9 sc; turn.

ROW 2: Sk sl st, sc in next 9 sts; ch 1, turn.

ROW 3: Sc in first 8 sts, sc dec in next st and in next sc on square in Step 3, sl st in next st on same square—9 sc; turn.

ROWS 4–8: Repeat Rows 2 and 3 twice more, then repeat Row 2 once more.

ROW 9: Sc in first 8 sts, sc dec in next st and in last st on square in Step 3, ch 1 loosely. Do not turn.

SECOND SQUARE

ROW 1 (RIGHT SIDE): Sc in edge of first 8 rows on square on Step 3, sc dec in edge of last row and in first sc on first edge triangle, sl st in next st on same triangle—9 sc; turn.

ROW 2: Sk sl st, sc in next 9 sts; ch 1, turn.

ROW 3: Sc in first 8 sts, sc dec in next st and in next st on first edge triangle, sl st in next st on same triangle— 9 sc; turn.

ROWS 4–8: Repeat Rows 2 and 3 twice more, then repeat Row 2 once more.

ROW 9: Sc in each st, sc in last st on first edge triangle— 10 sc; ch 1 loosely, turn.

Repeat Steps 2–5, working into appropriate square or triangle below, until scarf measures approximately 60" (152.5cm) long, or to desired length, ending by working Step 4.

STEP 6 (Ending Triangles)

FIRST ENDING TRIANGLE

ROW 1 (RIGHT SIDE): Sc in edge of first 8 rows on 2nd edge triangle, sc dec in edge of last row and in first st on square in Step 3, sl st in next st on same square—9 sc; turn.

ROW 2: Sk sl st, sc in next 7 sts, sk next st, hdc in last st— 8 sts; ch 1, turn.

ROW 3: Sk first st, sc in next 6 sts, sc, sc dec in next st and in next st on square in Step 3, sl st in next st on same square—7 sc; turn.

ROW 4: Sk sl st, sc in next 5 sts, sk next st, hdc in last st— 6 sts; ch 1, turn.

ROW 5: Sk first st, sc in next 4 sts, sc dec in next st and in next st on square in Step 3, sl st in next st on same square—5 sc; turn.

ROW 6: Sk sl st, sc in next 3 scs, sk next st, hdc in last st— 4 sts; ch 1, turn.

ROW 7: Sk first st, sc in next 2 sts, sc dec in next st and in next st on square in Step 3, sl st in next st on same square—3 sc; turn.

ROW 8: Sk sl st, sc in next st, sk next st, hdc in last st—2 sts; ch 1, turn.

ROW 9: Sk first st, sc dec in next st and in next st on square in Step 3—1 st; ch 1. Do not turn.

SECOND ENDING TRIANGLE

ROW 1 (RIGHT SIDE): Sc in edge of first 8 rows on square in Step 3, sc dec in edge of last row and in first st on first edge triangle, sl st in next st on same triangle—9 sc; turn.

ROWS 2–8: Work same as Rows 2–8 on first ending triangle, working 2nd half of sc dec and last sl st in first edge triangle.

ROW 9: Sk first st, sc-hdc dc in last st and in last st on first edge triangle—1 st. Do not fasten off.

CORKSCREW EDGING

*Ch 10, working in only 1 lp of chs, work 3 dc in 4th ch from hook, 3 dc in each of next 6 chs, ending triangle, sl st in edge of next row; repeat from * 6 more times—7 corkscrews with 21 dc each. Fasten off; weave in ends.

Working in edge of Base Triangles along opposite end of scarf, join yarn with a sl st in edge of first row on base triangle. Work corkscrew edging same as other end of scarf.

FASHION CROCHET

with
Margaret Hubert

"I have always loved to create very fashionable, up-to-date garments using the most simple of crochet techniques."

—MARGARET HUBERT

Margaret Hubert's son explains his mother's career by calling her "an overnight success after 40 years." Margaret began her career in the early 1960s—she owned her own yarn shop for twelve years, and she hasn't stopped since.

In addition to owning her own shop, Margaret and a partner owned a hand-knitting business, Mme DeFarge Handknits. Their garments were sold successfully in major department stores and boutiques from coast to coast and in many other countries. Unfortunately, along with success came the inevitable copies that sometimes sold in the same stores; Margaret's in the designer departments and the copies in the less expensive areas.

Margaret's career then moved to Bloomingdale's in White Plains, New York, where she was the needlework instructor. The yarn rep from a major yarn company noticed some things she had made using their yarns, and he encouraged her to design for them. In addition, he arranged for Margaret to meet with several magazine editors in New York, who bought her designs.

It was also while working in Bloomingdale's in the 1980s that Margaret met the craft editor at Van Nostrand Reinhold. Margaret eventually wrote four books for Van Nostrand, including *Weekend Knitting Projects*, *Weekend Crochet Projects*, *More Weekend Crochet Projects*, and *One-Piece Knits That Fit*. Although all of these books are no longer in print, Margaret still gets fan mail from knitters and crocheters who own copies of these books.

Eventually Margaret decided to retire from the yarn business, but she still enjoyed playing with yarn and stitches. She still taught classes locally and submitted designs to magazines, but most of her time was spent enjoying life, spending winters in Florida, coupled with a little traveling and golfing. Just when she thought her life was perfect, Margaret's husband died, and her life changed forever.

That Christmas her oldest son gave her a computer. She had no desire to own a computer, and she didn't want to learn to use it. Her son, however was determined that she learn, and a new life opened for Margaret. She soon found online lists, made friends all over the country, and was invited to teach. Her son helped her set up her own website (www.margarethubertoriginals.com) and a blog (www.margaret shooksandneedles.blogspot.com). Creative Publishing International, her current publisher, in fact, found her through her website, and offered her a book deal. Within the next three years, she had produced ten books, including *Knit or Crochet*, *Have It Your Way*, *Knits for Men*, *Plus Size Crochet*, *Hooked Hats*, and *Hooked Bags*. In-between books she has had designs published in many magazines.

Margaret is constantly called upon to teach, and she has traveled more in the past five years than during her entire life, attending fiber conferences and teaching in Australia and England as well in the United States from California to New York.

Finishing touches can make the difference between just a sweater and a true fashion garment. At left, Margaret chose to add black and gold spangles to a basic cardigan. At center and right, applied flowers and leaves turn a simple garment into a fashion statement.

HOW TO BE A MASTER OF FASHION CROCHET

Crochet fashion design has come a long way since the granny square skirts and ponchos of the 1970s. Today, top ready-to-wear fashion designers feature crochet garments and accessories in many of their runway presentations. Crochet has finally become recognized as something more than a technique to create afghans and doilies.

Not everyone who loves fashion might want to become a crochet fashion designer. While it may be easy to learn to crochet an afghan, it is not easy to become a fashion designer. Many schools and colleges offer involved courses in fashion designing, if that is a career choice. If, however, you love fashion and you long to try your hand at designing, here are some hints that might help you.

Becoming a fashion designer is not an easy process. Obviously, you need to have a love of fashion and be very skillful in the techniques of crochet. Then you need to think about why you want to be a designer: Do you want to design for yourself and your family and friends, or do you want to design for publication? And what do you want to design? Crochet fashion design is not exclusively for women's fashions. If you love to design for babies and children, that can become your specialty. And there is a need for good crochet design for men, too.

Fashion by its very nature comes and goes—and often very quickly. You need to spend time studying magazines in your chosen fashion area, watch videos of designer shows, see what TV stars are wearing on their shows (not what they wear on their evenings out when they are looking to attract the attention of the paparazzi), spend time wandering through retail stores to see what's new—and also take a good look at what is on the sale racks. That's a pretty good indication that a trend has run its course.

You also need to learn what fashion trends are really going to translate well into crochet. Crochet fabric is quite different than the woven fabrics used in ready-to-wear. You need to learn about all types of yarns that are available to the crocheter—from fuzzy eyelash to flat ribbons to metallics to bulky textured yarns to fine yarns. Buy a ball of a variety of yarns and spend a lot of time crocheting swatches. Learn to let the yarn tell you what it wants to become.

Although there are hundreds of beautiful crochet stitch patterns, not all of them are suitable to all types of yarn. Elaborate stitches cry out for a smooth, simple yarn. The fancier the yarn, the simpler the stitch needed to show it off.

Every fashion designer has to understand garment construction. You've probably been wearing a variety of clothing styles since you were a child, but have you studied how the garments in your wardrobe are actually made? If you've sewn a few garments, you probably already understand the basics. If not, head for the nearest fabric store and browse the pattern catalogs. Buy a few of the multi-size patterns. Take them home, open them, and iron the pieces flat. Study the included instruction sheets that show how the pieces are put together, and take note of where changes are made to adjust for different body sizes. You'll notice that as sizes get bigger, certain parts stay pretty much the same—for example, shoulder width and the back of the neck. The multi-size patterns are a textbook for designers to learn how to size a pattern. Pattern sizing just can't be done on a percentage basis.

Some really good help with sizing can be found on the Craft Yarn Council of America's website. This organization of yarn manufacturers, hook and needle makers, and publishers has created a section of suggested industry standards that are essential tools for the new designer. To access the site, go to www.yarnstandards.com.

The designer also needs to recognize that people come in all sizes and shapes, and that not every design is suitable for every body type.

What can be boring and tedious—but essential—is the writing out of instructions for making the designs you have created. Unless you are making one for a family member and don't need to provide anyone else with a pattern, you have to learn how to write instructions clearly and accurately. This includes a lot of math. You don't need to be a math expert, but you do need to keep a calculator handy and work out all the details required in making the garment.

The really exciting part of crochet fashion design is that it is in constant motion—what was in last week may be old news tomorrow. As Heidi Klum says on *Project Runway*, "In fashion, one day you're in, and the next day, you're out." This creates a challenge for designers to keep learning and experimenting.

At right, elaborate lace, based on a vintage design and applied to a wedding ensemble, creates a garment that combines contemporary lines with sweet nostalgia.

GLITTERING **GOLD**

Designed by Margaret Hubert

SKILL LEVEL

■■■□ Intermediate

SIZES
- S (M, L)
- Instructions are written for size S. Changes for sizes M and L are in parentheses. If only one number appears, it applies to all sizes.
- Finished bust 33 (37, 41)" (84 [94, 104]cm)

MATERIALS
- Lion Brand® *Vanna's Glamour* (96% acrylic, 4% metallic polyester, each approximately 1¾ oz [50g] and 202 yd [185m], ❷ fine/sport weight)
  - 1010 (1010, 1212) yd (925 [925, 1110]m) / 5 (5, 6) skeins in color 170 Topaz
- One size H-8 (5mm) crochet hook, or size needed to obtain gauge
- One size G-6 (4mm) crochet hook

GAUGE
12½ shells = 8" (20.5cm) using larger hook

I love to take high-fashion looks and translate them into something the average crocheter can make and wear in real life, and this garment is an example of my idea.

I wanted this garment to have an evening look, and to be simple but elegant. The bare shoulder look steps off the runway to create an easy-to-wear top with one graceful mesh sleeve.

In designing this top, I let the yarn itself do a lot to dictate the design. The slightly elastic quality of the yarn, imbued with gold flecks, lent itself to the fitted bodice and to the drape of the loosely flowing sleeve. I wanted the project to be easy to make and yet to look fantastic.

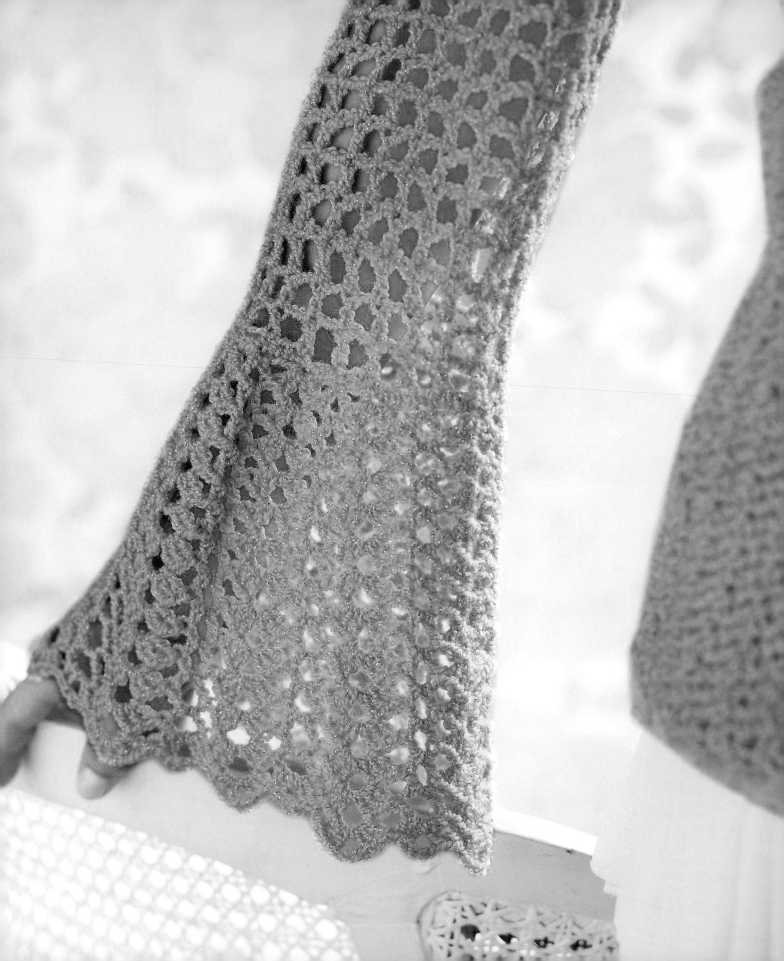

STITCH GUIDE

SHELL: Work (sc, ch 2, sc) in specified ch or sp.

BACK

With larger hook, ch 81 (90, 99).

FOUNDATION ROW: Sk 2 chs; *work shell in next ch, sk 2 chs, repeat from * across, ending last repeat with sk 2 chs, hdc in last ch—26 (29, 32) shells; ch 2 (counts as a hdc), turn.

ROW 1: *Work shell in ch-2 sp of next shell; repeat from * across, ending last repeat with hdc top of first 2 skipped chs; ch 2, turn.

ROW 2: *Work shell in ch-2 sp of next shell; repeat from * across, ending last repeat with hdc in top of beg ch-2; ch 2, turn.

ROW 3: *Work shell in ch-2 sp of next shell; repeat from * across, ending last repeat with hdc in hdc; ch 2, turn.

Repeat Rows 2 and 3 until piece measures 5 (5, 5½)" (12.5 [12.5, 14]cm) from beginning chain.

Change to the smaller hook and continue in the pattern as established for 2" (5cm) more to shape waistline; then change to larger hook and work in pattern as established until piece measures 14½ (15, 15½)" (37 [38, 39.5]cm) from beginning chain.

SHAPE ARMHOLE AND NECK

NOTE: Mark beginning of next row for armhole edge.

ROW 1: Sl st in hdc; *sl st in first sc of next shell, sl st in ch-2 sp and in next sc of same shell; repeat from * 3 times more; work even in pattern until 4 shells remain; ch 2, turn, leaving remaining 4 shells unworked—18 (21, 24) shells remain.

ROW 2: Sc in ch 2 sp of first shell; continue in pattern across row, ch 2, turn.

ROW 3: Work in pattern across to last sc, sk last sc, hdc in top of turning ch. You have decreased one shell at neck edge.

Repeat Rows 2 and 3 until 4 (4, 5) shells remain. Work even in pattern until armhole measures 7½ (8, 8½)" (19 [20.5, 21.5]cm). Fasten off.

FRONT

Work as for Back to shape armhole. At armhole, mark end of next row for armhole edge. Complete as for Back, working decreases at marked edge.

SLEEVE

With larger hook, ch 67 (70, 73).

ROW 1 (RIGHT SIDE): Dc in 7th ch from hook; *ch 2, sk 2 chs, dc in next ch; repeat from * across—21 (22, 23) ch-2 sps; ch 5 (counts as a dc and ch-2 sp), turn.

ROW 2: Sk first dc, dc in next dc; *ch 2, dc in next dc; repeat from * across, ending last repeat with dc in 3rd ch of ch-5; ch 5, turn.

Repeat Row 2 until piece measures 9" (23cm) from beginning chain. Turn work, but do not work turning ch.

SHAPE CAP

NEXT ROW: (Sl st in next dc, 2 sl st in ch-2 sp) 3 times, ch 5, work in pattern as established until 3 ch-2 sps remain at end of row; ch 5, turn, leaving remaining ch-2 sps unworked—15 (16, 17) ch 2 sps remain.

Continue in pattern until piece measures 6½ (7, 7½)" (16.5 [17.5, 19]cm) from beginning of sleeve cap shaping. At end of last row, turn, but do not work turning ch.

DECREASE ROW: Sk first dc, work 2 sl sts in ch-2 sp, sl st in next dc; ch 5, dc in next dc; continue in pattern across, leaving the last block unworked. Fasten off.

Sleeve Bell Bottom

Fold sleeve in half vertically with right sides facing. Sew seam from top to bottom, carefully matching stitches. Turn sleeve right side out and hold piece with starting chain at top. You will now work in rounds. Instructions are the same for all sizes.

RND 1: With smaller hook, join yarn with sl st in seam; ch 1, sc in sl st and work 69 more sc evenly spaced around, working in both ch–2 sps and in dc sts; join with a sl st in first sc.

RND 2: Ch 3; *sk 2 sc, work (2 dc, ch 2, 2 dc) in next sc, sk 2 sc, work (dc, ch 2, dc) in next sc; repeat from * around, ending last repeat with dc in same sc as beg ch–3, ch 2, join in top of beg ch—12 (2 dc, ch 2, 2 dc) groups and 12 (dc, ch 2, dc) groups.

RND 3: Change to larger hook; ch 3; *work (2 dc ch 2, 2 dc) in next ch–2 sp, work (dc, ch 2, dc) in next ch–2 sp; repeat from * around, ending last repeat with dc in ch 2–sp, ch 2, join with a sl st in top of beg ch–3.

RNDS 4–7: Repeat Rnd 2.

RNDS 8–11: Ch 3; *work (3 dc, ch 2, 3 dc) in next ch–2 sp, work (dc, ch 2, dc] in next ch–2 sp; repeat from * around, ending last repeat with dc in last ch 2–sp, ch 2, join with a sl st in top of beg ch–3.

RNDS 12–13: Ch 3, *work (3 dc, ch 3, 3 dc) in next ch–2 sp, work (dc, ch 3, dc) in next ch–2 sp; repeat from * around, ending dc in last ch–2 sp, ch 3, join with a sl st in top of beg ch–3.

RND 14: Ch 3, dc in same st as ch 3; *work (3 dc, ch 3, 3 dc) in next ch–3 sp, work (2 dc, ch 3, 2 dc) in next ch–3 sp; repeat from * around, ending 2 dc in last ch–3 sp, ch 3, join with a sl st in top of beg ch–3; fasten off.

FINISHING

Hold Front and Back with right sides together, and sew shoulder seam, carefully matching stitches. With right sides together, sew side seams.

Mark center of sleeve cap; with right sides together, pin Sleeve into armhole, placing center of sleeve cap at shoulder seam and sleeve seam at side seam. Ease sleeve cap into armhole and sew in place.

Neck Edging
Hold garment with neckline at top and with right side of work facing you. With smaller hook, join yarn with a sl st at underarm seam, ch 1, sc in joining, ch 3, sk next st; *sc in next st, ch 3, sk next st; repeat from * around entire neckline, join with a sl st in first sc. Fasten off.

Bottom Edging
Hold garment with bottom edge at top and right side of work facing you. With smaller hook, join yarn with a sl st at either side seam; ch 1, sc in joining; ch 3, sk next st; *sc in next st, ch 3, sk next st; repeat from * around, join with a sl st in first sc. Fasten off; weave in all yarn ends.

Ties (make 2)
Using 2 strands of yarn and smaller hook, ch 150; fasten off, leaving about 3" (7.5cm) of yarn. Thread yarn ends into a tapestry needle and weave into the chain to make a neat end. Draw one tie through 6th shell in from side seam on front and on back, tie at shoulder.

TUNISIAN CROCHET

with

Julia Bryant

Born in Southampton, a seaport on the southern coast of England, Julia Bryant learned to knit when she was four; and although she explored many other crafts, including weaving, cross-stitch, and embroidery, she was primarily a knitter for many years. Somewhere along the way she did learn to crochet, but initially it wasn't her favorite craft.

She was always trying something new in crafts and in life, so she boarded a ship with the idea of traveling around the world for a few years. Instead, she found the life that she was looking for in Toronto, Canada, where she now makes her home. And she found something more: her love for Tunisian crochet.

The first Tunisian pattern Julia made, from *Woman's Day* magazine, was for an afghan in a stained-glass motif. Julia dove into her yarn stash and got started. Once she had completed the squares, she decided that the project was too beautiful to be used as a blanket. So she turned her first Tunisian crochet project into a poncho, which she still wears.

Once she had finished the project, Julia was absolutely fascinated by Tunisian crochet, but she wasn't sure how to continue. She couldn't find any other patterns using the color inlay technique of that first pattern, so she started, for the first time in her life, to design her own garments and afghans, and she hasn't stopped since! She constantly finds better ways to create new and exciting projects. Her inspiration comes from everything around her: books, art galleries, fabric stores, and her travels, including trips to Morocco.

Julia's work has been shown in several exhibitions in Canada. A member of both the Crochet Guild of America and the Knitting Guild of America, Julia has taught for both organizations at their annual conferences. In addition, Julia belongs

to both a knitting and crochet guild in Toronto, where she teaches whenever possible. Because she finds teaching so rewarding, Julia often has classes in her home studio.

An occupational therapist by profession, Julia works with her clients in their homes and encourages them to get involved in the crafts that she loves. Her job is a challenging one, and her crafts provide the needed balance in her life. Julia finds that the crafts are a therapeutic tool for her clients, providing new leisure skills and helping to improve self-esteem.

HOW TO DO **TUNISIAN** CROCHET

Sometimes called afghan stitch, Tunisian is a technique that begins with a foundation chain as in regular crochet. Each row consists of two steps: the first step picks up stitches across the chain or row, leaving them all on the hook at the same time. The second step of each row works off all the loops, leaving one last loop on the hook.

Unlike regular crochet, the loop on the hook does count as a stitch.

To accommodate the number of stitches, an afghan or a Tunisian hook is used. These are much longer than regular crochet hooks and have a knob on the end like a knitting needle to keep the stitches from sliding off.

FOUNDATION ROW:

Ch the number specified in the pattern.

STEP 1: Sk first ch from hook; *insert hook through top lp only of next ch. Yo and draw lp through, forming a new lp on hook. [**FIG 1**]

Repeat from * across the chain, keeping all lps on hook. [**FIG 2**]

Do not ch or turn at the end of the row.

STEP 2: Yo and draw through first lp on hook; *yo and draw through 2 lps. [**FIG 3**]

Repeat from * across. At end one lp will rem on hook and is the first st of the next row. Do not ch or turn work.

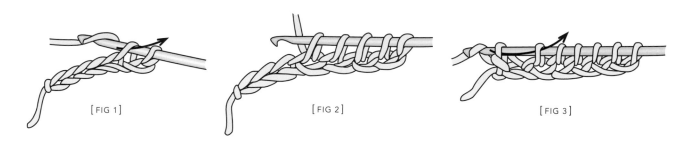

[FIG 1]   [FIG 2]   [FIG 3]

PATTERN ROW:

STEP 1: Insert hook in vertical bar of second st. [**FIG 4**]

Yo and draw through, adding a new lp on hook; *insert hook in vertical bar of next st and draw through, adding a new lp on hook; repeat from * across to last vertical bar. For a firmer side edge, on last bar insert hook through both vertical bar and thread behind it and work them together as one. [**FIG 5**]

STEP 2: Repeat Step 2 of Foundation Row. Repeat Steps 1 and 2 of Pattern Row until piece is desired length.

NOTE: Because the first lp on each row is not a full st, there will always be one more lp than the number of sts shown on the charts for each row.

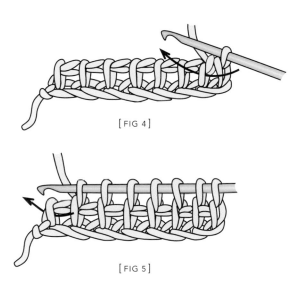

[FIG 4]

[FIG 5]

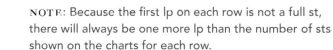

· · · · · · · TIP FROM THE MASTER · · · · · · ·

Count your stitches at the end of the first half of the row (left to right) before taking them off the hook, as it is very easy to lose one, especially when changing colors. Be sure to become very familiar with the basic Tunisian crochet before inlaying the colors and beads.

BEAD AND ROSES **COAT**

Designed by Julia Bryant

SKILL LEVEL
■■■□ Intermediate

SIZE
- Instructions are for a child's size 4.
- Finished chest 23" (58.5cm)
- Finished length 19" (48cm)
- Finished sleeve length 9" (23cm)

MATERIALS
- SandnesGarn *Lanett* (100% merino wool, each approximately 1¾ oz [50g] and 207 yd [190m], ①① super fine/sock weight)
  - 1449 yd (1330m) / 7 balls in color 1032 Gray
  - 207 yd (190m) / 1 ball in color 4119 Red
  - 207 yd (190m) / 1 ball in color 5846 Blue
  - 207 yd (190m) / 1 ball in color 7762 Dark Sage
- One size E-4 (3.5mm) afghan hook, or size needed to obtain gauge
- One size D-3 (3.25mm) crochet hook
- Yarn bobbins
- 413 size 4mm beads
- 6 buttons, ½" (13mm) wide
- Sewing needle and matching thread

GAUGE
30 sts and 26 rows = 4" (10cm)

CONTINUED ON PAGE 78

Little girls are just as interested in fashion as their mothers are. This simple coat, with its geometric floral borders and bold beaded stripes, is great fun to wear. I enjoy incorporating the flash and texture of beads in my work. These floral designs are actually worked into the piece, not embroidered on top.

I love making children's clothes, and I was especially pleased with the femininity of this garment. It's a great example of color and bead inlay.

CONTINUED FROM PAGE 76

BEADING INSTRUCTIONS
To add a bead, insert hook under next vertical bar, slide bead up behind hook, yo, draw yarn through bar, pushing bead through at same time (bead will sit on lp on hook). Work off lps in normal way.

SKIRT BACK

Thread 211 beads on gray yarn.

Beg at lower edge with afghan hook and gray, ch 121.

ROW 1: Insert hook in 2nd ch from hook and draw up a lp; *insert hook in next ch, draw up lp; repeat from * across—121 lps on hook; to work off lps, yo, draw through first lp on hook; ** yo, draw through 2 lps on hook; repeat from ** until 1 lp remains on hook. This last lp does not count as a st—120 sts.

ROWS 2–4: Sk first vertical bar; *insert hook under next vertical bar, draw up lp; repeat from * across; to work off lps, yo, draw through first lp on hook; ** yo, draw through 2 lps on hook; repeat from ** until 1 lp remains on hook.

ROW 5: Sk first vertical bar; (insert hook under next vertical bar, draw up lp) twice; *insert hook under next vertical bar, slide bead up, yo, draw lp through pushing bead through with yarn; (insert hook under next vertical bar, draw up lp) 3 times; repeat from * 28 times more; insert hook under next vertical bar, slide bead up, yo, draw lp through pushing bead through with yarn; (insert hook under next vertical bar, draw up lp) twice; to work off lps, yo, draw through 1 lp on hook; ** yo, draw through 2 lps on hook; repeat from ** until 1 lp rem on hook.

ROWS 6–7: Repeat Row 2.

NOTE: When changing colors on the following rows, do not carry second color over more than three stitches; use separate bobbins for each color as required.

ROW 8: Sk first vertical bar; insert hook under next vertical bar, draw up lp; *(insert hook under next vertical bar, with rose, draw up lp, insert hook under next vertical bar, with gray, draw up lp) 4 times; insert hook under next vertical bar, with gray, draw up lp, (insert hook under next vertical bar, with blue, draw up lp) twice; insert hook under next vertical bar, with gray, draw up lp, (insert hook under next vertical bar, with blue, draw up lp) twice; (insert hook under next vertical

Chart A
Skirt Back

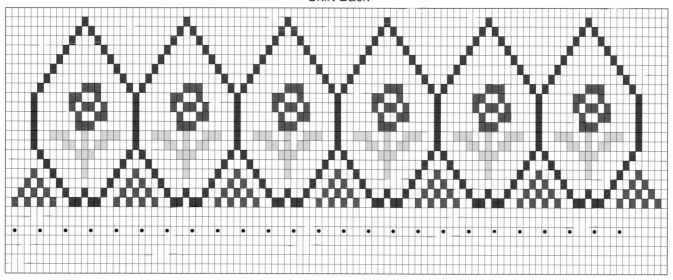

bar, with gray, draw up lp) twice; repeat from * 6 times more; (insert hook under next vertical bar, with rose, draw up lp, insert hook under next vertical bar, with gray, draw up lp) 4 times; work off lps, matching color to lp color.

ROWS 9–28: Continue to work according to Chart A above.

ROW 29: Sk first vertical bar; (insert hook under next vertical bar, draw up lp) 12 times; *insert hook under next vertical bar, yo, draw lp through, pushing 1 bead through with yarn, (insert hook under next vertical bar, draw up lp) 15 times; repeat from * 5 times more; insert hook under next vertical bar, yo, draw lp through, pushing 1 bead through with yarn, (insert hook under next vertical bar, draw up lp) 12 times; work off lps.

ROWS 30–31: Repeat Row 2.

ROWS 32–70: Repeat Rows 29–31 thirteen times.

ROWS 71–72: Repeat Rows 29 and 30.

ROW 73: Sk first vertical bar; *(insert hook under next vertical bar, draw up lp) twice; insert hook under next 2 vertical bars, draw up lp; repeat from * 14 times more; insert hook under next vertical bar, draw up lp, **insert hook under next 2 vertical bars, draw up lp, (insert hook under next vertical bar, draw up lp) twice; repeat from ** 14 times; work off lps—92 lps (91 sts). The last lp does not count as a st.

BACK YOKE

ROW 1: Sk first vertical bar; * insert hook under next vertical bar, draw up lp; repeat from * across; work off lps.

ROWS 2–8: Repeat Row 1.

ROW 9: Sk first vertical bar; (insert hook under next vertical bar, draw up lp) 3 times; *insert hook under next vertical bar, yo, draw lp through, pushing 1 bead through with yarn; (insert hook under next vertical bar, draw up lp) 3 times; repeat from * 21 times more; work off lps.

ROW 10: Repeat Row 1.

Chart B
Back Yoke

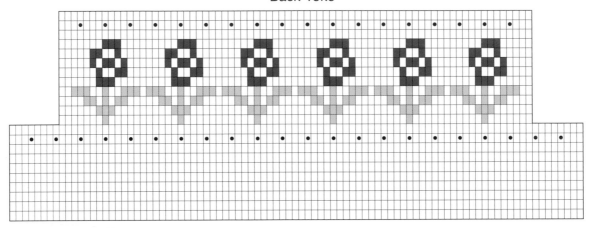

SHAPE ARMHOLES

ROW 11: Sk first vertical bar; (insert hook under next vertical bar, draw up lp, draw lp through lp on hook) 8 times; (insert hook under next vertical bar, draw up lp) 7 times; * insert hook under next vertical bar, with green, draw up lp, (insert hook under next vertical bar, with gray, draw up lp) 11 times; repeat from * 4 times more; insert hook under next vertical bar; with green draw up lp; (insert hook under next vertical bar, with gray, draw up lp) 7 times—76 lps (75 sts); leaving remaining bars unworked, work off lps. Note that the last lp does not count as a st.

ROWS 12–22: Work following Chart B above.

ROWS 23–46: Repeat Rows 11–22 of Chart B twice more.

ROWS 47–50: Repeat Row 1.

RIGHT BACK SHOULDER

ROW 51: Sk first vertical bar; (insert hook under next vertical bar, draw up lp) 19 times—20 lps (19 sts); leaving remaining bars unworked, work off lps.

ROW 52: Sk first vertical bar; bind off as follows: (insert hook under next vertical bar, draw up lp, draw lp through lp on hook) 19 times. Fasten off.

LEFT BACK SHOULDER

ROW 51: Sk next 36 vertical bars on Row 50; join gray in next vertical bar; (insert hook under next vertical bar, draw up lp) 19 times—20 lps; leaving remaining bars unworked, work off lps—19 sts.

ROW 52: Sk first vertical bar; bind off as follows: (insert hook under next vertical bar, draw up lp, draw lp through lp on hook) 19 times. Fasten off; weave in ends.

LEFT FRONT SKIRT

Thread 91 beads on gray yarn.

Beg at lower edge with afghan hook and gray, ch 57.

ROW 1: Insert hook in 2nd ch from hook, draw up lp; *insert hook in next ch, draw up lp; repeat from * across—57 lps on hook; to work off lps, yo, draw through 1 lp on hook; ** yo, draw through 2 lps on hook; repeat from ** until 1 lp remains on hook—56 sts.

ROW 2: Sk first vertical bar; *insert hook under next vertical bar, draw up lp; repeat from * across; work off lps.

ROWS 3–28: Work according to Chart C on page 81.

Chart C
Left Front Skirt

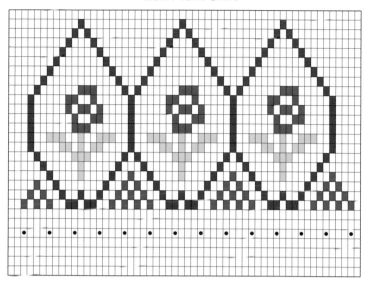

Chart D
Left Front Yoke

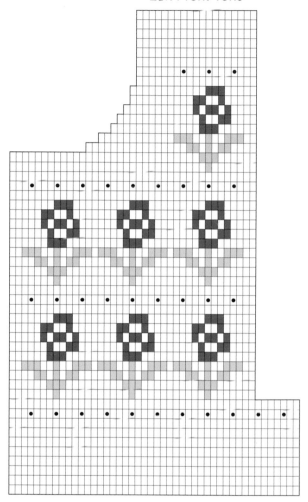

ROW 29: Sk first vertical bar; (insert hook under next vertical bar, draw up lp) 12 times; *insert hook under next vertical bar, slide bead up, yo, draw lp through pushing bead through with yarn; (insert hook under next vertical bar, draw up lp) 15 times; repeat from * once more; insert hook under next vertical bar, slide bead up, yo, draw lp through pushing bead through with yarn, (insert hook under next vertical bar, draw up lp) 11 times; work off lps.

ROWS 30–31: Repeat Row 2.

ROWS 32–70: Repeat Rows 29–31 thirteen times.

ROWS 71–72: Repeat Rows 29–30.

ROW 73: Sk first vertical bar; (insert hook under next vertical bar, draw up lp) 11 times; *insert hook under next 2 vertical bars, draw up lp, (insert hook under next vertical bar, draw up lp) twice; insert hook under next 2 vertical bars, draw up lp, insert hook under next vertical bar, draw up lp; repeat from * 4 times more;

(insert hook under next vertical bar, draw up lp) 10 times—47 lps (46 sts); work off lps.

LEFT FRONT YOKE
Work according to Chart D above, binding off stitches as indicated for armhole and neck. (See Back Yoke, Row 11 and Row 52.) Bind off shoulders. Weave in yarn ends.

**Chart E
Right Front Skirt**

**Chart F
Right Front Yoke**

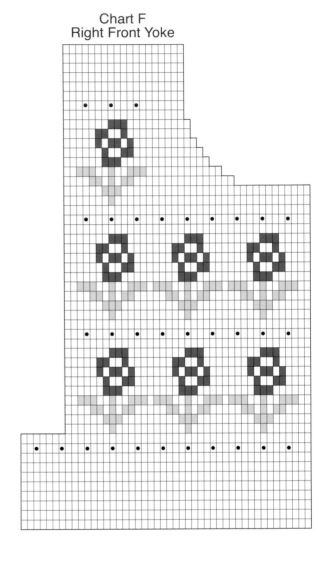

RIGHT FRONT SKIRT AND RIGHT FRONT YOKE

Referring to Charts E and F above, work following charts for Left Front Skirt and Left Front Yoke.

SLEEVES

Thread 10 beads on gray yarn.

Beg at lower edge with afghan hook and gray, ch 39.

ROW 1: Insert hook in 2nd ch from hook, draw up lp; *insert hook in next ch, draw up lp; repeat from * across—39 lps on hook; to work off lps, yo, draw through 1 lp on hook; **yo, draw through 2 lps on hook; repeat from ** until 1 lp remains on hook—38 sts.

ROW 2: Sk first vertical bar; *insert hook under next vertical bar, draw up lp; repeat from * across; work off lps.

ROWS 3–4: Repeat Row 2.

ROW 5: Sk first vertical bar; (insert hook under next vertical bar, draw up lp) twice; *insert hook under next vertical bar, slide bead up, yo, draw lp through pushing bead through with yarn, (insert hook under next vertical bar, draw up lp) 3 times; repeat from * 8 times more; insert hook under next vertical bar, slide bead up, yo, draw lp through pushing bead through with yarn; (insert hook under next vertical bar, draw up lp) twice; to work off lps, yo, draw through 1 lp on hook; ** yo, draw through 2 lps on hook; repeat from ** until 1 lp remains on hook.

ROWS 6–7: Repeat Row 2.

ROW 8: Sk first vertical bar, insert hook under next vertical bar, yo twice, draw both lps through (inc made); *insert hook under next vertical bar, draw up lp; repeat from * across to last bar, insert hook under last vertical bar, yo twice (inc made), draw both lps through—41 lps; work off lps.

ROW 9: Sk first vertical bar; *insert hook under next vertical bar, draw up lp; repeat from * across; work off lps (40 sts).

ROWS 10–51: Repeat Rows 8–9 twenty-one times.

ROW 52: Repeat Row 8—85 lps.

ROWS 53–62: Repeat Row 2—84 sts.

ROW 62: Sk first vertical bar; *insert hook under next vertical bar, draw up lp, bind off, drawing lp through lp on hook; repeat from * across. Fasten off; weave in yarn ends.

FINISHING

Pin out each piece to size on a padded surface and iron lightly under a damp cloth. Allow to dry completely before removing pins. With crochet hook and gray, hold pieces with wrong sides together and join side seams of Skirt/Yoke with single crochet. Join shoulder seams and then Sleeve seams in same manner, leaving top 1" (2.5cm) of seam open on Sleeves. Place end of Sleeve seam at side seam of Yoke, wrong sides together. With blue, crochet Sleeves into armholes.

Lower Edging

Hold Skirt with right side facing and starting ch at top; with crochet hook, join gray in one seam.

RND 1: Ch 1, sc in same sp; sc evenly around; join with a sl st in first sc.

RND 2: Ch 1, sc in each sc around; join with a sl st in first sc. Fasten off; weave in yarn ends.

Outer Band

Mark placement of 6 buttonholes evenly spaced on Right Front, placing first button ½" (13mm) below neck edge and last button 4" (10cm) from bottom edge.

Hold piece with right side facing and Right Front edge at top; with crochet hook, join gray with a sl st in end of first row, at lower corner of Right Front.

ROW 1: Ch 1, sc in same sp; working along Right Front edge, around neck opening, and across Left Front edge, sc evenly spaced across, working sc2tog in each corner of neck opening; turn.

ROW 2: Ch 1, sc in each sc across, working sc2tog in each corner of neck opening; turn.

ROW 3: Ch 1, sc in each sc to first button marker; ch 3, sk next 3 sc, (sc in each sc to next marker, ch 3, sk next 3 sc) 5 times; sc in each remaining sc; turn.

ROW 4: Ch 1, sc in each sc across, working 3 sc in each ch-3 sp; turn.

ROWS 5–6: Repeat Row 2. Fasten off.

Fronts and Back Neck Band

Hold piece with right side facing and lower edging at top; with crochet hook, join blue in first sc of lower border; ch 1, sc in same st; working around entire edge of Coat, sc evenly spaced around and working 3 sc at corners; join with a sl st in first sc. Fasten off.

Sleeve Edging

Hold one Sleeve with starting ch at top; with crochet hook, join blue in seam, ch 1, sc in same sp, sc evenly spaced around edge; join with a sl st in beg sc. Fasten off. Work second Sleeve edging in same manner.

With matching sewing thread, sew buttons opposite buttonholes.

FILET CROCHET

with
Hartmut Hass

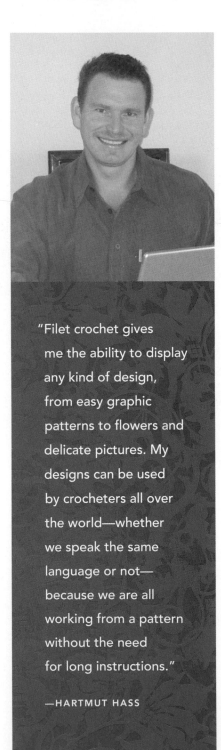

Hartmut Hass was born in Fuerstenberg, Germany, a town north of Berlin, which at that time was located in East Germany. After World War II, Germany had been divided into West and East Germany. West Germany was controlled by the Americans, English, and French and developed into a Western capitalist country. East Germany was controlled by the Soviet regime (in what is now the present-day Russian Federation) and remained under strict Communist control.

Throughout his childhood, Hardy (as he is called by his friends) had been exposed to a variety of crafts. His mother spent every evening knitting sweaters, crocheting, or embroidering tablecloths. When she started to teach Hardy's sisters to crochet, he decided that he would like to learn as well. Eventually he began to work on more difficult and exciting patterns. He was especially fascinated by patterns created with filet crochet, and this skill soon became the major outlet for his creative talents.

Although Hardy enjoyed crocheting, his real love as a child was sports, especially track and field, and he attended the university at Rostock, where he studied sports training. When Hardy was about ready to complete his studies his life turned around completely.

Living in East Germany under a totalitarian regime that dictated where you could go made him feel as if he were living in a cage. Hardy loved traveling and dreamed of seeing faraway places. Because Hungary was part of the Soviet domination, traveling there was not restricted as long as you had a visa. Hardy was able to obtain a visa and made plans to vacation in Budapest. Just before he was ready to leave, the East German government began revoking visas that had been issued to Hungary, deeming that the country had become too open to the West. The police were actually going door-to-door collecting visas. Hardy knew that he had this one chance to leave, and that he would not be able to return. It was a decision he had to make overnight, knowing that it was dangerous and that he

could end up in prison or shot by the police. In addition, even if he were able to leave, he would have to start over in a new culture—all of the years he had spent in school would become useless.

Then in a decisive moment, Hardy left East Germany and never looked back.

After his escape, Hardy had to earn a livelihood. He owned nothing more than his backpack and an extra sweater. He still had his love of crochet, so he sent a picture of some of his filet crochet work to Anne Burda, head of a large German publishing company. What had started as a hobby now became his livelihood. Burda has since published more than one hundred of Hardy's designs.

In addition to designing, Hardy became a swimming instructor, specializing in teaching disabled children. While visiting the United States, he found a position teaching swimming at a recreation center for the handicapped, and San Francisco became his home.

Teaching swimming may have become Hardy's profession, but crochet still remains his passion. His designs have appeared in books and on the covers of many magazines. Today, however, many of Hardy's special designs are saved for his website (www.hassdesign.com) where visitors can shop for Hardy's patterns (especially his beautiful filet crochet designs), find free tutorials, learn new techniques, and join his crochet-along classes.

At left, a delicate geometric pattern radiates from the center of this doily, which utilizes the filet crochet lacet stitch. At right, the filet table topper, sweetly reminiscent of the Victorian era, combines floral motifs with bunches of grapes, all accented with a lacy border.

HOW TO DO **FILET** CROCHET

Filet crochet is a beautiful imitation of filet lace, a needle lace known in Italy as early as the 1500s. It is worked in a grid pattern of open squares and filled squares. Historians believe the first version may have been worked on fishing nets. It has been popular with crocheters since the 1850s, and it is often used for tablecloths, bedspreads, doilies, and centerpieces as well as for fashion garments. Though usually worked in crochet cotton, filet crochet can be done with any weight yarn.

The crochet is usually worked by following charts, which are much easier to follow than written instructions.

READING THE CHARTS

On our charts, a blank square stands for an open mesh, and a dotted square stands for a closed mesh.

An open mesh is made with a double crochet, then 2 chains, then another double crochet. The chart showing open meshes will look like this.

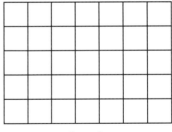

[FIG 1]

To begin a row, form the first double crochet and ch–2 space by working a ch–5 at the end of the preceding row. This ch–5 equals a double crochet and a ch–2 space. To end the row, work the final double crochet into the third chain of the ch–5 turning chain.

A single closed mesh is made by 4 double crochet stitches: one on each side and 2 in the middle. To work a single closed mesh over an open mesh on the previous row, work: double crochet in next double crochet, 2

double crochet in ch–2 space, double crochet in next double crochet. To work a closed mesh over a closed mesh on the previous row, work: double crochet in next 4 double crochet.

For several closed mesh units worked together in a row, work the first unit as a single closed mesh—4 double crochet made. For each additional closed mesh unit in the group, work as follows: (working over an open mesh) work 2 double crochet in the ch–2 space, double crochet in the next double crochet—3 double crochet made; or (working over a closed mesh) work a double crochet in each of the next 3 double crochet—3 double crochet made.

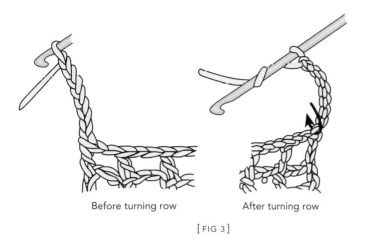

Before turning row   After turning row

[FIG 3]

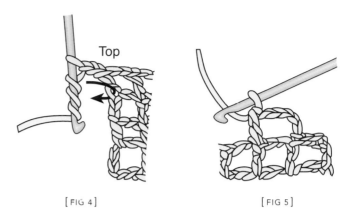

Top

[FIG 4]   [FIG 5]

Note that when closed mesh units are worked together in a group across on a row, the first unit has 4 double crochet and each following unit has only 3 double crochet.

A chart showing closed meshes will look like this.

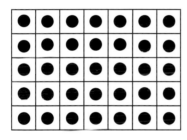

[FIG 2]

INCREASING AND DECREASING

In some designs, you will be increasing or decreasing the number of closed meshes or open meshes at the edges.

Increases are made by working additional chains, as specified in the pattern, in the turning chain at the end of a row to add blocks for the next row. [FIG 3]

To add closed meshes at the end of the working row, work a ch 2, then a double triple crochet (yo 3 times) in the same place as the last double crochet was made. [FIG 4]

Decreases at the beginning of a row are worked by turning without chaining. Then skip the first double

crochet of the previous row, and slip stitch across each chain and in each double crochet until you reach the first block that will be worked. [FIG 5]

A decrease at the end of a row is made by working the last block shown on the chart then turning, leaving the following blocks unworked.

LACETS

A lacet is a decorative stitch that is shown on the charts by this symbol.

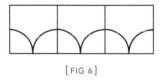

[FIG 6]

A lacet covers two open meshes or closed meshes, and is worked like this: double crochet in next double crochet, ch 3, skip next 2 stitches, single crochet in next stitch, ch 3, skip next 2 stitches, double crochet in next stitch). To work the next row above a lacet, double crochet in first double crochet of lacet, ch 5, double crochet in next double crochet.

WORKING FROM THE CHARTS

The first row of each chart is read from right to left, and the second row from left to right. Continue alternating directions with each row.

FILET CROCHET **TABLE RUNNER**

Designed by Hartmut Hass

SKILL LEVEL
■■■☐ Intermediate

SIZE
Approximately 27" x 43"
(68.5cm x 109cm)

MATERIALS
- J&P Coats® *Royale*® Size 20 Fine Crochet Thread (100% mercerized cotton, each approximately 400 yd [365m]) 1600 yd (1460m) / 4 balls in color 201 White
- One size 10 (1.30mm) steel crochet hook, or size needed to obtain gauge

GAUGE
10 squares x 10 squares = 2½" x 2½" (6.5cm x 6.5cm)

STITCH GUIDE
Double triple crochet (dtr):
Yo 3 times, insert hook in specified ch and draw up a lp, (yo and draw through first 2 lps on hook) 4 times—dtr made.

NOTES
- See How to Do Filet Crochet on page 86.
- The chart for this project shows small open (empty or blank) squares, closed or solid blocks (those with dot), plus large open squares and lacets (large square with loops in the lower half, as in Row 26).

CONTINUED ON PAGE 90

I designed this table runner just using basic stitches because I discovered a long time ago that in filet crochet sometimes simple is actually better. I wanted to make something that shows the pattern nicely and yet looks elegant. I chose to make a table runner because crocheters are always looking for patterns like this, and there aren't many out there. I think it will be the perfect truly elegant accent for any beautiful wood table.

CONTINUED FROM PAGE 88

Directions for working these different units are described in How to Do Filet Crochet.

- As you work the first two rows, check the chart as you go along to learn how to read the chart. Then you will be able to follow the chart without needing row-by-row written directions.

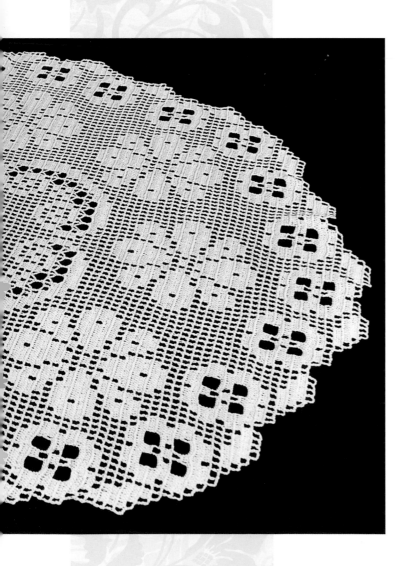

TABLE RUNNER

Ch 213.

ROW 1 (WRONG SIDE): Dc in 9th ch from hook and in next 12 chs; (ch 2, sk next 2 chs, dc in next ch) twice; dc in next 6 chs, ch 9, sk next 5 chs, dc in next 4 chs; ch 9, sk next 5 chs, dc in next 7 chs; (ch 2, sk next 2 chs, dc in next ch) 4 times; dc in next 21 chs; (ch 2, sk next 2 chs, dc in next ch) 15 times; dc in next 21 chs, (ch 2, sk next ch, dc in next ch) 4 times; dc in next 6 chs; ch 9, sk next 5 chs, dc in next 4 chs; ch 9, sk next 5 chs, dc in next 7 chs; (ch 2, sk next 2 chs, dc in next ch) twice; dc in next 12 chs, ch 2, sk next 2 chs, dc in next ch; ch 8, turn.

ROW 2 (RIGHT SIDE): Dc in first dc, 2 dc in next ch–2 sp, dc in next 7 dc; (ch 2, sk next 2 dc, dc in next dc) twice; (ch 2, sk next ch–2 sp, dc in next dc) twice; dc in next 5 dc, sk first ch of next ch–9 sp, sc in next 7 chs, sk last ch; ch 2, sk next 4 dc and first ch of next ch–9 sp, sc in next 7 chs, sk last ch and next dc; dc in next 6 dc, (ch 2, sk next ch–2 sp, dc in next dc) 4 times; (ch 2, sk next 2 dc, dc in each of next 7 dc) twice, ch 2, sk next 2 dc, dc in next dc; (ch 2, sk next ch–2 sp, dc in next dc) 15 times; (ch 2, sk next 2 dc, dc in each of next 7 dc) twice; ch 2, sk next 2 dc, dc in next dc; (ch 2, sk next ch–2 sp, dc in next dc) 4 times; dc in next 5 dc, sk first ch of next ch–9 sp, sc in next 7 chs, sk last ch, ch 2, sk next 4 dc and first ch of next ch–9 sp, sc in next 7 chs; sk last ch and next dc; dc in next 6 dc, (ch 2, sk next ch–2 sp, dc in next dc) twice; (ch 2, sk next 2 dc, dc in next dc) twice; dc in next 6 dc, dc in next 3 skipped chs at beginning of Row 1; ch 2, dtr in same ch as last dc made. Ch 8, turn.

ROWS 3–150: Work following chart.

ROWS 151–161: Work following chart, fastening off and rejoining thread as necessary to complete rows.

ROWS 162–173: Turn piece upside down. With right side facing you and beginning chain at top, turn chart upside down. Working in unused loops of beginning chain, join thread in first unused loop of chain at base of first double crochet in upper right-hand corner. Following chart, work Rows 162–173, fastening off and rejoining thread as necessary to complete rows. At end of Row 173, fasten off; weave in all thread ends.

FILET CROCHET TABLE RUNNER CHART

DOUBLE-ENDED CROCHET

with

Darla J. Fanton

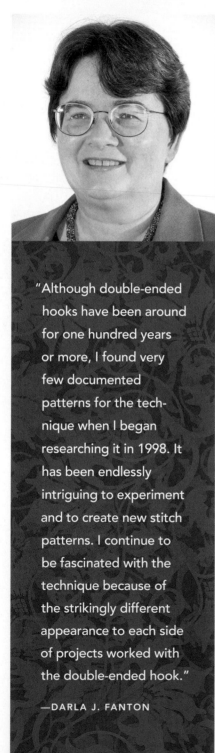

"Although double-ended hooks have been around for one hundred years or more, I found very few documented patterns for the technique when I began researching it in 1998. It has been endlessly intriguing to experiment and to create new stitch patterns. I continue to be fascinated with the technique because of the strikingly different appearance to each side of projects worked with the double-ended hook."

—DARLA J. FANTON

Darla doesn't remember a time when she didn't have some type of needlework in her hands. Growing up on a farm in central Iowa with few neighbor kids nearby, yarn and thread became her playmates, and innovation in design became a requirement.

Darla's earliest needlework was limited to embroidering designs on pillowcases and dishtowels, followed by making simple quilts. In high school she decided to learn to knit, which was complicated by the fact that she didn't know anyone who could knit. She ended up teaching herself from a book that unfortunately lacked complete instructions, resulting in a self-developed, slightly unorthodox style. This experience also taught Darla the value of complete instructions.

After Darla married, and her husband started working on his Doctor of Veterinary Medicine degree, she looked around for a quieter form of needlework to pass the evenings while her husband studied. Although he never complained about the clicking knitting needles, in their tiny apartment they seemed loud and distracting to her. Crochet became her next needlework focus.

It was her husband who encouraged her to send her designs to craft magazines, and for more than fifteen years Darla had more than one thousand designs published in all areas of needlework, including plastic canvas, counted cross-stitch, quilting, knitting, and crocheting.

In 1998, Darla's career took a different turn, prompted by a request her sister made. Almost twenty-five years earlier her sister saw a wooden, hand-carved, double-ended crochet hook at a craft fair in Arkansas. Having never seen one before, she decided to buy it; however, she soon discovered that there were very few designs available for this hook. She did succeed in making one afghan. When the two sisters got together, Darla's sister discovered that Darla had also purchased a double-ended hook, because she, too, was intrigued by the unusual design. Bemoaning the fact that she could only make one pattern, her sister

Darla uses the double-ended technique to create colorful afghans, but she also designs striking wearables.

challenged Darla, "You're a designer. Why don't you create something new for me so I can use this hook again?"

Darla took up the challenge, and after a few hours she was "hooked;" in fact, she was "doubly hooked!" Soon her double-ended hook projects started to appear in magazines and craft booklets. Darla became known as the designer who revived a form of crochet that had been nearly unheard of for the last quarter of a century.

Today Darla is invited to teach at conferences and fiber events all over the country. She continues to design for yarn companies, magazines, and her own pattern line, Designs by Darla J. With a company motto of "Continuing the Rich Tradition of Crochet," she enjoys exploring what can be accomplished by traditional crochet and specialty techniques, such as the double-ended hook, and sharing her discoveries with her students.

Darla uses the double-ended technique to create colorful afghans, but she also designs striking wearables.

HOW TO WORK CROCHET
WITH A **DOUBLE-ENDED HOOK**

Working with a double-ended hook creates a look and feel that combine elements of both crochet and knitting. It creates a soft fabric almost like knitting, but requires only one needle to manipulate. It is similar to Tunisian crochet because you are picking up stitches on a long hook and then working them off. It's different in that you usually work with at least two colors, and work first with one end of the hook, turn, and then work from the opposite end. This produces a unique two-sided, totally reversible fabric with each side having a different dominant color and, in some patterns, a distinctly different look to the stitches themselves. A bonus is that the fabric edges do not roll or curl as they have a tendency to do in Tunisian crochet.

Like its cousin the afghan hook (also known as Tunisian crochet or tricot) the double-ended hook is known by several names. While Boye refers to it as a Cro-Hook™, Susan Bates simply calls it a double-ended hook. The act of using the tool has been called cro-hooking, cro-knitting, double-hooking, Crochenit™, and, most recently, Crochet on the Double™. At first glance it looks like an afghan hook—a long crochet hook with a knob at one end. But look again: Instead of a knob there is a hook on the other end, too!

NOTE: The phrase "Crochet on the Double" is a trademark of The Needlecraft Shop, "Cro-Hook" is a trademark of the Boye Needle Co, and "Crochenit" is a trademark of Mary Middleton.

There are two basic methods of picking up loops: either by working under the vertical bar or working under the horizontal bar. All double-hook patterns are combinations of these two methods, with the addition of various methods of increases and decreases to form a variety of stitches.

METHOD 1:
WORKING UNDER THE VERTICAL BAR
Pattern multiple: any number of stitches

ROW 1: With double-ended hook and first color, ch 20; working through back lp only, insert hook in 2nd ch from hook, yo and draw through, leaving another lp on hook; *insert hook through back lp of next ch, yo and draw through; repeat from * across foundation ch, leaving all lps on hook. [FIG 1]

You will now have 20 lps (or sts) on the hook. Slide all sts to opposite end of hook and turn.

ALTERNATE ROW 1 VARIATION: An alternate method of picking up stitches is by working in the bottom bumps of

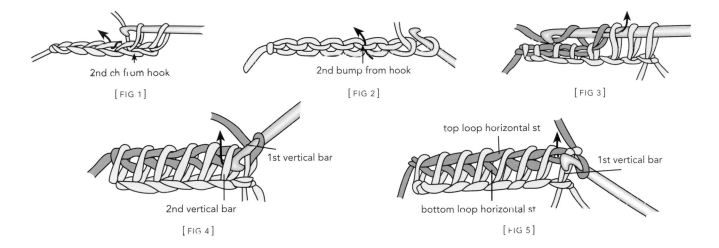

[FIG 1] 2nd ch from hook

[FIG 2] 2nd bump from hook

[FIG 3]

[FIG 4] 1st vertical bar / 2nd vertical bar

[FIG 5] top loop horizontal st / bottom loop horizontal st / 1st vertical bar

the foundation chain, which results in a finished look that more closely matches the appearance of the final (bind-off) row. **[FIG 2]**

For this method, ch the indicated number with a slightly looser tension than normal, then gently roll the chain toward you, exposing the backside of the chain. Insert hook through 2nd bump from hook, yo and draw through; *insert hook through bump of next ch, yo and draw through; repeat from * across foundation chain leaving all lps on hook. Keeping the chain looser makes it easier to insert the hook through the bump.

TIP: Use a standard crochet hook one size larger to work the foundation chain in order to maintain a looser tension, then switch to the double-ended hook as you begin to pick up sts.

ROW 2: To work lps off hook: on left end of hook make a slip knot with 2nd color; working from left to right draw slip knot through first lp on hook; *yo and draw through next 2 lps (1 lp of each color); repeat from * across until one lp of 2nd color remains on hook. Do not turn. **[FIG 3]**

ROW 3: Working from right to left with 2nd color, ch 1, sk first vertical bar; *insert hook under next vertical bar, yo and draw through, keeping lp on hook. **[FIG 4]**

Repeat from * across. You should have 20 sts on the hook. Slide all sts to the opposite end of the hook and turn.

ROW 4: To work lps off with a color that is already in use: pick up first color yarn at left end of hook, yo and draw

through first lp on hook; *yo and draw through 2 lps on hook (one lp of each color); repeat from * until 1 lp remains on hook.

ROW 5: Repeat Row 3 with first color.

ROW 6: Repeat Row 4 with 2nd color.

Repeat Rows 3–6 until piece reaches desired length, ending by working a Row 4. At this point you will have worked loops off with the first color and will be ready for the final row.

FINAL ROW: With first color, ch 1, sk first vertical bar; *insert hook under next vertical bar, yo and draw through vertical bar and lp already on hook; repeat from * across. Fasten off.

SECOND METHOD: WORKING IN THE HORIZONTAL STITCH

Pattern multiple: any number of stitches

ROW 1: Work as for Vertical Bar method.

ROW 2: Work as for Vertical Bar method.

ROW 3: Stop and look at your work. You will see the vertical bars with the 1st color that you worked with in the first sample. Notice that between the vertical bars there are horizontal sts or bars with the 2nd color. Working from right to left with 2nd color, ch 1, sk first vertical bar; *insert hook under the top lp of the next horizontal st, yo and draw through, keeping lp on hook repeat from * across. You should have 20 sts on hook; slide all sts to opposite end of hook and turn. **[FIG 5]**

Unless the pattern states otherwise, when picking up a stitch in a horizontal stitch, insert hook under the top lp only of the horizontal stitch.

ROW 4: To work lps off with a color that is already in use, pick up first color yarn at left end of hook, yo and draw through first lp on hook; *yo and draw through 2 lps on hook (1 lp of each color); repeat from * until 1 lp remains on hook.

ROW 5: Working from right to left with first color, ch 1, sk first vertical bar; *insert hook under top lp of next horizontal st, yo and draw through, keeping lp on hook; repeat from * across—20 sts on hook. Slide sts to opposite end of hook and turn.

ROW 6: Repeat Row 4 with 2nd color.

Repeat Rows 3–6 until piece reaches desired length, ending by working a Row 4. At this point you will have worked lps off with the 1st color and will be ready for the final row.

FINAL ROW: With first color, ch 1, sk first vertical bar; *insert hook under top lp of next horizontal st, yo and draw through, yo and draw through both lps on hook; repeat from * across. Fasten off.

DESIGN TIPS

1. With just these two stitches you can have fun designing your own projects.

2. Look at your two swatches. You will notice that working under the vertical bar creates a fabric that is thicker and requires more rows to reach the same length as working in the horizontal stitches. Working in the horizontal stitch results in a fabric that is softer and probably requires an extra stitch or two to reach the same width as using the vertical bars.

3. To get started, crochet a test swatch using the yarns you plan to use for the project. Measure this swatch to determine how many stitches you will need to achieve the width you want. You can work your project in one piece, in panels or blocks. You can edge your projects with any traditional crochet stitches you would like or with an edging worked with the double-ended hook.

4. If you are going to work in panels or blocks, decide if you want to join them by alternating Side A and Side B of each panel or with the same side facing. If alternating, you should have an odd number of panels; if the same side is facing, it is crocheter's choice whether to go odd or even. Decide the width you would like and the number of panels. Then divide width by number of panels. For example, if you want the finished piece 49" (124.5cm) with 7 panels; each panel would need to be 7" (18cm) wide. Don't forget to allow for the panel edging.

5. Most projects seem to have better balance if you begin and end with the darkest color—but as with all rules there are exceptions. Don't be afraid to experiment! Variegated yarns can yield some interesting results. And don't limit yourself to just two colors.

INCREASING AND DECREASING

There are several ways to work increases and decreases. These can be done both when you are working stitches off the hook and when you are picking stitches up again.

If each time you work a decrease you also work a compensating increase, the stitch count will remain the same and the edges should remain straight.

Some examples of increases:

- Work a yo before picking up the next st.
- Pick up more than 1 st in the same place.
- Pick up a st in the horizontal st and the vertical bar right next to it.
- When working the lps off the hook, add extra chs to provide a location to pick up additional stitches on the next pickup row.

Some examples of decreases:

- Simply skip a stitch.
- When working lps off the hook, draw through 3 (or more) lps instead of the usual 2.
- When picking up lps under the vertical bars, insert the hook under 2 or more vertical bars and draw the yarn through all of them at once.

MORE TIPS FOR WORKING THE DOUBLE-ENDED CROCHET TECHNIQUE

- Most people find it easiest to hold the double-ended hook with your hand above the hook, as if holding a knife.

- If you have trouble with the loops sliding off the unused end of the hook, you may want to cap the end of the hook. A knitting needle protector or a clean wine cork works well for sizes through K-10½ (6.5mm); for larger hooks wrap a hair elastic around the unused end.

- Since you will usually be working with two skeins of yarn at the same time, in order to keep your yarn from tangling, rotate the hook first from right to left and then from left to right.

- Turn the hook only when you have picked up all the loops for that row, never after you have worked off the loops.

- If you are ready to begin working loops off the hook and can't remember if you have turned the hook, give the yarn on the left side a tug; if it is attached to the loop on the hook you have not yet turned.

- You will have one loop left on your hook after working off the loops. If you need to lay your work aside at this point, slip a safety pin or split-ring marker into that loop to prevent it from pulling out.

- Unless instructed otherwise, you will be picking up loops using the same color yarn you just used to work off the previous row of loops.

- A method for keeping your edges neat when working with more than two colors of yarn is to carry the unused strands along the side edge by working over them before the ch-1 at the beginning of a pickup row or before the yarn over on a work-off row.

- Giving the yarn not in use a slight tug before beginning a pickup row will also help keep your edges neat.

- When working panels or blocks to be joined later, you may find it helpful to mark the final row with a safety pin. This way it will be easier later to ensure that all panels are joined with the final row in the same position.

- If you find the yarn sticking on the hook, try polishing the hook with wax paper, or clean aluminum or plastic hooks with warm, soapy water.

- With this technique it is very easy to combine yarns of different weights or textures. You can achieve some interesting effects using two very different yarns.

LILACS AND ROSES **BABY AFGHAN**

Designed by Darla J. Fanton

SKILL LEVEL
■■□□ Easy

SIZE
- Approximately 38" x 38" (96.5cm x 96.5cm)
- Afghan is very stretchy lengthwise. If desired, afghan may be blocked to measure 37" x 46" (94cm x 117cm).

MATERIALS
- Cascade Yarns *Cherub DK* (55% nylon, 45% acrylic, each approximately 1¾ oz [50g] and 190 yd [174m], light/DK weight)
  - 760 yd (696m) / 4 balls in color 16 Lilac
- Cascade Yarns Cherub Kaleidoscope DK (55% nylon, 45% acrylic, each approximately 1¾ oz [50g] and 190 yd [174m], ③ light/DK weight) 950 yd (870m) / 5 balls in color 993 Lavender/Rose Variegated
- One size K-10½ (6.5mm) 14" (35.5cm) double-ended crochet hook or circular double-ended crochet hook, or size needed to obtain gauge
- One size I-9 (5.5mm) crochet hook (for edging only)
- Tapestry needle

GAUGE
19 sts and 31 rows = 4" (10cm) using larger hook

Because the double-ended hook creates a soft fabric with a different look to each side, it is particularly well suited to afghans, especially warm and cuddly baby afghans.

Once you've made one project using the double-ended crochet technique, you'll want to make many more. While the instructions look very complicated, the technique is really simple and fun to do. The results are sure to please everyone.

STITCH GUIDE

HALF DOUBLE CROCHET DECREASE (HDC DEC): Yo, insert hook in next st and draw up a lp, insert hook in next st and draw up a lp, yo and draw through all 4 lps on hook—hdc dec made.

AFGHAN

NOTE: When picking up a lp in a horizontal st, insert hook under top lp only.

ROW 1: With double-ended hook and variegated yarn, ch 163; working through bumps on back of ch (see Fig 1), pick up a lp in 2nd bump from hook and each remaining bump, leaving all lps on hook. Slide all sts to opposite end of hook and turn—163 lps on hook. **[FIG 1]**

2nd bump from hook

[FIG 1]

ROW 2: To work lps off hook: place lilac on hook with slip knot, working from left to right draw slip knot through first lp; *yo, draw through 2 lps (one lp of each color) (see Fig 2); repeat from * across until one lp remains on hook. Do not turn. **[FIG 2]**

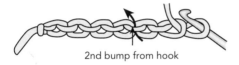

[FIG 2]

ROW 3: To pick up lps, with lilac and working right to left; ch 1, sk first 2 vertical bars; *pick up lp in next horizontal st (see Fig 3), pick up lp under next vertical bar (see Fig 4), sk next vertical bar; repeat from * across. Slide all sts to opposite end of hook and turn—163 lps on hook. **[FIGS 3, 4]**

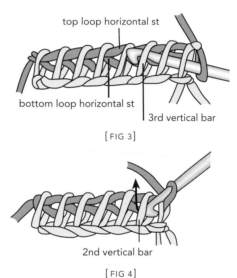

top loop horizontal st

bottom loop horizontal st

3rd vertical bar

[FIG 3]

2nd vertical bar

[FIG 4]

ROW 4: Pick up variegated yarn; yo, draw through one lp; *yo, draw through 2 lps (one lp of each color); repeat from * across until one lp remains on hook. Do not turn.

ROW 5: Repeat Row 3 with variegated yarn.

ROW 6: Repeat Row 4 with lilac.

ROWS 7–264: Repeat Rows 3–6, 64 times more, then repeat Rows 3 and 4 once more.

ROW 265: Bind off in the following manner; with variegated yarn, and working right to left, ch 1, sk first vertical bar; *insert hook in next horizontal st, yo, draw through st and lp on hook (sl st made); repeat from * across, transfer final lp to regular hook for first side edging. Fasten off lilac.

EDGINGS

NOTE: Edgings are worked with standard crochet hook with the predominantly lilac side of afghan always facing you.

First Side Edging

With variegated yarn and working in ends of rows, evenly space 133 sc along first long edge, placing last sc in end of foundation ch—133 sc. Fasten off.

Second Side Edging

Join variegated yarn with sc in opposite end of foundation ch; evenly space an additional 132 sc along 2nd long edge, placing last sc in end of Row 265—133 sc. Do not fasten off, continue working in rounds.

Afghan Edging

RND 1: Ch 2, 2 hdc in same st as last sc worked; *hdc in next 7 sts; hdc dec in next 2 sts; (hdc in next 3 sts; hdc dec in next 2 sts) 29 times; hdc in next 7 sts; 3 hdc in next st to turn corner; working along side, hdc in next 131 sts**; 3 hdc in next st; repeat from * to **; join with a sl st in 2nd ch of beginning ch-2—3 hdc in each corner with 131 hdc along each edge between corners. Fasten off variegated yarn.

RND 2: Join lilac with a sl st in center st of any corner group; ch 3, 4 dc in same st as joining; *(ch 1, sk next st, dc in next st) 66 times; ch 1, sk next st**; work 5 dc in center st of next corner group; repeat from * around, ending last repeat at **; join with a sl st in 3rd ch of beginning ch-3—5 dc in each corner with 66 dc and 67 ch-1 sps along each edge between corners. Fasten off lilac.

RND 3: Join variegated yarn with sc in center st of any corner group, 2 sc in same st; *sc in next 2 sts; (dc in st 1 rnd below next ch-1 sp, sc in next dc) 67 times; sc in next dc**; 3 sc in center st of next corner group; repeat from * around, ending last repeat at **; join with a sl st in first sc—3 sc in each corner with 67 dc and 70 sc along each edge between corners. Fasten off.

FINISHING

With tapestry needle, weave in all yarn ends. Block as desired.

TASSELS

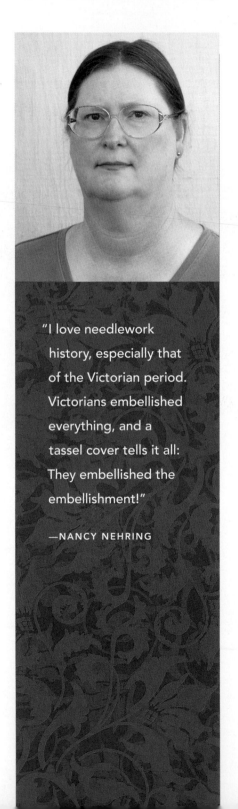

with
Nancy Nehring

"I love needlework history, especially that of the Victorian period. Victorians embellished everything, and a tassel cover tells it all: They embellished the embellishment!"

—NANCY NEHRING

Nancy Nehring leaned to crochet and to master all types of needlework from her grandmother. Her relationship with the past, however, doesn't stop there. She is fascinated with old needlework, especially Victorian crochet patterns, and these have had a strong influence on her work.

Nancy's fascination with the history of crochet began when she worked as a research chemist for the United States Geological Survey studying hot springs and volcanoes. And as it turns out, her background in scientific research helped her solve some crochet puzzles. She had found a collection of old crocheted buttons, but there were no instructions for making the buttons. Without documentation, the techniques for making these buttons would be lost, so she determined to teach herself how to make them. By employing reverse engineering, she carefully took each button apart until she was able to make a reasonable facsimile. To do this, she had to teach herself how to recognize crochet and other needlework stitches in a range of threads and tensions done both left- and right-handed. By the time she had completed her first book, *50 Heirloom Buttons to Make,* Nancy was hooked; she loved examining old needlework, researching old needlework techniques, and passing on what she had learned—just as she had done when she worked as a chemist.

Today Nancy designs crochet patterns and writes articles that have appeared in many books and magazines. Many of her pieces are intended to be replicas of original designs. When she became interested in Irish crochet, she realized that she would never be able to replicate a garment exactly because the tiny threads used years ago are no longer manufactured. Using thread at the larger limits of what might have been used in the 1840s, Nancy created an Irish crochet dress sized for an 18" (45.5cm) doll. The dress took her more than three hundred hours and three years to complete, but it won the PieceWork Needleworker of

the Year award. In addition, Nancy is well known as a collector of crochet hooks, and she has a collection of more than four hundred hooks that tell the history of crochet as well.

Believing there is no point in studying the past unless we share the information we learn, Nancy spends a great deal of her time traveling around the world teaching. Whether she is giving classes in "Designing for Larger Sizes," "Couture Techniques for Knit and Crochet," "Buttons, Frogs, and Tassels," or her ever-popular "Make Your Own Wooden Crochet Hook," her classes are filled with students eager to learn all that Nancy knows and is willing to impart to them.

At left, a collection of crocheted button covers, some styles dating from the Victorian era, showcases the variety of techniques that Nancy has used.
At center, glass beads and metallic yarns add sparkle to elegant crocheted tassels.
At right, the designer's award winning Irish crochet doll dress.

HOW TO MAKE CROCHETED TASSELS

Crocheted tassels have been around ever since crochet became popular in the mid-1800s. Tassels ideally fit the Victorian sense of style, which was to embellish everything in sight. Patterns for crocheted tassels have never been common but have been occasionally published ever since Mademoiselle Riego de la Branchardiere published the pattern for a fuchsia tassel in 1849.

Crocheted tassels usually take one of two forms. In one form, a conventional tassel made from strands of fiber held together with a neck wrap is covered with a decorative crocheted covering. The covering might be lace worked in a bell shape or might take a fanciful shape such as petals of a flower to go over a tassel representing the stamens. In the second form, the entire tassel is crocheted. Crocheted chains that might incorporate bobbles, beads, and other embellishments are suspended from a flat or spherical top.

You can mix a variety of materials in a tassel, including metallic or fuzzy yarns. When making a garment or an item for home décor, use yarn from the project for the body of the tassel and then add metallics, beads, and other glitzy embellishments. Edging patterns with small repeats can be modified for tassel covers by working in the round and by adding a few chain stitches between repeats to the lower rounds so that the cover flares slightly.

Here's how to make the basic version of a tassel:

Cut a piece of cardboard ½" (13mm) longer than the length desired for the tassel.

Place a 12" (30.5cm) piece of yarn or cord across the top for the tie and wind yarn around the cardboard and over the tie until you have the desired thickness. [FIG 1]

Draw the tie up tightly and knot securely. Cut the yarn at the bottom of the cardboard and slide off the cardboard. [FIG 2]

Cut another 12" (30.5cm) piece of yarn or cord and wrap tightly about 1" (2.5cm) below the top of the tassel. Wrap several times then tie a secure knot. Trim the ends of the cord and the bottom of the tassel as desired. [FIG 3]

A tassel on a garment can be removed and repaired later if needed. The yarn will have "aged" the same as the garment through use and cleaning and will match perfectly.

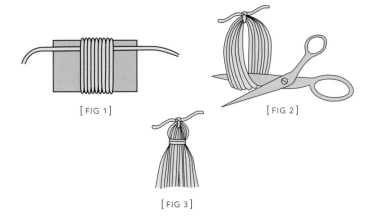

[FIG 1]   [FIG 2]

[FIG 3]

TIP FROM THE MASTER

Use expensive yarns in your tassel. Tassels are small and don't cost much even if an expensive yarn is used. A luscious tassel makes the entire project look richer.

VICTORIAN FLOWER **TASSEL**

Designed by Nancy Nehring

Tassels are great embellishments for all sorts of projects: garments, home décor, crafts. They add flow, color, and movement. Tassels are fast to make and can be made from so many different fibers that it's easy to make one that coordinates with your project.

SKILL LEVEL
■■□□ Easy

SIZE
- Approximately 6" (15cm) long x ⅝" (16mm) diameter

MATERIALS
- DMC® *Size 5 Pearl Cotton* (100% mercerized cotton, each approximately 27 yd [25m])
  - 108 yd (100m) / 4 skeins in color 642 Dark Beige Gray
- One size 7 (1.65mm) steel crochet hook, or size needed to obtain gauge
- 3–5 small, wired flower picks
- 8 size 4mm pink freshwater pearls
- 16 size 13/0 pink seed beads
- Fine sewing or beading needle and matching sewing thread
- 6" x 3" (15cm x 7.5cm) piece of cardboard

GAUGE
20 sc (first 2 rounds of Top) = ⅝" (16mm) diameter

TASSEL

Ch 4; join with a sl st to form a ring.

RND 1: Ch 1, work 10 sc in ring; join with a sl st in beg sc—10 sc.

RND 2: Ch 1, work 2 sc in each sc around; join as before—20 sc.

RNDS 3–9: Ch 1, sc in each sc around; join as before.

OVERSKIRT

RND 10: Ch 4 (counts as first tr), in same st as joining work (tr, ch 1, 2 tr)—beg shell made; sk next 4 sc; * in next sc work shell of (2 tr, ch 1, 2 tr), sk 4 sc; repeat from * twice more, join with a sl st in 4th ch of beginning ch-4—4 shells made.

RND 11: Sl st in next tr and into ch-1 sp; ch 4 (counts as a tr), in same sp work (tr, ch 2, 2 tr)—beg shell made; dc between shell just worked into and next shell on Rnd 10; *in next ch-1 sp work shell of (2 tr, ch 1, 2 tr), dc between shell just worked into and next shell; repeat from * twice more; join with a sl st in 4th ch of beginning ch-4.

RNDS 12 AND 13: Sl st in next tr and into ch-1 sp, work beg shell; dc in next dc between shells; *work (2 tr, ch 1, 2 tr) shell in sp of next shell, dc in next dc, repeat from * twice more; join in 4th ch of beg ch-4.

RND 14: Sl st in next tr and into ch-1 sp; ch 4 (counts as a tr), in same sp work (2 tr, ch 1, 3 tr)—beg shell made; dc in next dc; *in next ch-1 sp work a shell of (3 tr, ch 1, 3 tr), dc in next dc; repeat from * twice more; join with a sl st in top of beg ch-4.

RNDS 15–18: Sl st in next 2 tr and into ch-1 sp, work beg shell as for Rnd 14, dc in next dc; *work (3 tr, ch 1, 3 tr) shell in next ch-1 sp, dc in next dc; repeat from * twice more; join in 4th ch of beg ch-4 sp.

RND 19: Ch 1, sc in same tr as joining, sc in each of next 2 tr, 2 sc in ch-1 sp, sc in each of next 3 tr; sc in next dc between shells; *sc in each tr of next shell, and work 2 sc in ch-1 sp of same shell; sc in next dc between shells; repeat from * twice more, join with a sl st in first sc of rnd. Fasten off; weave in thread ends. Set piece aside.

Hanging Cord and Tie

With pearl cotton, leave a 6" (15cm) loose yarn end and make an 8" (20.5cm) long chain for the hanging cord, leaving a 6" (15cm) loose yarn end. Thread loose ends into a needle and weave back into the cord for a few inches. Trim excess. Set aside. Measure a 12" (30.5cm) length of pearl cotton for tie and set aside.

Tassel Base and Underskirt

Place hanging cord chain across top of cardboard. Wrap all remaining pearl cotton lengthwise around cardboard, allowing the wraps to pile on top of one another and to cover the hanging cord. This forms the underskirt.

When cardboard is full, tie the ends of the hanging cord together firmly and turn the knot so that it is under the wraps. Slide the cardboard out from under the wraps.

Holding on to the hanging cord, fold the wraps down over the hanging cord and gather the wraps into a bundle about ³⁄₄" (2cm) below the hanging cord. Wrap the 12" (30.5cm) length of reserved pearl cotton firmly around the bundle several times and then tie a firm knot. Trim ends of knotted strand to 1" (2.5cm).

Attaching Beads

With needle and thread and referring to photo for placement, sew beads to each of the 4 valleys and each of the 4 points around lower edge of overskirt. To attach beads, secure thread at point or valley, string a seed bead, a pearl, and another seed bead on thread, tie a knot in the thread, then run needle and thread back through the beads and pearl to the skirt. Run the thread invisibly on the wrong side to the next bead placement, and attach beads in the same manner. At end, secure thread on wrong side and cut thread.

ASSEMBLING

Draw the hanging cord of the tassel base up through the center of the lace overskirt and through the hole formed at the center of the Top. Pull overskirt down over wrapped lengths of underskirt.

Twist flower picks around neck of tassel where wraps are tied. Use 3 picks to cover two-thirds of the neck if the tassel will be visible from only one side (used against a flat surface) or 5 picks to encircle the entire neck if the tassel will be visible from all sides.

Cut bottom loops of skirt apart to create fringe, and trim evenly.

BULLION STITCH

with
Bonnie Pierce

"The desire to replicate an antique Christening gown made almost entirely of bullions started me on my love of bullions. I love the raised texture of the stitch and how it makes a piece seem smooth and textural at the same time."

—BONNIE PIERCE

"If you think you can, or if you think you can't, you are right" has been Bonnie Pierce's philosophy throughout her life.

When she was four, she thought she could learn to embroider, and she did. She so loved the feel of yarn through her fingers that she was soon darning her father's wool socks before she was old enough to attend school.

At eleven, Bonnie thought she could teach herself to knit, and she did. At sixteen, she tried to teach herself to crochet. Although she wasn't able to do it "properly," she determined to figure out a way to crochet. Holding both the yarn and the hook in her right hand, she taught herself what she needed to know. By the time Bonnie was ready to go off to college, she had won several awards in local fairs for her work, including an award for being the fastest knitter.

Then tragedy struck, and Bonnie's philosophy was severely tested. After graduation from high school, Bonnie was critically injured in a car accident where she was thrown from the car, injuring her head. For the next year, Bonnie could remember nothing of her life before the accident. She had to relearn to read and write as well as to knit and crochet.

Despite these obstacles, Bonnie went off to college anyway because, as she says, "I didn't know I couldn't." She graduated with honors from Eastern Washington University four years later with a degree in child psychology and elementary education. She married her college sweetheart, moved to Vancouver, Washington, and worked in the teaching field for several years before she left to raise her three children.

Almost thirty years ago, Bonnie decided to crochet a Christening gown for her daughter Katie. She found an old pattern completely made of bullions. Once again Bonnie knew she could. She taught herself to do the bullion stitch and completed the dress made with more than one hundred bullions.

Now that Bonnie had mastered the bullion, the stitch that many experienced crocheters call the "most difficult crochet stitch," she soon learned that few patterns were available using it, so Bonnie created her own. When she decided to make crochet squares using the bullion stitch, she made her own squares, many of which were eventually published in Bonnie's first book, *24 Blocks on a Roll*. It was for this book that Bonnie developed and named the "bent bullion" and the "pearl bullion" stitches.

Because Bonnie loves to share her love of bullions, she features them on her website, www.elegantcrochet.com, which contains free patterns for squares along with instructions for bullions. Her patterns are downloaded and used around the world. She has heard from people in many countries, such as Malaysia, where no patterns like hers exist. Her bullion stitch patterns were featured in the Bar Mitzvah outfits that one of Bonnie's fans made for all thirteen of her grandchildren. Bonnie's squares have appeared in afghans for the mothers, widows, and children of fallen United States soldiers. She participates in many crochet charity projects, such as afghans for hospice and preemie hats and blankets for a neonatal ward, but her finest bullion squares are reserved for afghans for the homeless.

Bonnie has exhibited her crochet and won awards in Israel, Australia, and Wales as well as many spots in the United States. Her work has been displayed at the Lacis Museum of Lace in Berkeley, California, and at the Museum of Arts and Design in New York City for the "Non-Conformist Crochet" demonstration. In 2004, Bonnie was named *Piecework* magazine's Crocheter of the Year.

Bonnie Pierce's beloved bullion stitch is versatile enough to create a delicate metallic thread butterfly (left), make tiny rosebuds to accent a baby's bonnet (center), or even to become the focal point of an heirloom afghan (right).

HOW TO DO THE CROCHETED BULLION STITCH

The bullion stitch is historically an elaborate coiled embroidery stitch done with pure gold metal, used to enrich formal garments as far back as the time of the ancient Romans. Gold bullion embroidery is still used on official garments of high-ranking government officials and military officers.

The same coil technique has been adapted to crochet, creating an interesting textual element. The crocheted bullion stitch (sometimes called the roll stitch) takes practice to master, but once learned it is easy and fun to do.

If you can you make a half double crochet, you will be able to make a bullion stitch. The process is actually the same; think of a bullion stitch as an hdc gone crazy. Practice adding a yo or two to an hdc, because bullions are worked like an hdc but with a lot more yarn overs. Before starting the Blooming Bullions Pillow Cover (see page 112), you'll want to practice the stitch. Use a smooth worsted-weight yarn (weight 4) and a fairly large hook: an H-8 (5mm) or an I-9 (5.5mm). Bullion stitches are always worked on the right side of a piece. Some yarns lend themselves well to bullion stitches. Don't use the end of a fresh skein of yarn to make a bullion stitch—it is kind of crinkly and will just make you split a stitch. Use smooth yarn from the middle of the skein.

Make certain that the space from the hook to the flat spot allows you room enough to maneuver. Make your yarn overs around the shaft of the hook, not the narrow part by the hook. The wrapped yarns should slide easily on your hook. When bullions are completed, roll them gently with your fingers to tighten them up a bit. The yarn overs should lie parallel to each other firmly enough to look like satin stitch embroidery. Use a tapestry needle to "clean up" your bullion, tacking the ch-3 behind the bullions.

Be careful when blocking bullions; don't hold your iron directly over the bullion but rather work around it. Always use a damp pressing cloth or use the steam setting on your iron from a distance of about 8" (20.5cm). Your work can be smoothed and shaped somewhat while blocking.

· · · · · TIPS FROM THE MASTER · · · · ·

Always use a firm, smooth yarn that doesn't split. Keep the yarn overs fairly loose (they should slide easily on the hook) and even.

For the final yarn over, the one that you will draw through all the others, tuck the yarn fairly tightly under the hook. Point the hook facing down, and pull it straight through the yarn overs on the hook as smoothly as you can. You can wiggle the hook a bit while holding the work with your left hand, pinching the base and long underside of the bullion stitch to steady it.

You'll notice a long vertical piece of yarn at the left of each completed bullion stitch. Be sure the tension of this vertical piece is neither too tight nor too loose. Some patterns tell you to work a final chain stitch after completing a bullion, to lock the yarn over rolls in place. Others eliminate this step. Either way works fine. After making a few bullions, use your fingers to straighten and even out the yarn over rolls gently.

Have patience! Nice, full, even bullions can take quite a bit of practice. It's worth the time and effort because they add such a special dimension to your work. If your bullions don't look great at first, then you are right on track! The old Victorian patterns stated that you should expect to fail numerous times when attempting to make the bullion stitch. Each time you fail brings you closer to success. The best advice I can give you is to relax and have fun with the bullion stitches. They do get easier with practice.

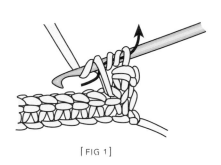

[FIG 1]

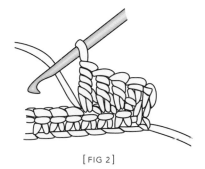

[FIG 2]

THE PRACTICE SWATCH

Ch 21.

ROW 1: Sc in 2nd ch from hook and in each rem ch—20 sc; ch 2 (counts as first hdc of following row), turn.

ROW 2 (RIGHT SIDE): Yo, insert hook in next st and draw up a lp, yo and draw through all 3 lps on hook: one hdc made. Now we will start increasing the number of yos. Yo twice, insert hook in next st and draw up a lp, yo and draw through all 4 lps on hook. **[FIG 1]**

Make the yarn overs fairly loose and even, and make them well up on the shaft of the hook, not on the shaped throat coming from the hook. Now it's going to get a little more difficult, but don't get discouraged. Yo 3 times, insert hook in next stitch and draw up a lp to the same height as the yos, now draw that lp through the 5 yos. **[FIG 2]**

Try to draw the lp through all the yos in one swooping motion—this does take practice. It's fine to use your fingers to pull the yos off one by one until you master the swooping movement, but if you use this method be sure to keep the same tension on each loop. Keep working across the row, adding one more yo each time, until you really get the rhythm of the stitch.

When you make the flower in the center of the pillow cover, you will be making bullions with 15 yos! So keep practicing, and you'll do them just fine.

BLOOMING BULLIONS **PILLOW COVER**

Designed by Bonnie Pierce

SKILL LEVEL
◼◼◼◻ Advanced

SIZE
Approximately 18" x 18"
(45.5cm x 45.5cm)

MATERIALS
- Lion Brand® Yarn *Vanna's Choice*® (100% acrylic, each approximately 3½ oz [100g] and 170 yd [156m], ❹ medium/worsted weight)
  - 340 yd (312m) / 2 skeins in color 860-123 Beige (A)
  - 340 yd (312m) / 2 skeins in color 860-100 White (B)
- One size G-6 (4mm) crochet hook, or size needed to obtain gauge
- One size I-9 (5.5mm) crochet hook (for cording)
- Size 14 steel tapestry needle or plastic yarn needle
- One 18" x 18" (45.5cm x 45.5cm) purchased pillow

GAUGE
16 sc = 4" (10cm) using smaller hook

I chose the pillow to showcase the bullion stitch, as it makes an attractive addition to a room. The bullions are arranged in such a way that they appear lacelike while still being textural.

STITCH GUIDE

BULLION STITCH (BST): Yo loosely and evenly as many times as stated in pattern; insert hook in specified st, yo and draw up a lp even with lps on hook, yo and draw through all lps on hook in one motion.

WRAPPED SC (WRSC): Insert hook in specified st or sp, yo and draw up a lp; working from left to right, take yarn from back of work, wrap it around front of loops and to back again, yo and draw through both lps on hook. This gives a corded effect.

PILLOW COVER

CENTER FRONT MESH SQUARE

With smaller hook and Color A, ch 46.

ROW 1 (RIGHT SIDE): Sc in 2nd ch from hook and in each remaining ch—45 sc; ch 1, turn.

ROW 2: Sc in first sc; (ch 5, sk next 3 sc, sl st in next sc) 10 times; ch 5, sk next 3 sc, sc in last sc—11 ch-5 lps; ch 2, turn.

ROW 3: Dc in first sc; (sl st in next ch-5 lp, ch 5) 10 times; sl st in last ch-5 lp, dc in last sc—10 ch-5 lps; ch 1, turn.

ROW 4: Sc in first dc; (ch 5, sl st in next ch-5 lp) 10 times; ch 5, sc in last dc—11 ch-5 lps; ch 2, turn.

ROWS 5–26: Repeat Rows 3 and 4.

ROW 27: Sc in first sc; (3 sc in next ch-5 lp, sc in next sl st) 10 times, sc in last sc—42 sc. Fasten off; weave in yarn ends. Mark Row 27 as Top.

On a padded surface, pin piece out to measure 12" (30.5cm) square. Lightly steam block; let dry completely before removing pins.

FRONT BORDER

Hold blocked mesh square with right side facing you and Row 27 at top; with smaller hook, join Color A with a sl st in first sc in upper right-hand corner.

RND 1 (RIGHT SIDE): Ch 1, 3 sc in same sc—corner made; work 40 sc evenly spaced across row to last sc, work 3 sc in last sc for corner; working in ends of rows across next side, work 40 sc evenly spaced; working across bottom edge in unused lps of beg ch, work 3 sc in first unused lp for corner; work 40 sc evenly spaced across to last lp, work 3 sc in last lp for corner; working in ends of rows across last side, work 40 sc evenly spaced to first sc; join with a sl st in first sc. You should have 40 sc along top, bottom, and each side, plus 3 sc in each of the four corners.

RND 2: Sl st in next sc (center sc of corner), ch 3 (counts as a dc on this and following rnds), in same st work (dc, ch 2, 2 dc) for first corner; *dc in each sc to center sc of next corner, in center sc work (2 dc, ch 2, 2 dc); repeat from * twice more; dc in each sc to beg ch-3, join with a sl st in 3rd ch (top) of beg ch-3.

RNDS 3–5: Sl st in next dc and into ch-2 corner sp; ch 3, work (dc, ch 2, 2 dc) for corner in same sp; dc in each dc around, working (2 dc, ch 2, 2 dc) in each ch-2 corner sp; join with a sl st in top of beg ch-3.

RND 6: Ch 3 (counts as a dc), dc in next dc, ch 2 for corner; *dc in each dc to next ch-2 sp, ch 2 for corner; repeat from * twice more, dc in each st to beg ch-3; join with a sl st in top of ch-3.

BACK MESH SECTION

RND 1: Continuing to work around front edge, sl st in next dc and into ch-2 corner, ch 5 (counts as a dc and ch-2 sp on this and following rnds), sk next 2 dc, dc in next dc; (ch 2, sk next 2 dc, dc in next dc) 18 times, ch 2 for corner, dc in next dc; (ch 2, sk next 2 dc, dc in next dc) 19 times; repeat from * twice more; ch 2, join with a sl st in 3rd ch of beg ch-5.

RNDS 2–4: Ch 5; *dc in next st, ch 2; repeat from * around; join with a sl st in 3rd ch of beg ch-5.

RNDS 5–7: Ch 4 (counts as a dc and ch-1 sp); *dc in next st, ch 1; repeat from * around; join in 3rd ch of beg ch-4. At end of Rnd 7, fasten off; weave in yarn ends.

Cording

Hold piece with right side of Front facing you; with larger hook, working in front of Rnd 7 of Front Border, join Color A with a sl st in any corner ch-2 sp on Rnd 6; ch 1, work 5 wrsc in same corner sp; *wrsc in each skipped dc on Rnd 6 to next ch-2 corner sp, work 5 wrsc in ch-2 sp;

repeat from * twice more, work wrsc in each remaining skipped dc on Rnd 6, join with a sl st in first wrsc. Fasten off; weave in yarn ends.

CENTER FLOWER MOTIF

RND 1: With smaller hook and Color B, make a loose slip knot on hook; draw the hook up a bit to open up the knot lp, since you will be working the first round into it; (ch 3, work a 10-yo Bst, sl st in lp) 5 times; join with a sl st in 3rd ch of beg ch-3. The 5 Bsts you have just made are called bent Bsts, because the sl st pulls the Bst into a slightly curved shape. Pull gently on the beginning yarn end to draw the center slip knot loop closed.

RND 2: Ch 3, work a 10-yo Bst; *sl st in next ch-3 sp, work 15-yo Bst; repeat from * 3 times more, join with a sl st in first ch-3 sp, sl st in next ch-3 sp—5 bent Bsts.

RND 3: *Ch 4, work a 10-yo Bst, sl st in same ch-3 sp, ch 4, work 15-yo Bst, sl st in next ch-3 sp; repeat from * 4 times more—10 bent Bsts.

RND 4: *Sl st in next ch-4 sp, ch 3; repeat from * around—10 ch-3 sps.

RND 5: Sl st in next ch-3 sp; *ch 3, work 15-yo Bst, sl st in same ch-3 sp, ch 3, 15-yo Bst, sl st in next ch-3 sp; repeat from * 9 times more; join with a sl st in first ch-3 sp—20 bent Bsts. Fasten off; weave in yarn ends.

SCALLOP (Make 8)

RND 1: With smaller hook and Color A, ch 12. Fasten off, leaving a 12" (30.5cm) end for sewing to front mesh square later.

RND 2: With smaller hook, join Color B with a sl st in first ch, ch 1, sc in same ch as joining; work a 5-yo Bst in next ch, ch 1; work a 6-yo Bst in next ch, ch 1; work a 7-yo Bst in next ch, ch 1; work an 8-yo Bst in next ch, ch 1; work a 9-yo Bst in next ch, ch 1; work a 10-yo Bst in next ch, ch 1, work an 11-yo Bst in next ch, ch 1; work a 12-yo Bst in next ch, ch 1; in next ch work (13-yo Bst, ch 1) 3 times; in next ch work (14-yo Bst, ch 1, 15-yo Bst), ch 1; work a 15-yo Bst and a sl st in last ch—14 Bsts. Fasten off; weave in Color B yarn ends.

REVERSE SCALLOP (Make 8)

RND 1: With smaller hook and Color A, ch 12. Fasten off, leaving 12" (30.5cm) end for sewing to mesh square later.

RND 2: With larger hook, join Color B with a sl st in first ch, ch 3, work a 15-yo Bst and a sl st in same ch as joining; turn; sl st in next ch-3 sp, turn; in next ch work (15-yo Bst, ch 1, 14-yo Bst); ch 1, in next ch work (13-yo Bst, ch 1) 3 times; 12-yo Bst in next ch, ch 1, 11-yo Bst in next ch; ch 1, 10-yo Bst in next ch, ch 1; 9-yo Bst in next ch, ch 1, 8-yo Bst in next ch, ch 1, 7-yo Bst in next ch, ch 1, 6-yo Bst in next ch, ch 1, 5-yo Bst in next ch, ch 1, sc in last ch—14 Bsts. Fasten off; weave in Color B yarn ends.

LEAF (Make 4)

With smaller hook and Color A, ch 6; work sl st and sc in 2nd ch from hook, 5-yo Bst in next ch, ch 1; 6-yo Bst in next ch, ch 1; 7-yo Bst in next ch, ch 1; in back lp of next ch work (8-yo Bst, ch 1) 5 times; working in unused lps on opposite side of beg ch, 7-yo Bst in next lp, ch 1; 6-yo Bst in next lp, ch 1; 5-yo Bst in next lp, ch 1; sc in next lp, sl st in last ch. Fasten off, leaving a long yarn end for sewing to Front Mesh Square later.

FINISHING

Following layout shown in photo, using the steel tapestry needle or yarn needle, and yarn to match each motif, sew Center Flower Motif and Leaves to Center Mesh Section. Sew Scallops to Center Mesh Section with Color A, being sure each Scallop is turned in the correct direction as shown in photo.

Place completed pillow cover over purchased pillow, carefully adjusting stitches at corners.

For back drawstring, with smaller hook and Color B, make a chain to measure 56" (142cm). With tapestry needle, weave yarn ends back into chain. To close the back section, weave drawstring alternately over and under stitches of last round of Back Mesh Section, drawing up as needed to fit pillow and securely knotting drawstring. Tie remaining ends into a bow.

OVERLAY CROCHET

with
Melody MacDuffee

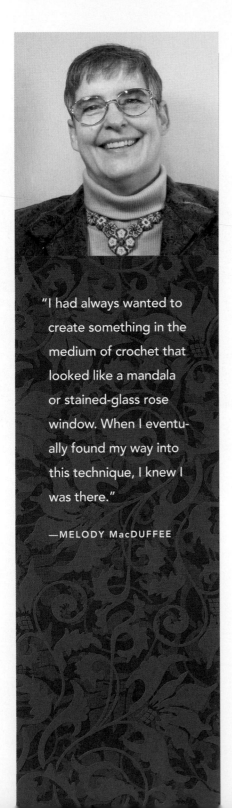

"I had always wanted to create something in the medium of crochet that looked like a mandala or stained-glass rose window. When I eventually found my way into this technique, I knew I was there."

—MELODY MacDUFFEE

Melody and her sister taught themselves to crochet when they were twelve. It was love at first stitch. From that hour on, despite a few casual flings with embroidery, cross-stitch, needlepoint, and knitting, she knew that crochet would be her medium. Even so, from the beginning she was concerned about what she felt were the constraints of crochet. She got tired of the horizontal and concentric striping that was typical of most of the designs she was seeing at the time. To achieve the complex multicolored effects she wanted seemed to require changing colors every few stitches. That would mean weaving in and tying off hundreds and hundreds of tails, a task she did not relish.

What she wanted to produce were vivid mandalas, jewel-like stained-glass windows, and the magical views seen through a kaleidoscope's lens. And she wanted to produce this with a crochet hook. She explored various techniques to see whether she could produce the sought-after effects. Most of them led to dead ends, so she continued enjoying other types of crochet.

She soon became interested in working cables in crochet. It didn't occur to her that this was the technique that would lead her to the breakthrough she had been hoping for. Gradually, over the course of several decades, after a lot of experimentation with color changes, her work in cable crochet gave birth to something that looked new and different. It's really not new, just an extension of something that's been around for a long time: Overlay crochet, densely textured cable crochet with color changes on every row or round. Since the long stitches cover up the horizontal rows or concentric rounds behind them, they make any unwanted ones disappear like magic. And since those same long stitches constitute frequent interruptions in the lines of color belonging to each round or row, one gets the illusion that colors change every few stitches, but without the labor. Melody had developed her own technique for overlay crochet.

Melody has been publishing her work since 1989, when she entered an

afghan contest sponsored by a crochet magazine and earned an honorable mention. Since that time, almost two hundred of her designs, ranging from fine Irish lace to colorful doilies to afghans, have appeared inside and on the covers of magazines and books.

She currently spends a fair amount of time traveling around the country, teaching the overlay technique to crocheters from New York to Alaska. Examples of Melody's work have been exhibited in juried shows in several states, and she has published several books on the overlay technique.

Although she spends a lot of her time designing jewelry, teaching jewelry-making techniques, and writing freelance articles, her heart is in overlay crochet. Using this technique, she can create complex mandalas that satisfy her ongoing cravings for intricately (and infinitely) repeating patterns in rich, saturated, riotous color. And that's what makes her the happiest.

In addition to working with overlay crochet, Melody uses her design skills and color sense to create jewelry (left). Strategic color changes of the overlay technique create colorful medallions seen in everything from pillow toppers to purses.

HOW TO DO OVERLAY CROCHET

Overlay crochet involves creating a background fabric of single crochet, always worked with the right side facing you. The single crochet stitches are always worked in the back loops only of the previous rows or rounds, leaving the front loops free to become anchor points for a variety of long, often complex, stitches and clusters of stitches that "overlay" the single crochet background fabric.

The back loop of a stitch is always the loop at the top of the stitch that is farthest away from you. **[FIG 1]**

back loop

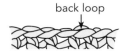

[FIG 1]

Front post stitches are used often to add texture and dimension to overlay projects. Whether the post stitch is worked with a dc, tr, or taller stitch, it is always worked by inserting the hook from front to back to front again around the post (vertical part) of the stitch. **[FIG 2]**

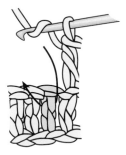

[FIG 2]

A number a special stitches that may be unfamiliar are used in working overlay projects. Here is a stitch guide to explain how each one is worked:

STITCH GUIDE

Long sc (Lsc): Insert hook in specified st or sp and draw up a lp to height of current rnd, yo and draw through 2 lps on hook—Lsc made.

2 sc decrease (2scdec): *Insert hook in first specified st and draw up a lp; repeat from * in second specified st, once; yo and draw through all 3 lps on hook—2scdec made.

2 tr decrease (2trdec): *Yo twice, insert hook in first specified st and draw up a lp, (yo and draw through 2 lps on hook) twice; repeat from * in second st once; yo and draw through all 3 lps on hook—2trdec made.

2 dtr decrease (2dtrdec): *Yo 3 times, insert hook in first specified st and draw up a lp, (yo and draw through 2 lps on hook) 3 times; repeat from * in second st once; yo and draw through all 3 lps on hook—2dtrdec made.

Front Post tr (FPtr): Yo twice, insert hook from front to back to front around post of specified st and draw up a lp, (yo and draw through 2 lps on hook) 3 times—FPtr made.

Front Post dtr (FPdtr): Yo 3 times, insert hook from front to back to front around post of specified st and draw up a lp, (yo and draw through 2 lps on hook) 4 times—FPdtr made.

Front Post trtr (FPtrtr): Yo 4 times, insert hook from front to back to front around post of specified st and draw up a lp, (yo and draw through 2 lps on hook) 5 times—FPtrtr made.

Front Post 2 tr decrease (FP2trdec): *Yo twice, insert hook from front to back to front around post of first specified st and draw up a lp, (yo and draw through 2 lps on hook) twice; repeat from * in second st once; yo and draw through all 3 lps on hook—FP2trdec made.

Front Post 2 dtr decrease (FP2dtrdec): *Yo 3 times, insert hook from front to back to front around post of first specified st and draw up a lp, (yo and draw through 2 lps on hook) 3 times; repeat from * in second st once; yo and draw through all 3 lps on hook—FP2dtrdec made.

Front Post 2 trtr decrease (FP2trtrdec): *Yo 4 times, insert hook from front to back to front around post of first specified st and draw up a lp, (yo and draw through 2 lps on hook) 4 times; repeat from * in second st once; yo and draw through all 3 lps on hook—FP2trtrdec made.

OVERLAY MANDALA **PILLOW COVER**

Designed by Melody MacDuffee

SKILL LEVEL

◼◼◼▭ Experienced

SIZE

Approximately 15" (38cm) diameter

MATERIALS

- DMC® *Six Strand Embroidery Floss* (100% cotton, each approximately 8.75 yd [8m])
  - 44 yd (40m) / 5 skeins in color 3760 Medium Wedgewood (blue)
  - 44 yd (40m) / 5 skeins in color 816 Garnet (red)
  - 53 yd (48m) / 6 skeins in color 921 Copper (orange)
  - 44 yd (40m) / 5 skeins in color 977 Light Golden Brown (yellow)
  - 44 yd (40m) / 5 skeins in color 500 Very Dark Blue Green (dark green)
  - 44 yd (40m) / 5 skeins in color 3848 Medium Teal Green (turquoise)
  - 35 yd (32m) / 4 skeins in color 3346 Hunter Green (lime green)
  - 44 yd (40m) / 5 skeins in color 780 Ultra Very Dark Topaz (brown)
- One size 7 (1.65mm) steel crochet hook, or size needed to obtain gauge
- One 15" x 15" (38cm x 38cm) purchased pillow

CONTINUED ON PAGE 122

Overlay crochet lets me create the impression of frequent color changes on each round without actually having to start with a new thread every few stitches and weave in all those ends.

This was actually my first successful overlay design, the first one to really get the look I'd been after. It's still my favorite.

CONTINUED FROM PAGE 120

GAUGE

Rnds 1–7 = 2½" (6.5cm)
diameter

NOTES

- A number of special stitches
  that may be unfamiliar to you
  are used in working overlay
  projects. An explanation
  of those stitches appears
  under Stitch Guide on
  pages 118–119.
- Always work sts in back
  lps only throughout unless
  otherwise instructed.
- All rnds are worked on right
  side. To join a new color,
  simply pull a lp of new color
  (or join with a sl st) in specified
  st unless otherwise instructed.

PILLOW COVER

With blue, ch 6; join with a sl st to form a ring.

RND 1 (RIGHT SIDE): With red, work 8 sc in ring—8 sc; join
with a sl st in first sc.

RND 2: With dark green, work 2 sc in each st around—16
sc; join as before.

RND 3: With blue, (2 sc in next st, sc in next st) 8
times—24 sc; join. Fasten off; weave in ends.

RND 4: Join red with a sl st in any st, (sc in next st, 2 dc in
front lp of st on Rnd 1 straight down from current st, sk
st on Rnd 3 behind 2 dc just made; sc in next 2 sts, 2 sc
in next st, sc in next st) 4 times—32 sts; join. Fasten off;
weave in ends.

RND 5: Join orange in sc 2 sts before any 2 dc pair, (sc in
next sc, tr in front lp of st on Rnd 1 before next 2 dc pair,
sc in next 2 dc, tr in front lp of st on Rnd 1 after same 2
dc pair, sc in next 5 sc) 4 times—40 sts; join. Fasten off;
weave in ends.

RND 6: Join yellow in sc 2 sts before first tr, (sc in next sc,
dtr in same st on Rnd 1 as tr made on Rnd 5, sk tr on Rnd
5 behind dtr just made, sc in next 2 sc, dtr in same st on
Rnd 1 as next tr made on Rnd 5, sk tr on Rnd 5 behind dtr
just made, sc in next 2 sc, 2 sc in each of next 2 sc, sc in
next sc) 4 times—48 sts; join. Fasten off; weave in ends.

RND 7: Join dark green in st before first dtr, (sc in next
dtr, sc in next 3 sts, 7 trtr in front lp of st on Rnd 2 most
directly centered between last dtr and next dtr: fan made)
4 times—44 sts; join. Fasten off; weave in ends.

RND 8: Join yellow in last trtr of any fan, (sc in next sc, 2 sc
in each of next 2 sc, sc in next sc, sc in next 3 trtr, 2trdec
in front lps of previous and next yellow dtrs on Rnd 6, sk
trtr on Rnd 7 behind 2trdec just made, sc in last 3 trtr) 4
times—52 sts; join. Fasten off; weave in ends.

RND 9: Join orange in last sc, (sc in next 8 sts, 2 sc in next
st, 2dtrdec in front lp of yellow st on Rnd 6 before st with
first leg of 2trdec on Rnd 8 and in front lp of yellow st on
Rnd 6 just after st with 2nd leg of same 2trdec, sk 2trdec
on Rnd 8 behind 2dtrdec just made, 2 sc in next st, sc in
next 2 sts) 4 times—60 sts; join. Fasten off; weave in ends.

RND 10: Join red in last sc, (sc in next 2 sc, 2 sc in each of next 2 sts, sc in next 6 sts, 2dtrdec in front lps of same yellow sts on Rnd 6 with first and 2nd legs of 2dtrdec on Rnd 9, sk 2dtrdec on Rnd 9 behind 2dtrdec just made, sc in next 4 sts) 4 times—68 sts; join. Fasten off; weave in ends.

RND 11: Join blue in last sc, sc in each st around; join. Fasten off; weave in ends.

RND 12: Join turquoise in 2nd sc, (sc in next 2 sts, 2scdec in same st and in next st, sc in same st as 2nd leg of 2scdec, sc in next st, ch 4, sl st in front lp of 2nd dark green trtr of next fan on Rnd 7, ch 4, sk next 4 sts on Rnd 11, sc in next 5 sts, ch 4, sl st in 6th dark green trtr of same fan on Rnd 7, ch 4, sk next 4 sts on Rnd 11) 4 times—40 sc and 8 (ch 4, sl st, ch 4) sps; join. Fasten off; weave in ends.

RND 13: Join lime green in 2nd sc on Rnd 11 (same st as Rnd 12 beg joining), (on Rnd 12 work: sc in next 2 sts, 2 sc in next st, sc in next 2 sts; on Rnd 11 work: sc in 4 blue skipped sts) 8 times—80 sts; join. Fasten off; weave in ends.

RND 14: Join yellow in last sc, (sc in next 6 sts, ch 3, sl st in front lp of red st on Rnd 10 at center of turquoise "V" worked on Rnd 12, ch 3, sk next 4 sts on Rnd 13) 8 times—48 sc and 8 (ch 3, sl st, ch 3) sps; join. Fasten off; weave in ends.

CENTER

With orange, ch 5; join with a sl st to form a ring.

RND 1 (RIGHT SIDE): Work 10 sc in ring: 10 sc; join with a sl st in first sc.

RND 2: [Work (sc, hdc, dc, tr, dtr, tr, dc, hdc, sc) in next st, sl st in next st] 5 times—5 petals; join as before. Fasten off; weave in ends.

RND 3: Join lime green in first sc, (sc in next 3 sts, 3 sc in dtr, sc in next 3 sts, sk next sc, Lsc in center ring, sk next sl st and next sc) 5 times—50 sts; join. Fasten off; weave in ends.

NOTE: *Joining sc on next round are made by holding flower upside down behind main piece with wrong sides together and working through back lps of both pieces.*

RND 15: Join brown in 3rd sc on Rnd 14; *sc in next 2 sts, holding a flower behind main piece with wrong sides together, work joining sc in next st on Rnd 14 and in first sc of 3 sc at flower petal tip at same time, (work joining sc in next ch on Rnd 14 and in next sc on flower [previous sc worked on Rnd 3] at same time) twice; ch 2, sk next 3 sts on Rnd 14 (ch, sl st and ch) and next 3 sts on flower (ch, Lsc and ch), (work joining sc in next ch on Rnd 14 and in next sc on next petal of same flower at same time) twice; work joining sc in next sc on Rnd 14 and in next sc on flower (3rd sc of 3 sc on Rnd 3 of flower at tip of next petal) at same time, sc in next 2 sts on Rnd 14; repeat from * 7 times more—80 sc and 8 ch-2 sps; join. Fasten off; weave in ends.

RND 16: Join red in last sc, (sc in next 2 sts; holding flower extended outward wth the right side of work facing you and working on Rnd 3 of flower: sk 2nd sc of 3 sc on Rnd 3 of flower at tip of petal; *sc in next 3 sts, sk next 3 sts [sc, Lsc and sc], sc in next 3 sts**; 3 sc in next st [2nd sc of 3 sc at tip of next petal]; repeat from * 4 times more, ending last repeat at **; sk last sc on flower [2nd sc of 3 sc at tip of petal]; sc in next 2 sts on Rnd 15) 8 times—296 sc; join. Fasten off; weave in ends.

RND 17: Join yellow in last sc; *sc in next st, sk next 2 sts, sc in next 2 sts; **sk next st, sc in next 3 sts, 3 sc in next st, sc in next 3 sts, sk next st**; sc in next 4 sts, 3 sc in next st, sc in next 4 sts; repeat from ** to ** once; sc in next 2 sts, sk next 2 sts, sc in next st; repeat from * 7 times more—280 sts; join. Fasten off; weave in ends.

RND 18: Join turquoise in next to last sc; *2scdec in next 2 sts, sc in next 6 sts, (3 sc in next st, sc in next 9 sts) twice, 3 sc in next st, sc in next 6 sts; repeat from * 7 times more—320 sts; join with a sl st in first 2scdec. Fasten off; weave in ends.

NOTE: Joining sc on next round are worked through wrong side of back lps of corresponding sts on previous flower when working on side of next flower.

RND 19: Join dark green in first sc of 3-sc cluster on Rnd 18 at center tip of any flower; (3 sc in next st, sc in next 11 sts, 3 sc in next st, sc in next 7 sts, sl st in 2scdec, sc in next st; working in next 5 sts on new flower and in 6th through 2nd sc of previous flower [work joining sc in corresponding sts] 5 times; working now on right side of new flower only, sc in next st [first sc of previous 7 sc], 3 sc in next st, sc in next 11 sts) 8 times—360 sc, counting joining sc, and 8 sl sts; join with a sl st in first sc. Fasten off; weave in ends.

RND 20: Join brown in first sc of 3-sc cluster on Rnd 19 at center tip of any flower, (3 sc in next st, sc in next 14 sts, ending in center sc of 3-sc cluster, sk next 4 sc [2 sc before and 2 sc after joining sc], sc in next 14 sts) 8 times—248 sts; join as before. Fasten off; weave in ends.

RND 21: Join yellow in first sc of any 3-sc cluster, (3 sc in next st, sc in next 13 sts, 3 tr in 5th sc of 5 dark green joining sc on Rnd 19, sk next 4 sts on Rnd 20 behind 3 tr just made, sc in next 13 sts) 8 times—256 sts; join. Fasten off; weave in ends.

RND 22: Join blue in first sc of any 3 sc cluster, (3 sc in next st, sc in next 13 sts, dtr in same dark green joining sc on Rnd 19 as 3 tr on Rnd 21, placing it before first yellow tr, sk st on Rnd 21 behind dtr just made, sc in next 3 tr, dtr in same dark green joining sc as last dtr worked, placing it after 3rd yellow tr, sk st on Rnd 21 behind dtr just made, sc in next 13 sts) 8 times—272 sts; join. Fasten off; weave in ends.

RND 23: Join turquoise in first sc of any 3-sc cluster, (3 sc in next st, sc in next 7 sts, sk next st, sc in next 6 sc, sc in

next dtr, *dtr in same dark green joining sc on Rnd 19 as dtr on Rnd 22, placing it between first and 2nd yellow tr on Rnd 21, sk sc on Rnd 22 behind dtr just made**; sc in next sc; repeat from * to **, placing this dtr between 2nd and 3rd yellow tr on Rnd 21; sc in next dtr, sc in next 6 sts, sk next st, sc in next 7 sts) 8 times—272 sts; join. Fasten off; weave in ends.

RND 24: Join lime green in first sc of any 3-sc cluster, (3 sc in next st, sc in next 15 sts; *trtr in same dark green joining sc as dtr in Rnd 23, placing it before first turquoise dtr, sk dtr on Rnd 23 behind trtr just made**; sc in next sc; repeat from * to **, placing this trtr after 2nd turquoise dtr; sc in next 15 sts) 8 times—288 sts; join. Fasten off; weave in ends.

RND 25: Join dark green with sc in front lp of 2nd sc of 3-sc cluster on Rnd 19 at center tip above any flower; *ch 5, sc in 9th st before next trtr, sc in next 2 sts, FPdtr around post of first yellow tr of next 3 yellow tr on Rnd 21, sk st on Rnd 24 behind FPdtr just made, sc in next 13 sts, FPdtr around post of 3rd yellow tr of same 3 yellow tr on Rnd 21, sk st on Rnd 24 behind FPdtr just made, sc in next 3 sts, ch 5**; sl st in front lp of 2nd sc of 3-sc cluster on Rnd 19 at center tip above next flower; repeat from * 7 times more, ending last repeat at **—176 sts and 16 ch-5 sps; join. Fasten off; weave in ends.

RND 26: Join turquoise in first sc, (sc in each of next 5 chs, sc in next 5 sts; *FPtr around post of next blue dtr on Rnd 22, sk st on Rnd 25 behind FPtr just made**; sc in next 9 sts; repeat from * to ** once; sc in next 5 sts, sc in next 5 chs, sk next sc) 8 times—248 sts; join. Fasten off; weave in ends.

RND 27: Join blue in next to last sc, (2scdec in next 2 sts, sc in next 4 sts, 2 sc in next st, sc in next 6 sts; reaching back with hook *FPtr around post of next turquoise dtr on Rnd 23, sk st on Rnd 26 behind FPtr just made**; sc in next 5 sts; repeat from * to ** once; sc in next 6 sts, 2 sc in next st, sc in next 4 sts) 8 times—256 sts; join with a sl st in first 2scdec. Fasten off; weave in ends.

RND 28: Join brown in last sc, (sc in next 2scdec, sc in next 14 sts; *FPtr around post of next lime green trtr on Rnd 24, sk st on Rnd 27 behind FPtr just made** sc in next st;

repeat from * to ** once; sc in next 14 sts) 8 times; join with a sl st in first sc. Fasten off; weave in ends.

RND 29: Join yellow in last sc, (working in front lp of st below, Lsc in next 3 turquoise sc on Rnd 26, sk 3 sc on working row behind the 3 Lsc, sc in next 27 sts, Lsc in next 2 turquoise sc on Rnd 26, skipping sc behind these sts) 8 times; join with a sl st in first Lsc. Fasten off; weave in ends.

RND 30: Join orange in sc before any 5 Lsc, (sc in next 5 Lsc, sc in next 2 sts, 2 sc in next st, sc in next 21 sts, 2 sc in next st, sc in next 2 sts) 8 times—272 sts; join with a sl st in first sc. Fasten off; weave in ends.

RND 31: Join red in last sc, (dc in next 5 sts, 2 hdc in next st, sc in next 12 sts, 2scdec in next 2 sc, 2scdec in same st as 2nd leg of 2scdec and in next sc, sc in next 12 sts, 2 hdc in next st) 8 times—280 sts; join with a sl st in first dc. Fasten off; weave in ends.

RND 32: Join brown in 6th st before first st, (tr in front lp of first yellow Lsc of next 5 yellow Lsc groups on Rnd 29, sk st on Rnd 31 behind tr just made, sc in next 13 sts, reaching back with hook, tr in front lp of last Lsc in same group of 5 Lsc worked on Rnd 29, sk st on Rnd 31 behind tr just made, sc in next 9 sts, FP2trdec around posts of next 2 brown FPtr on Rnd 28, sk both 2scdec on Rnd 31 behind FP2trdec just made, sc in next 9 sts) 8 times—272 sts; join with a sl st in first tr. Fasten off; weave in ends.

RND 33: Join blue in st before last st, (tr in front lp of blue sc on Rnd 27 before st where first yellow Lsc of next 5 yellow Lsc on Rnd 29 was worked, sk st on Rnd 32 behind tr just made, sc in next 15 sts, tr in front lp of blue sc on Rnd 27 after st where 5th yellow Lsc of same 5 yellow Lsc on Rnd 29 was worked, sk st on Rnd 32 behind tr just made, sc in next 8 sts, FP2dtrdec around posts of next 2 blue dtr on Rnd 22, sk st on Rnd 32 behind FP2dtrdec just made, sc in next 8 sts) 8 times; join as before. Fasten off; weave in ends.

RND 34: Join turquoise in st before last st, (dtr in front lp of turquoise sc on Rnd 26 before st where next blue tr on Rnd 33 was worked, sk st on Rnd 33 behind dtr just made, sc in next 3 sts, 2 sc in next st, sc in next 9 sts, 2 sc in next st, sc in next 3 sts, dtr in front lp of turquoise sc on Rnd 26 after st where next blue tr on Rnd 33 was worked, sk st on Rnd 33 behind dtr just made, Lsc in next 7 brown sc on Rnd 32, FP2dtrdec around posts of next 2 turquoise FPtr on Rnd 26, sk st on Rnd 33 behind FP2dtrdec just made, sc in next 7 brown sc on Rnd 32) 8 times—288 sts; join with a sl st in first dtr. Fasten off; weave in ends.

RND 35: Join dark green st before last st, (trtr in dark green sc on Rnd 25 before st where next turquoise dtr on Rnd 34 was worked, sk st on Rnd 34 behind trtr just made, sc in next 21 sts, trtr in front lp of dark green sc on Rnd 25 after st where next turquoise dtr on Rnd 34 was worked, sk st on Rnd 34 behind trtr just made, sc in next 3 sts, 2 sc in next st, sc in next 2 sts, FP2trtrdec around posts of next 2 dark green dtr on Rnd 25, sk st on Rnd 34 behind FP2trtrdec just made, sc in next 2 sts, 2 sc in next st, sc in next 3 sts) 8 times—304 sts; join with a sl st in first trtr. Do not fasten off.

RND 36: Sc in each st around; join with a sl st in first sc. Fasten off; weave in ends.

FINISHING

Sew finished piece to front of purchased pillow.

EDGES OF PILLOW

BEAD CROCHET

with

Lydia Borin

"I am a beadwork historian, and when I realized this stitch was crochet, not knitting, I had to learn more. I found bags using this "swag" stitch were most popular from 1860 to 1880 and resurfaced in the 1970s. It is exciting to make a bag or jewelry today based on an obscure stitch that has been in existence for at least 160 years. "

—LYDIA BORIN

Born in Beaumont, Texas, Lydia Borin grew up in New Mexico. Her interest in the arts began at age four, when she made dolls with her grandmother's buttons, and she continued to experiment with various crafts throughout her life. From the age of nine, until she was fourteen, she spent her summers on Native American reservations in the Southwest.

While her husband was in the military, Lydia traveled extensively in both Europe and Asia. In 1980, Lydia and her husband retired to Florida, where Lydia, an oil painter for more than twenty-five years, switched to a career in fiber arts. She learned beading, weaving, stitchery, crochet, knitting, hand spinning, macramé, and many other crafts. She mastered beading and bead crochet, publishing three books, including *Beadwrangler's Hands-on Crochet with Beads and Fiber*. She taught many classes, including beading classes, at the local university in Florida.

In order to reach a larger audience, Lydia started her website, www.bead wrangler.com. The website became her teaching arena, offering free projects, beadwork samplers, storytelling, history, creature making, and much more. She then added two teaching sites: www.beadcrochet.com and www.beadknit.com. Her viewers began to request kits, and she created another site, www.7beads.com, where viewers can purchase not only her kits but also all of the kit components, including beads, fiber, needles and other tools.

Lydia remains a mentor to many bead and fiber artists. She continues her beadwork history studies, learning through making samplers and researching historical information.

OPPOSITE: In the centuries-old tradition of using beads as decoration, Lydia Borin adds glittering beads to crochet to create striking accessories from headpieces to evening bags to jewelry.

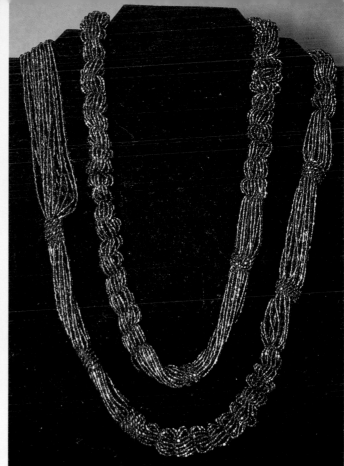

HOW TO DO BEAD CROCHET

Bead crochet is an exciting method of crocheting with yarn or thread in which beads are added as you crochet. You can string the beads onto the yarn/thread before starting to crochet or while crocheting. There are several special stitches used in bead crochet, such as the bead chain, bead loop, and bead single crochet. The beads generally fall to the back of the stitches, but they can also be oriented on the front of the stitches with minor changes. Beads can be added one at a time or in groups, such as in a bead loop.

To learn the technique of bead crochet, work the necklace project on page 130. The beads are strung onto the thread before the necklace is started. The necklace starts with a single crochet foundation instead of a foundation chain. Each of the two necklace sections is worked in three strips with loops of beads worked in the bead single crochet stitches, each strip worked onto the previous strip.

This necklace has a soft, sensual, undulating appearance, much like an exotic ribbon. A large focal bead joins two front sections together, and a small focal bead is set below a button on the opposite end with a beaded loop on the other, which makes for a dynamic finish.

The necklace has a single crochet foundation, swag stitch body and netting embellishment to the large focal bead. It can be made longer, shorter, wrapped tighter or looser, or more strips can be added; the swag is a diverse and exciting stitch. The swag section rows can be set vertical or turned horizontal.

Experiment with this stitch and add a new repertoire to your bead crochet.

STITCH GUIDE

To work a bead chain (bch), slide 1 bead up to hook, yarn over and draw through lp on hook, securing bead.

To work a bead single crochet (bsc), insert hook in specified stitch, yarn over and draw up a lp (2 lps on hook), slide bead up to hook, yarn over and draw through both lps on hook, securing bead.

To work a bead lp (bdlp), work a bsc, sliding appropriate number of beads (more than one) up to hook before last

yarn over. A "bdlp" is added in parentheses to any bsc with more than one bead in that stitch. Example: bsc (5 bdlp).

NOTE: Use forefinger of opposite hand to hold beads while last yarn over is completed.

A swag strip requires one row of bead lps and one row of stitches worked into bead lps to connect the lps. At the end of the bead lp row, turn, bch the number of stitches required to reach the height of the bead lps in the previous row. Insert the hook in the center of the bead lp with half of the beads on each side of the hook. Yo and draw up a lp, yo and draw through both lps on hook: sc made. Both rows (one of bead lps and one of stitches worked into bead lps) are repeated to form a swag strip.

CRYSTALISE **NECKLACE**

Designed by Lydia Borin, The Beadwrangler

SKILL LEVEL

◼◼◼◻ Intermediate

SIZE
Approximately 29" (73.5cm) long (including focal bead)

MATERIALS
- On the Surface *New Metallics 2-Ply Metallic Gimp Thread* (each approximately 100 yd [92m])
  - 100 yd (92m) / 1 spool in color 15 Aquamarine
- One size 12 (1.00mm) steel crochet hook, or size needed to obtain gauge
- 2 hanks (each approximately 30g), size 11/0 clear seed beads
- 2 crystal cube focal beads (with square center opening), sizes 12mm and 30mm
- Size 7 or 8 tapestry needle
- Size Medium twisted flexible wire needle (or dental floss threader)

GAUGE
8 bdlps = 1" (2.5cm); 3 swag strips (6 rows) = 1" (2.5cm).

I designed this project because it includes more than one technique; crocheters can make adjustments for a longer or shorter necklace, add a focal bead, make bead crochet netting for attachment of the focal bead to the swag pieces, and make a button and loop closure. I love the versatility of this necklace, and these techniques can be used for many other projects as well.

STITCH GUIDE

FOUNDATION SINGLE CROCHET (FSC): Ch 2, insert hook in 2nd ch from hook, yo and draw up a lp, yo and draw through one lp on hook (ch made at base of fsc), yo and draw through both lps on hook—first fsc completed. *Insert hook in ch at base of previous fsc, yo and draw up a lp, yo and draw through one lp on hook (ch made), yo and draw through both lps on hook—fsc completed. Repeat from * as many times as needed to work required number of fsc.

BEAD CHAIN (BCH): Slide 1 bead up to hook, yo and draw through lp on hook, securing bead.

BEAD SINGLE CROCHET (BSC): Insert hook in specified stitch, yo and draw up a lp (2 lps on hook), slide bead up to hook, yo and draw through both lps on hook, securing bead.

BEAD LOOP (BDLP): Bead lps are formed when working bsc, sliding appropriate number of beads (more than one) up to hook before last yarn over. A "bdlp" is added in parentheses to any bsc with more than one bead in that stitch. Example: bsc (5 bdlp).

NOTE: Use forefinger of opposite hand to hold beads while last yarn over is completed.

SWAG STRIP: This technique requires one row of bead lps and one row of stitches worked into bead lps to connect lps. At the end of the bead lp row, turn, then work number of bch stitches to reach the height of the bead lps in the previous row. Insert the hook in the center of the bead lp with half of the beads on each side of the hook; yo and draw up a lp, yo and draw through both lps on hook— sc made. Both rows (one of bead lps and one of stitches worked into bead lps) are repeated to form a swag strip.

GENERAL INSTRUCTIONS

The necklace is composed of two sections, with each section having three swag strips. One section is shorter than the other. Bead crochet netting is created on the straight end of each section, which is then attached to opposite corners of a focal bead, pulling the whole necklace together. The necklace closure is made at the other end of the sections, made up of a button-and-loop closure. A small focal bead is placed onto one of the ends, and the swag strips are stitched together at that end to form a button. The lp closure is made at the end of the other section with a bead crochet lp that is set over the button and bead to complete the closure. Having one section longer and one shorter sets the focal bead at an asymmetrical angle, resulting in a very attractively balanced necklace.

STRING BEADS

Use a twisted flexible wire needle (the eye collapses as the beads pass through) to string the beads directly onto crochet thread before crocheting. Add about 2 yards (183cm) of beads each time you run out, allowing you to finish a swag strip before needing more beads. When you run out of beads, fasten off, leaving a 3" (7.5cm) tail of thread. String more beads, insert the hook from the wrong side to the right side, place a slip knot on the hook, pull the slip knot and hook through to the wrong side, ch 1, and the new thread is attached. Stitch over the fastened-off thread at the end of a strip. Add new thread to work the closures.

HINT: Use a soft hair curler with a clip to wrap the excess thread strung with beads when storing.

NECKLACE SECTIONS

Each swag section is composed of 3 strips of bead lps between rows of thread stitches. String the beads onto the thread before starting.

FIRST SECTION
Foundation Row: Fsc 236 sts—236 sc; ch 1, turn.

ROW 1: Work bsc (10 bdlp) in first st, sl st in next st; *bsc (10 bdlp) in next st, sl st in next st; repeat from * across—118 bsc and 118 sl sts; tu rn.

ROW 2: Bch 3, sc between 5th and 6th bead in center of first bdlp; *ch 1, sc between 5th and 6th bead in center of next bdlp; repeat from * across—118 sc and 117 chs; ch 1, turn.

ROW 3: Work bsc (10 bdlp) in first sc, sl st in next ch; *bsc (10 bdlp) in next sc, sl st in next ch; repeat from * across to last 3 sts—116 bsc and 116 sl sts; ch 1, turn, leaving last 3 sts unworked.

ROW 4: Repeat Row 2—116 sc and 115 chs.

ROW 5: Repeat Row 3—114 bsc and 114 sl sts.

ROW 6: Repeat Row 2—114 sc and 113 chs; ch 1, turn. Do not fasten off.

Netting

ROW 1: Work bsc in first 12 sts—12 bsc; join with a sl st in first bsc. Do not turn. Work now progresses in rounds.

RND 1: Ch 1, sc in same st as joining, 3 bch; *sc in next st, bch 3; repeat from* around—12 sc and 12 bch 3; join with a sl st in first sc.

RND 2: Ch 1 loosely; *sc in center ch of next 3-bch, 3 bch; repeat from * around; join with a sl st in first sc.

RNDS 3 AND 4: Repeat Rnd 2, twice more. At end of Rnd 4, fasten off, leaving a 12" (30.5cm) tail.

SECOND SECTION

Foundation Row: Fsc 150 sts—150 sc; ch 1, turn.

ROWS 1–6: Work same as Rows 1–6 on First Section—Row 1: 75 bsc and 75 sl sts; Row 2: 75 sc and 74 chs; Row 3: 73 bsc and 73 sl sts; Row 4: 73 sc and 72 chs; Row 5: 71 bsc and 71 sl sts; Row 6: 71 sc and 70 chs.

Netting

Work same as Netting on First Section.

Attaching Netting to Focal Bead

Set the two sections with netting on each side of the large focal bead. Thread a needle with tail from one section. Place the focal bead in the center of the netting with netting encasing one corner of bead. Firmly stitch the center of the netting over the center of the focal bead so the netting lies flat on both sides of the bead and the thread is taut. Secure thread and weave in ends. Repeat for the other section on the opposite corner of the focal bead.

CLASP

BUTTON CLOSURE

Put a small focal bead over the other end of the First Section and push it down over the section until it will go no farther. With needle and thread, stitch back and forth through a few stitches on the same end until the thread is taut. Stitch back and forth between stitches at the end of the section, pulling bead lps close together until it looks like a rounded ball, securing the bead onto the section past the formed "button." Stitch through a few stitches next to the bead until the thread is taut. Fasten off; securely weave in ends.

NOTE: The clasp receives the most wear, so make sure the stitches will not come out.

LOOP CLOSURE

String some beads onto the thread and join with a sl st in first st on Foundation Row at the other end of the Second Section. Chain approx 27 (or number of chains required to wrap around below the small focal bead), sl st in next st on Foundation Row on Second Section to form a loop. Check to see if the chains fit over the small focal bead and do not come off too easily. Add or remove some chains until the correct length is achieved; turn; sl st in first sl st, bsc in each ch around, sl st in last sl st made, working on other side of ch, bsc in each ch around. Fasten off; securely weave in ends.

With wear, loop closure may stretch and become too big to stay in place over focal bead on button closure. If this happens, stitch through beginning and end of loop at base of loop next to strip of necklace to make loop smaller.

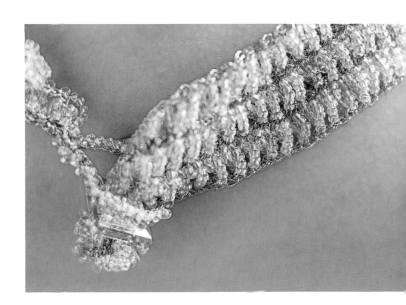

BRUGES CROCHET

with
Tatyana Mirer

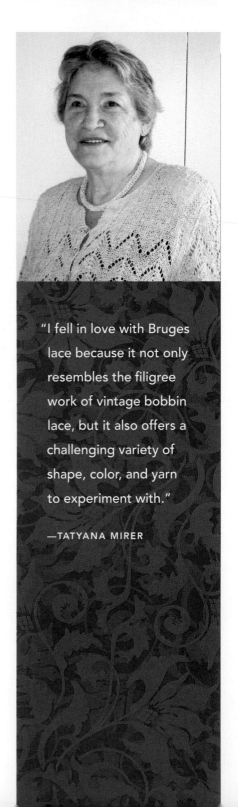

B orn in Moscow, Russia, Tatyana Mirer feels that her passion for crochet must have come from her grandmother, who decorated her home with crocheted and embroidered pieces.

Tatyana was very young when her grandmother died, so she never learned any of these skills from her directly. However, Tatyana still remembers the lovely starched doilies and tablecloths as well as the embroidered pillows and handkerchiefs in her grandmother's home.

Eager to learn to crochet, Tatyana was delighted when her school taught the basic crochet stitches to the girls. She fell in love with the skill and was able to re-create some of her grandmother's samples. Crochet had become her hobby.

Tatyana graduated from the Moscow Design Institute, formerly called the Moscow Institute of Light Industry, with a bachelor's degree in fashion design. At the beginning of her professional career she worked for a manufacturer of women's wear. Later she was employed at the Central Research Institute for the Sewing Industry and was co-author of a book, *Women Clothes Sewing Technology*, published in Moscow.

When her two boys were young, Tatyana wanted to change careers so that she would have more time for the children. She decided to turn her crochet hobby into her profession. She began teaching crochet to both children and adults, and soon she started selling her designs to Russian magazines. To improve her crochet skills, she completed a two-year program at the Moscow Art University.

In 1991, the family emigrated to the United States, and Tatyana, not sure what kind of job she might find in New York, took a sewing and patternmaking course at the Fashion Institute of Technology (FIT) to update her knowledge. Luckily, she found a job where she could use her crochet knowledge and skills: She now designs and makes various crochet pieces for the fashion industry,

The crocheted Bruges technique appears in fashions ranging from a trendy top to a flowing skirt to an ultra-feminine cape.

while continuing her teaching and freelance designing. A number of her pieces have made the front covers of current knit and crochet magazines. In addition, she was hired by the Moscow Publishing Company, MIR, to translate into Russian two of Sasha Kagan's books: *The Sasha Kagan Sweater Book* and *Big and Little Sweaters*.

While Tatyana is an expert in all fields of crochet as well as knitting, her favorite technique is crocheted Bruges lace, which she first discovered in 1974 while still living in Russia. She has collected many pieces as well as patterns of braids and motifs. Today most of her teaching is on the Bruges technique, and the many awards won by her students attest to her success in introducing Bruges crochet to contemporary crocheters.

Bruges crocheted strips are shaped into a crisp summer purse or a simple yet elegant dress accented with a ribbon bow.

HOW TO MAKE CROCHETED BRUGES LACE

Bruges crochet was originally developed as a method of imitating expensive antique bobbin lace. Bobbin lace needs equipment such as wooden bobbins, a special round pillow, thin metal pins, complex paper patterns, and lengthy training and experience to produce professional results.

The original Bruges style of true bobbin lace involved creating braids, motifs, and net patterns and joining them to create a specific design.

Crocheted Bruges lace resembles the original Bruges bobbin lace, incorporating the same design elements, but it is made with a crochet hook. The braid that is such an important part of the lace is crocheted along with the connecting links that give it the desired shape.

An important advantage of crocheted Bruges lace over every other kind of handmade lace is that a large piece can be assembled out of small pieces, which can be worked separately.

Many crochet historians have researched the history of Bruges crochet lace, but no written records of its existence have been found before 1930, though the skill may have been handed down from crocheter to crocheter long before that date.

Traditionally, crocheted Bruges lace has been made with both cotton and linen threads in white, but today's designers are experimenting with new yarns and new color combinations.

The basics of making the crocheted tape that are the foundation of Bruges crochet are simple. The center of the tape is composed of rows of double crochet stitches, which can vary from three to five or more, depending on the desired width of the tape. Each row is separated by a number of turning chains, which also can vary depending on the project. These turning chains are often called "arches" in Bruges patterns.

BASIC BRUGES TAPE

Ch 10.

ROW 1: Dc in 6th ch from hook and in each rem ch: 5 dc; ch 5, turn.

ROW 2: Dc in each dc, ch 5, turn.

Repeat Row 2 for desired length of tape.

REVERSIBLE **MAGICAL WAVE** STOLE

Designed by Tatyana Mirer

SKILL LEVEL
■■■□ Intermediate

SIZE
Approximately 76" x 25" (193 cm x 63.5 cm)

MATERIALS
- Phildar *Phil'Douce 3½* (75% acrylic, 20% kid mohair, 5% wool, each approximately 1¾ oz [50g] and 186 yd [170m] 〖2〗 fine sport) 1488 yd (1360m) / 8 balls in color Plum
- One size G-6 (4mm) crochet hook, or size needed to obtain gauge

GAUGE
16 dc = 3½" (9cm)
9 rows = 4" (10cm)
4 dc = ⅞" (2.2cm)

NOTE
- The stole is made in four parts that are joined as you work.
- The two center parts, Part 1 and Part 2, are made first, then Part 3 and Part 4 are made and joined.

My lace projects are all inspired by classic bobbin lace patterns as well as by patterns gleaned from various sources. For example, an ancient Egyptian robe painted on a sarcophagus I saw in the Metropolitan Museum of Art in New York gave me the idea for one of my Bruges lace designs. I designed this stole because I wanted to present a beautiful design in a simple form.

STITCH GUIDE

ARCH: An arch is a ch-5 sp.

SINGLE CROCHET JOINING (SC JOINING): Dc in each of next 4 sts, ch 2; (insert hook in next adjacent arch, yo and draw up a lp through arch) 3 (4, 5) times for curve, yo and draw through all 4 (5, 6) lps on hook; ch 3, turn.

PART 1

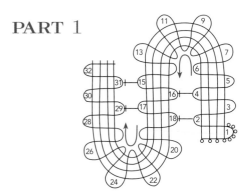

ROW 1: Ch 9, dc in 6th ch from hook (beg 5 skipped chs count as beg arch) and in each of next 3 chs; ch 5—arch made; turn.

ROW 2: Dc in each of next 4 dc; ch 5, turn.

ROWS 3–12: Repeat Row 2.

ROW 13: Dc in each of next 4 dc, ch 2; do not turn, but rotate piece to work along left edge, in each of 4 adjacent arches just made, work (yo and draw up a lp), yo and draw through all 5 lps on hook—sc joining curve made; ch 3, turn.

ROW 14: Dc in each of next 4 dc; ch 5, turn.

ROW 15: Dc in each of next 4 dc; ch 2, yo, insert hook in opposite arch and draw up a lp, (yo and draw through 2 lps on hook) twice—dc joining made; ch 2, turn.

ROWS 16 AND 17: Repeat Rows 14 and 15.

ROWS 18–25: Dc in each of next 4 dc; ch 5, turn.

ROW 26: Repeat Row 13.

ROWS 27 AND 28: Repeat Rows 14 and 15.

ROWS 29 AND 30: Repeat Rows 14 and 15 again.

ROWS 31–37: Repeat Row 2.

Repeat Rows 13–37 for pattern, ending on Row 18, when you will have 20 sc joining curves on one side and 10 on the other side. Do not cut yarn.

PART 2

ROWS 1–12: Dc in each of next 4 dc; ch 5, turn.

NOTE: Mark arch at beginning of Row 1 for strip joining.

ROW 13: Dc in each of next 4 dc; ch 2, work sc joining curve as before; ch 3, turn.

ROW 14: Dc in each of next 4 dc; ch 5, turn.

ROW 15: Dc in each of next 4 dc; ch 2, work dc joining as before; ch 2, turn.

ROWS 16 AND 17: Repeat Rows 14 and 15.

ROW 18: Dc in each of next 4 dc; ch 5, turn.

NOTE: See Joining Diagram on page 142.

You will now begin to join this lower section (Part 2) to the rest of the completed top section (Part 1).

ROW 19: Dc in each of next 4 dc; ch 2, yo 3 times, insert hook in same arch as last dc joining and draw up a lp, (yo and draw through 2 lps on hook) 3 times; yo 3 times, insert hook in same arch as last dc joining of Part 1 (top section) and draw up a lp, (yo and draw through 2 lps on hook) 3 times; yo and draw through all 3 lps on hook—2-dtrc joining made; draw up a lp in next free arch on Part 1, yo and draw through both lps on hook—sc joining made; ch 2, turn.

ROW 20: Dc in each of next 4 dc; ch 5, turn.

ROW 21: Dc in each of next 4 dc; ch 2, draw up a lp in next free arch on Part 1, yo and draw through 2 lps on hook—sc joining made; ch 2, turn.

ROWS 22: Dc in each of next 4 dc; ch 5, turn.

ROW 23: Dc in each of next 4 sts; ch 5, turn.

ROWS 24–28: Repeat Rows 13–17.

ROWS 29–34: Dc in each of next 4 dc; ch 5, turn.

ROWS 35–40: Repeat Rows 13–18.

ROW 41: Dc in each of next 4 dc; ch 2, work sc joining in opposite arch from Part 1; ch 2, turn.

ROW 42: Dc in each of next 4 dc; ch 5, turn.

ROW 43: Repeat Row 41.

ROW 44: Repeat Row 42.

Repeat Rows 22–44 eighteen times more.

Repeat Rows 22–40 once; at end of last row do not ch 5—20 waves made.

Hold first and last row with right sides together and sl st through last row and unused lp of beg ch to join. Fasten off.

Join yarn with a sl st in arch of Row 2, ch 4, sc in center of last sc joining, ch 4, sl st in last arch made. Fasten off.

Filler Cluster

Join yarn with a sl st in any arch of an open space between Part 1 and Part 2, ch 4; *yo 3 times, insert hook into next arch, (yo and draw through 2 lps on hook) 3 times; repeat from * 6 times more (8 lps on hook); yo and draw through all 8 lps on hook; ch 1. Fasten off.

Repeat Filler Cluster in each remaining open space between Part 1 and Part 2.

PART 3

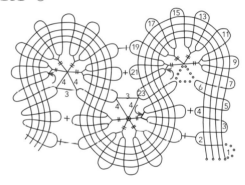

ROW 1: Ch 9, dc in 6th ch from hook and in each of next 3 chs; ch 5, turn.

ROW 2: Dc in each of next 4 dc; ch 5, turn.

ROWS 3–20: Repeat Row 2—10 arches on each side and one unconnected turning chain.

ROW 21 (JOINING ARCHES): Dc in each of next 4 sts; ch 2, draw up a lp in next arch, yo 4 times, draw up a lp in each of next 2 arches, (yo and draw through 2 sts on hook) 3 times— joining trc cluster made (5 lps on hook); *yo twice, draw up a lp in each of next 2 arches, (yo and draw through 2 lps on hook) 3 times; repeat from * once more (7 lps on hook), yo and draw through 3 lps on hook; (yo and draw through 2 lps on hook) twice; yo and draw through rem 3 lps on hook— trc cluster joining made; ch 2, turn.

ROW 22: Dc in each of next 4 dc; ch 5, turn.

ROW 23: Dc in each of next 4 sts; ch 6, sc in center of previous trc-cluster joining (between 2nd and 3rd trc); ch 4, sc in next free arch; ch 3, sl st into 2nd ch of beg ch-6; ch 2, turn.

ROW 24: Repeat Row 22.

ROW 25: Dc in each of next 4 dc; ch 2, work sc joining in opposite arch; ch 2, turn.

ROW 26: Repeat Row 22.

ROW 27: Dc in each of next 4 dc; ch 2, dc joining in opposite arch; ch 2, turn.

ROWS 28–37: Dc in each of next 4 dc; ch 5, turn—5 arches after last joining.

Repeat Rows 21–37 thirty times more, then repeat Rows 21–27 once—16 waves made. Do not cut yarn.

Strip

ROWS 1–4: Dc in each of next 4 dc; ch 5, turn.

ROW 5: You will now join this Part 3 section to the Part 1 side of the previously made unit. Dc in each of next 4 dc; ch 2, yo 3 times, insert hook in 4th arch and draw up a lp; (yo and draw through 2 lps on hook) 4 times—dtrc joining made; ch 2, turn.

ROW 6: Dc in each of next 4 dc; ch 5, turn.

ROW 7: Dc in each of next 4 sts; ch 2, sc joining in next opposite arch of Part 1; ch 2, turn.

ROW 8 (CORNER): Dc in each of next 4 dc; ch 2, draw up a lp in each of next 3 arches for curve; yo twice and draw up a lp in same arch as last dc joining of Strip, (yo and draw through 2 lps on hook) twice; yo twice and draw up a lp in next unused arch on Strip, (yo and draw through 2 lps on hook) twice (6 lps on hook); yo and draw through all 6 lps on hook: corner made; ch 3, turn.

ROW 9: Dc in each of next 4 dc; ch 2, dtr joining in dc joining of opposite 2 arches of Part 1; ch 2, turn.

ROW 10: Dc in each of next 4 dc; ch 2, yo and draw up lp in last arch used for corner joining, yo and draw through all 3 lps on hook: hdc joining made; ch 2, turn.

ROW 11: Dc in each of next 4 dc; ch 2, dtr joining in same arch as last dtr joining made; ch 2, turn.

ROW 12: Dc in each of next 4 dc; ch 2, sc joining in next unused opposite arch; ch 2, turn.

ROW 13: Dc in each of next 4 dc; ch 2, sc joining in next unused opposite arch of Part 1; ch 2, turn.

ROW 14: Dc in each of next 4 dc; ch 2, hdc joining in next unused opposite arch; ch 2, turn.

ROW 15: Dc in each of next 4 dc; ch 2, sc joining in next unused opposite arch of Part 1; ch 2, turn.

ROWS 16–19: Dc in each of next 4 dc; ch 2, dtr joining in opposite dc joining; ch 2, turn.

ROW 20: Dc in each of next 4 dc; ch 2, hdc joining in next unused opposite arch; ch 2, turn.

ROW 21: Dc in each of next 4 dc; ch 2, sc joining in next unused opposite arch of Part 1; ch 2, turn.

Continue joining in same manner across, ending with the corner as for Row 8. Place first and last rows with right sides together and join with a sl st. Fasten off.

Work Part 4 Strip as for Part 3 Strip, joining it to Part 2 and working Row 5 joining in 4th arch from beg arch of Part 2.

Edging
Join yarn with a sc in any arch; *work 7 sc in each arch and work one or more sc as needed between arches; repeat from * around; join with a sl st in first sc. Fasten off; weave in all yarn ends.

TOP

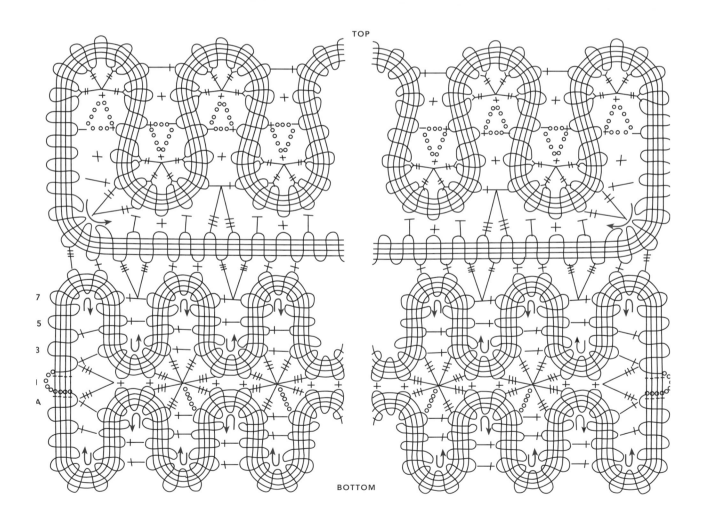

BOTTOM

PAINTED CROCHET

with
Ferosa Harold

Ferosa Harold, a crocheter from the island of Trinidad and Tobago, taught herself to crochet when she was sixteen. She began by making doilies that she gave as gifts to friends and family. Eventually, as other people saw her work and wanted doilies for their home as well, Ferosa began taking on commissioned assignments.

In 1998, when Ferosa lost her job, she decided to make a career of crochet. She planned to do commissioned work and to teach crochet. Unfortunately, the commissioned work was slow, and not many people were interested in learning to crochet.

At that time, there were few crochet publications available on the island, limiting Ferosa's contact with the crochet world. Her father-in-law, however, who lived in Canada, came home for a visit and, knowing how much Ferosa loved crochet, brought her a crochet magazine. That magazine opened a whole world to Ferosa and put her into contact with other crocheters around the world.

She found ads for places in the United States where she could buy crochet books, and when she contacted one of them, while talking to the customer service person she asked whether the company ever bought designs from outside designers. She was given the name of the acquisition editor and told to e-mail photos of her designs.

Ferosa didn't have a computer or Internet access, but she was able to get one relative to take some pictures of her work and another to e-mail the necessary information to the editor. It didn't take long for the editor to contact Ferosa and ask her to submit designs and instructions for publication in the company's books and magazines.

Ferosa did not know how to type or have any idea what the Internet or a computer could do, nor had she ever written the instructions for a pattern. She

had, however, taught herself to crochet, and she was not afraid to teach herself all of the other skills necessary to become a published designer. Her first booklet, *Irish Lace Doilies*, was published in 2001. Since that time, Ferosa has published more than fifteen booklets and has had more than forty of her designs published in various crochet publications.

Although Ferosa works in many crochet areas, her favorite type of crochet is painted crochet, a technique used for making crochet projects by using various colors to give a multicolored look. The technique has actually been around for a long time, but there is not much documentation on when this type of crochet started. When Ferosa sent her first proposal to a publisher, the acquisition committee wanted to know how Ferosa painted her doilies to get her effect. She had to explain that it wasn't paint but changing colors of thread that gave the painted effect.

Today Ferosa continues to pass on her knowledge of crochet through her website, www.ferosahcrochet.com. Here you will find all of her books, including the ones that she now self-publishes, along with the crochet lessons she has developed. One Saturday each month she appears at a local craft store, offering help to anyone encountering problems with a pattern or a crochet stitch. Two Saturdays a month, she teaches crochet to children at a home for abandoned children.

HOW TO DO PAINTED CROCHET

Painted crochet is a term that describes a technique used to produce gradual or dramatic color changes by using three threads held together and varying the color combinations. It is usually done with fine threads, such as sewing threads.

For the most dramatic results, four colors are used, and three spools of each color are required. The three strands are held together at all times. Thread designed for hand or machine sewing is usually used because of the size and wide spectrum of colors available.

GRADUAL COLOR CHANGES

Dropping one strand of one color and adding one strand of the next color creates gradual color changes. Begin with 3 strands of the first color; work the desired number of rows or rounds. Drop one strand of the first color and add one strand of the next color; repeat this process as indicated in the instructions.

CHANGING COLORS

When working with double crochet, triple crochet, or double triple crochet, drop one strand of the color you're working with, add one strand of the next color, and draw the threads through the last two loops of the stitch at the end of the specified row or round. For changing color with a slipstitch, add the new color and then make the slipstitch.

HIDING THREAD ENDS

Cut thread of dropped color about 2–3" (5–7.5cm) after adding the next color. Crochet dropped thread end in with first stitch of next row or round, then trim excess thread. Because the thread is so fine, this method will not add bulk to the work.

DESIGNING YOUR OWN PROJECT

The thread painting technique can be used with just about any pattern. To determine the number of rows or rounds to be worked in each color combination, follow these examples.

Example:

Let's say the chosen project consists of 66 rows or rnds, and you wish to use six colors.

The 3 spools of the first color should be counted as one when doing your calculations.

The next 5 colors x 3 spools = 15

15 + 1 = 16

You have 16 color changes for your project.

Divide the rows or rnds by the number of colors:

66 ÷ 16 = 4, with 2 extra rows

Each color combination will be worked for 4 rows. Working 5 rows of the first and last color combinations can be used for the 2 extra rows.

HEARTS AND ROSES **CENTERPIECE**

Designed by Ferosa Harold

I didn't choose to make this design; it chose me.

SKILL LEVEL
■■■■ Experienced

SIZE
Approximately 25" (63.5cm)
diameter

MATERIALS
- Coats *Rayon Machine
  Embroidery Thread 40 weight*,
  Article D63 (100% rayon, each
  approximately 200 yd [183m])
  - 600 yd (549m) / 3 spools in
    color 308A Ultra Violet (A)
  - 600 yd (549m) / 3 spools in
    color 9 Yale Blue (B)
  - 600 yd (549m) / 3 spools in
    color 510 Radiant Blue (C)
  - 600 yd (549m) / 3 spools in
    color 177 Kerry Green (D)
  - 600 yd (549m) / 3 spools in
    color 321A Sun Yellow (E)
  - 600 yd (549m) / 3 spools in
    color 324A Kumquat (F)
  - 600 yd (549m) / 3 spools in
    color 35A Fuchsia (G)
- One size 10 (1.30mm) steel
  crochet hook, or size needed
  to obtain gauge
- Safety pins (for markers)

GAUGE
One Rose = 1½" (4cm)
diameter

CONTINUED ON PAGE 148

CONTINUED FROM PAGE 147

NOTES
- Entire piece is worked with 3 strands of thread held together.
- The letter following each color name, above, is used to indicate that color in pattern. If pattern states (AAA) for example, work with 3 strands of Ultra Violet; (AAB) means 2 strands of Ultra Violet and one strand of Yale Blue. This method describes color combinations for each round.

STITCH GUIDE

SHELL (SH): In specified st, work (2 dc, ch 2, 2 dc).

BEGINNING SHELL (BEG SH): In specified st, work (ch 3, dc, ch 2, 2 dc).

DOUBLE SHELL (DSH): In specified st, work (2 dc, ch 2) twice, 2 dc in same st.

BEGINNING DOUBLE SHELL (BEG DSH): In specified st, work (ch 3, dc) then (ch 2, 2 dc) twice.

V STITCH (V-ST): In specified st, work (dc, ch 3, dc).

BEGINNING V-ST (BEG V-ST): In specified st, work (ch 6, dc).

LARGE V-ST: In specified st, work (dc, ch 5, dc).

JOINED DOUBLE CROCHET (JDC): (Yo, insert hook in specified st, yo and draw up a lp, yo and pull through 2 lps on hook) twice, yo and pull through rem 3 lps on hook.

PICOT (P): Ch 3, sl st in last sc made.

FAN ST: In picot work (dc, p) 5 times, dc in same picot.

CENTERPIECE

There are 25 roses made individually for this project. Because of the color changes, it is advisable to make all 25 roses before starting Doily; see below.

FIRST ROSE

With aaa, ch 6; join with a sl st in first ch to form a ring.

RND 1 (AAA) (RIGHT SIDE): Ch 1, work 12 sc in ring, join with a sl st in first sc.

RND 2 (AAA): Ch 1, sc in same sc as joining; *ch 3, sk next sc, sc in next sc; repeat from * around, ch 3, sl st in first sc. Fasten off.

RND 3 (BBB): Attach threads with a sl st in first ch-3 sp, ch 1; *in ch-3 sp work (sc, hdc, 3 dc, hdc, sc): petal made; repeat from * around; sl st in first sc.

RND 4 (BBB): Sl st in back lp of sc between petals, ch 1, sc in same place as sl st; *ch 4, sc in next sc between next 2 petals; repeat from * around; sl st in first sc. Fasten off.

RND 5 (CCC): Attach threads with a sl st in first ch-4 sp, ch 1; *in ch-4 sp work petal of (sc, hdc, 5 dc, hdc, sc); repeat from * around; sl st in first sc.

RND 6 (CCC): Reaching in back of rose, sl st in sp between petals, ch 1, sc in same place as sl st; *ch 5, sc between next two petals; repeat from * around; sl st in first sc. Fasten off.

RND 7 (DDD): Attach threads with a sl st in first ch-5 sp, ch 1; *in ch-5 sp work petal of (sc, hdc, 7 dc, hdc, sc); repeat from * around; sl st in first sc.

RND 8 (DDD): Reaching behind row, sl st in sp between petals, ch 1, sc in same place as sl st; *ch 6, sc between next 2 petals; repeat from * around; sl st in first sc. Fasten off.

RND 9: (EEE): Attach threads with a sl st in first ch-6 sp, ch 1; *in ch-6 sp work (sc, hdc, 9 dc, hdc, sc) for petal; repeat from * around; sl st in first sc.

RND 10 (EEE): Behind rose, sl st in sp between petals, ch 1, sc in same place as sl st; *ch 7, sc between next 3 petals; repeat from * around; sl st in first sc. Fasten off.

RND 11 (FFF): Attach threads with a sl st in first ch-7 sp, ch 1, *in ch-7 sp work (sc, hdc, 11 dc, hdc, sc) for petal; repeat from * around; sl st in first sc.

RND 12 (FFF): Behind rose, sl st in sp between petals, ch 1, sc in same place as sl st; *ch 8, sc between next 2 petals; repeat from * around; sl st in first sc. Fasten off.

RND 13 (GGG): Attach threads with a sl st in first ch-8 sp, ch 1; *in ch-8 sp work (sc, hdc, 13 dc, hdc, sc); repeat from * around; sl st in first sc. Fasten off and mark this as first rose.

Make 24 more roses, working only Rnds 1–12; do not work Rnd 13 until instructions state to attach roses to Doily center.

DOILY

RND 1 (AAA): Attach threads with a sl st to 7th dc of any petal in Rnd 13 of first rose, ch 1, sc in join; *ch 10, sc in 7th dc of next petal; repeat from * around, ch 10; sl st in first sc.

RND 2 (AAA): Ch 1, sc in joining; *in ch-10 sp work (8 sc, p, 7 sc**, sc in next sc); repeat from * around, end at ** on last repeat; sl st in first sc.

RND 3 (AAA): Beg V-st; *ch 6, V-st in p, ch 6, sk 7 sc** V-st in next sc; repeat from * around, end at ** on last repeat; sl st in 3rd ch of beg ch-6.

RND 4 (AAA): Sl st in ch-3 sp, beg sh; *ch 5, 8 dc in next V-st, ch 5**, sh in next V-st; repeat from * around, end at ** on last repeat; sl st in 3rd ch of ch-3.

RND 5 (AAB): Sl st in dc and ch–2 sp, beg sh; *ch 3, (dc in next dc, ch 1) 7 times, dc in next dc, ch 3**, sh in sh; repeat from * around, end at ** on last repeat; sl st in 3rd ch (base of pineapple formed) of ch–3.

RND 6 (AAB): Sl st in dc and in ch–2 sp, beg dsh; *ch 5, (sc in ch–1 sp, ch 3) 6 times, sc in next ch–1 sp, ch 5**, dsh in next sh; repeat from * around, end at ** on last repeat; sl st in 3rd ch of ch–3.

RND 7 (AAB): Sl st in dc and in ch–2 sp, beg sh; *ch 3, sh in next ch–2 sp, ch 5, (sc in ch–3 sp, ch 3) 5 times, sc in next ch–3 sp, ch 5**, sh in next ch–2 sp; repeat from * around, end at ** on last repeat; sl st in 3rd ch of ch–3.

RND 8 (ABB): Sl st in dc and in ch–2 sp, beg sh; *ch 3, sc in ch–3 sp, ch 3, sh in sh, ch 5, (sc in ch–3 sp, ch 3) 4 times, sc in next ch–3 sp, ch 5**, sh in next sh; repeat from * around, end at ** on last repeat; sl st in 3rd of ch–3.

RND 9 (ABB): Sl st in dc and in ch–2 sp, beg sh; *(ch 3, sc in ch–3 sp) twice, ch 3, sh in next sh, ch 5, (sc in ch–3 sp, ch 3) 3 times; sc in next ch–3 sp, ch 5**, sh in next sh; repeat from * around, end at ** on last repeat; sl st in 3rd ch of ch–3.

RND 10 (ABB): Sl st in dc and in ch–2 sp, beg sh; *ch 3, sk 1 ch–3 sp, V–st in next ch–3 sp, ch 3, dsh in sh, ch 5; (sc in next ch–3 sp, ch 3) twice, sc in next ch–3 sp, ch 5 **, dsh in next sh; repeat from * around, end at ** on last repeat, 2 dc same sp as beg sh, ch 2; sl st in 3rd ch of ch–3.

RND 11 (BBB): Sl st in dc and in ch–2 sp, beg sh, *ch 3, 8 dc in V–st, ch 3, sh in next ch–2 sp, ch 3, sh in next ch–2 sp, ch 5, sc in next ch–3 sp, ch 3, sc in next ch–3 sp, ch 5, sh in next ch–2 sp, ch 3**, sh in next ch–2 sp; repeat from * around, end at ** on last repeat; sl st in 3rd ch of ch–3.

RND 12 (BBB): Sl st in dc and in ch–2 sp, beg sh; *ch 3, (dc in next dc, ch 1) 7 times, dc in next dc, ch 3, sh in sh, ch 3, sc in ch–3 sp, ch 3, sh in sh, ch 5, sc in ch–3 sp, ch 5, sh in sh, ch 2, sc in ch–3, ch 2**; sh in sh; repeat from * around, end at ** on last repeat; sl st in 3rd ch of ch–3.

RND 13 (BBB): Sl st in dc and ch–2 sp, beg sh; *ch 5, (sc in ch–1 sp, ch 3) 6 times, sc in next ch–1 sp, ch 5, sh in sh, ch 5, sc in sc, ch 5; sh in sh, sh in next sh, ch 5, sc in sc, ch 5**, sh in sh; repeat from * around, end at ** on last repeat; sl st in 3rd ch of ch–3.

RND 14 (BBC): Sl st in dc and ch–2 sp, beg sh; *ch 5, (sc in ch–1 sp, ch 3) 5 times, sc in next ch–1 sp, ch 5, sh in sh, ch 7, sc in sc, ch 7; (2 dc in sh) twice, ch 7**, sh in next sh; repeat from * around, end at ** on last repeat; sl st in 3rd ch of ch–3.

RND 15 (BBC): Sl st in dc and ch–3 sp, beg dsh; *ch 5, (sc in ch–1 sp, ch 3) 4 times, sc in next ch–1 sp, ch 5, dsh in sh, (ch 5, sc in next ch–7 sp) 4 times, ch 5**, dsh in sh; repeat from * around, end at ** on last repeat; sl st in 3rd ch of ch–3. Fasten off.

NOTE: On the rnd just completed, note that there is a group of 5 ch-5 sps between each pair of pineapples. You will be joining a rose to the 3 center sps of each group of 5 sps, following the directions below:

Roses
Complete and join 6 roses to Doily center as follows:

RND 13: On this rnd you will complete and join 6 roses. Attach (ggg) threads with a sl st to any ch–8 sp of Rnd 12 of an unfinished rose, ch 1; *(in ch–8 sp work sc, hdc, 13 dc, hdc, sc) 3 times; in next ch–8 sp work (sc, hdc, 7 dc); on Centerpiece sk 1 ch–5 sp between pineapples, sc in next ch–5 sp, finish petal with (7 dc, hdc, sc); in next ch–8 sp work (sc, hdc, 7 dc), sc in next ch–5 sp, finish petal with (7 dc, hdc, sc) twice; sl st in first sc. Fasten off.

RND 16 (BBC): Attach threads with a sl st to first ch–2 sp of dsh on left of any rose, beg sh; *ch 3, sh in next ch–2 sp, ch 5, (sc in ch–3 sp, ch 3) 3 times, sc in next ch–3 sp; ch 5, (sh in next ch–2 sp, ch 3) twice, tr in free ch–5 sp, ch 6, sc between 3rd and 4th petals of rose, ch 20, sc between 6th and first petal, ch 6, tr in next free ch–5 sp, ch 3**, sh in next ch–2 sp; repeat from * around, end at ** on last repeat; sl st in 3rd ch of ch–3.

RND 17 (BCC): Sl st in dc and ch–2 sp, beg sh; *ch 3, sc in ch–3 sp, ch 3, sh in sh, ch 5; (sc in ch–3 sp, ch 3) twice, sc in next ch–3 sp, ch 5, sh in sh, ch 3, sc in ch–3 sp, ch 3, sh in sh, ch 5, sc in ch–6 sp, ch 5; in ch–20 sp work (sh, ch 3, V–st, ch 3, sh), ch 5, sc in ch–6 sp, ch 5**, sh in sh; repeat from * around, end at ** on last repeat; sl st in 3rd ch of ch–3.

RND 18 (BCC): Sl st in dc and in ch–2 sp, beg sh; *ch 5, sc in sc, ch 5, sh in sh, ch 5; sc in ch–3 sp, ch 3, sc in next ch–3 sp, ch 5, sh in sh, ch 5, sc in sc, ch 5, sh in sh, ch 5, sk 1 ch-5 sp, sc in next ch–5 sp; ch 5, sh in sh, ch 3, 8 dc in V–st, ch 3, sh in sh, ch 5, sc in ch–5 sp, ch 5**, sh in sh; repeat from * around, end at ** on last repeat; sl st in 3rd ch of ch 3.

RND 19 (BCC): Sl st in dc and in ch–2 sp, beg sh; *ch 7, sc in sc, ch 7, sh in sh, ch 5, sc in ch–3 sp, ch 5, sh in sh, ch 7, sc in sc, ch 7, sh in sh, ch 5; sk 1 ch–5 sp, sc in next ch–5 sp, ch 5, sh in sh, ch 2, (dc in next dc, ch 1) 7 times; dc in next dc, ch 2, sh in sh, ch 5, sc in next ch–5 sp, ch 5**, sh in sh; repeat from * around, end at ** on last repeat; sl st in 3rd ch of ch–3.

RND 20 (CCC): Sl st in dc and in ch–2 sp, beg sh; *ch 9, sc in sc, ch 9; (dsh in sh) twice, ch 9, sc in sc, ch 9, sh in sh, ch 5, sk 1 ch–5 sp, sc in next ch–5 sp, ch 5, sh in sh, ch 5; (sc in ch–1 sp, ch 3) 6 times, sc in next ch 3 sp, ch 5, sh in sh, ch 5, sc in ch–5 sp, ch 5**, sh in sh; repeat from * around, end at ** on last repeat; sl st in 3rd ch of ch–3.

RND 21 (CCC): Sl st across to ch–9 sp, beg sh in ch–9 sp; *ch 5, sc in sc, ch 5, sh in ch–9 sp, ch 5, sk 1 ch–2 sp, 2 dc in next ch–2 sp, ch 1, 2 dc in next ch–2 sp, ch 5, sh in ch–9 sp, ch 5, sc in next sc, ch 5, sh in ch–9 sp, ch 7, sk 1 ch–5 sp, sc in next ch–5 sp, ch 5, sh in sh, ch 5, (sc in ch–3 sp, ch 3) 5 times, sc in next ch–3 sp, ch 5, sh in sh, ch 5, sc in ch–5 sp, ch 7**, sh in ch–9 sp; repeat from * around, end at ** on last repeat; sl st in 3rd ch of ch–3.

RND 22 (CCC): Sl st in all sts of beg sh and into ch–5 sp, beg sh; *ch 2, sc in sc, ch 2, sh in ch–5 sp, ch 9, jdc in next two ch–5 sps, ch 9, sh in ch–5 sp, ch 2, sc in sc, ch 2, sh in next ch–5 sp, ch 9, jdc in ch–7 and ch–5 sps, ch 3, sh in sh, ch 5, (sc in ch–3 sp, ch 3) 4 times, sc in next ch–3 sp, ch 5, sh in sh, ch 3, jdc in ch–5 and ch–7 sps**, ch 9, sh in ch–5 sp; repeat from * around, end at ** on last repeat; ch 4, dtr in 3rd ch of ch–3.

RND 23 (CCD): Ch 1, sc in join; *[ch 7, jdc in next two shs, (ch 7, sc in next ch sp) twice] twice, ch 5, sh in sh, ch 5, (sc in next ch–3 sp, ch 3) 3 times, sc in next ch–3 sp, ch 5, sh in sh, ch 5, sc in next ch–3 sp**, ch 5, sc in next ch sp; repeat from * around, end at ** on last repeat; ch 2, dc in first sc.

RND 24 (CCD): Beg sh; *(ch 5, sc in ch–7 sp) twice, ch 5, sh in next ch sp, (ch 5, sc in next ch sp) twice, ch 5, sh in next ch sp, ch 5, sc in next ch sp, ch 5, sh in next sh, ch 5 (sc

in next ch–3 sp, ch 3) twice, sc in next ch–3 sp, ch 5, sh in sh, ch 5, sc in next sp, ch 5**, sh in next sp; repeat from * around, end at ** on last repeat; sl st in 3rd ch of ch–3.

RND 25 (CCD): Sl st in dc and ch–2 sp, beg sh; *ch 5, sk 1 ch–5 sp, large V–st in next ch–5 sp, ch 5, dsh in sh, ch 5, sk 1 ch–5 sp, large V–st in next ch–5 sp, ch 5, sh in sh; (ch 5, sc in next ch–5 sp) twice, ch 5, sh in sh, ch 5, sc in ch–3 sp, ch 3, sc in next ch–3 sp, ch 5, sh in sh, (ch 5, sc in next ch–5 sp) twice, ch 5**, sh in sh; repeat from * around, end at ** on last repeat; sl st in 3rd ch of ch–3.

RND 26 (CDD): Sl st in dc and ch–2 sp, beg sh; *(ch 3, 8 dc in large V–st, ch 3, sh in ch–2 sp, ch 3, sh in next ch–2 sp, ch 3, 8 dc in large V–st, ch 3, sh in sh, (ch 5, sc in ch–5 sp) 3 times, ch 5, sh in sh, ch 5, sc in ch–3 sp, ch 5, sh in sh, (ch 5, sc in ch–5 sp) 3 times, ch 5**, sh in sh; repeat from * around, end at ** on last repeat; sl st in 3rd ch of ch–3.

RND 27 (CDD): Sl st in dc and ch–2 sp, beg sh; *ch 3, (dc in next dc, ch 1) 7 times, dc in next dc, ch 3, sh in sh, ch 3, sc in ch–3 sp, ch 3, sh in sh, ch 3; (dc in next dc, ch 1) 7 times, dc in next dc, ch 3, [sh in sh, (ch 5, sc in next ch–5 sp) 4 times, ch 5**, sh in sh] twice; repeat from * around, end at ** on last repeat; sl st in 3rd ch of ch–3.

RND 28 (CDD): Sl st in dc and ch–2 sp, beg sh; *ch 5, (hdc in ch 1 sp, ch 3) 6 times, hdc in next ch–1 sp, ch 5, sh in sh; (ch 3, sc in ch–3 sp) twice, ch 3, sh in sh, ch 5, (hdc in ch–1 sp, ch 3) 6 times, hdc in next ch–1 sp, ch 5, sh in sh, (ch 5, sc in ch–5 sp) twice, sh in next ch–5 sp, sc in next ch–5 sp, ch 5, sc in next ch 5 sp, ch 5, 2 dc in next sh, ch 1, 2 dc in next sh, (ch 5, sc in next ch–5 sp) twice, sh in next ch–5 sp, sc in next ch–5 sp, ch 5, sc in next ch–5 sp, ch 5**, sh in sh; repeat from * around, end at ** on last repeat; sl st in 3rd ch of ch–3.

RND 29 (DDD): Sl st in dc and ch–2 sp, beg sh; *ch 5, (hdc in ch–3 sp, ch 3) 5 times, hdc in next ch–3 sp, ch 5, sh in sh, ch 3, sk 1 ch–3 sp, V–st in next ch–3 sp, ch 3, sh in sh, ch 5, (hdc in ch–3 sp, ch 3) 5 times, hdc in next ch–3 sp, ch 5, sh in sh, (ch 5, sc in next ch–5 sp) twice, ch 5, sh in sh, (ch 5, sc in next ch–5 sp) twice, ch 5, sc in ch–1 sp, (ch 5, sc in next ch–5 sp) twice, ch 5, sh in sh, (ch 5, sc in next ch –5 sp) twice, ch 5**, sh in sh; repeat from * around, end at ** on last repeat; sl st in 3rd ch of ch 3.

RND 30 (DDD): Sl st in dc and ch–2 sp, beg sh; *ch 5, (sc in ch 3 sp, ch 3) 4 times, sc in next ch–3 sp, ch 5, sh in sh, ch 3, 8 dc in V–st, ch 3, sh in sh, ch 5, (sc in ch–3 sp, ch 3) 4 times, sc in next ch–3 sp, ch 5, sh in sh, (ch 5, sc in ch–5 sp) twice, ch 5, dsh in sh, (ch 5, sc in ch–5 sp) 4 times, ch 5, dsh in sh, ch 5, sk one ch–5 sp, (sc in ch–5 sp, ch 5) twice**, sh in sh; repeat from * around, end at ** on last repeat; sl st in 3rd ch of ch–3.

RND 31 (DDD): Sl st in dc and ch–2 sp, beg sh; *ch 5, (sc in ch–3 sp, ch 3) 3 times, sc in next ch–3 sp, ch 5, dsh in sh, ch 2, (dc in dc, ch 1) 7 times, dc in next dc, ch 2, dsh in sh, ch 5, (sc in ch–3 sp, ch 3) 3 times, sc in next ch–3 sp, ch 5, sh in sh, (ch 5, sc in ch–5 sp) twice, ch 5, sh in ch–2 sp, ch 3, sh in next ch–2 sp, ch 5, sk one ch–5 sp, (sc in next ch–5 sp, ch 5) 3 times, sh in ch–2 sp, ch 3, sh in next ch–2 sp, ch 5, sk one ch–5 sp, (sc in next ch–5 sp) twice**, sh in sh; repeat from * around, end at ** on last repeat; ch 2, sl st in 3rd ch of ch–3.

RND 32 (DDE): Sl st in dc and ch–2 sp, beg sh; *ch 5, (sc in ch–3 sp, ch 3) twice, sc in next ch–3 sp, ch 5, sh in ch–2 sp, ch 3, sh in next ch–2 sp, ch 5, (sc in ch–1 sp, ch 3) 6 times, sc in next ch–3 sp, ch 5, sh in ch–2 sp, ch 3, sh in next ch 2 sp, ch 5, (sc in ch–3 sp, ch 3) twice, sc in next ch–3 sp, ch 5, sh in sh, (ch 5, sc in ch–5 sp) twice, ch 5, sh in sh, ch 3, sc in ch–3 sp, ch 3, sh in sh, ch 5, sk one ch–5 sp, (sc in next ch–5 sp, ch 5) twice, sh in sh, ch 3, sc in ch–3 sp, ch 3, sh in sh, ch 5, sk one ch–5 sp; (sc in next ch–5 sp, ch 5) twice**, sh in sh; repeat from * around, end at ** on last repeat; sl st in 3rd ch of ch–3.

RND 33 (DDE): Sl st in dc and ch–2 sp, beg sh; *ch 5, sc in ch–3 sp, ch 3, sc in next ch–3 sp, ch 5, sh in sh, ch 3, sc in ch–3 sp, ch 3, sh in sh, ch 5, (sc in ch–1 sp, ch 3) 5 times, sc in next ch–3 sp, ch 5, sh in sh, ch 3, sc in next ch–3 sp, ch 3, sh in sh, ch 5, sc in ch–3 sp, ch 3, sc in next ch–3 sp, ch 5, sh in sh, (ch 5, sc in ch–5 sp) twice, ch 5, sh in sh, ch 5, sc in sc, ch 5, sh in sh, ch 5, sk one ch–5 sp, sc in next ch–5 sp, ch 5, sh in sh, ch 5, sc in sc, ch 5, sh in sh, ch 5, sk 1 ch–5 sp, (sc in next ch–5 sp, ch 5) twice**, sh in sh; repeat from * around, end at ** on last repeat; sl st in 3rd ch of ch–3.

RND 34 (DDE): Sl st in dc and ch–2 sp, beg sh; *ch 5, sc in ch–3 sp, ch 5, sh in sh, (ch 3, sc in ch–3 sp) twice, ch 3, sh in sh, ch 5, (sc in ch–3 sp, ch 3) 4 times, sc in next ch–3 sp, ch 5, sh in sh, (ch 3, sc in ch–3 sp) twice, ch 3, sh in

sh, ch 5, sc in ch–3 sp, ch 5, sh in sh, (ch 5, sc in ch–5 sp) twice, ch 5, sh in sh, ch 7, sc in sc, ch 7, sh in sh, ch 5, sh in sh, ch 7, sc in sc, ch 7, sh in sh, ch 5, sk one ch–5 sp, (sc in next ch–5 sp, ch 5) twice**, sh in sh; repeat from * around, end at ** on last repeat; sl st in 3rd ch of ch–3.

RND 35 (DEE): Sl st in dc and ch–2 sp, beg sh; *sh in sh, (ch 3, sc in ch–3 sp) 3 times, ch 3, sh in sh, ch 5, (sc in ch–3 sp, ch 3) 3 times, sc in next ch–3 sp, ch 5, sh in sh, (ch 3, sc in ch–3 sp) 3 times, ch 3, (sh in sh) twice, (ch 5, sc in ch–5 sp) twice, ch 5, sh in sh, ch 9, sc in sc, ch 9, (sh in sh) twice, ch 9, sc in sc, ch 9, sh in sh, ch 5, sk 1 ch–5 sp, (sc in next ch–5 sp, ch 5) twice**, sh in sh; repeat from * around, end at ** on last repeat; sl st in 3rd ch of ch–3.

RND 36 (DEE): Sl st in dc and ch–2 sp, ch 3, dc in ch–2 sp; *2 dc in next ch–2 sp, (ch 5, sc in ch–3 sp) 4 times, ch 5, sh in sh, ch 5, (sc in ch–3 sp, ch 3) twice, sc in next ch–3 sp, ch 5, sh in sh, (ch 5, sc in ch–3 sp) 4 times, ch 5, (2 dc in sh) twice, (ch 5, sc in ch–5 sp) 3 times, ch 5, sh in ch–9 sp, ch 5, sc in sc, ch 5, sh in ch–9 sp, ch 7, sh in ch–9 sp, ch 5, sc in sc, ch 5, sh in ch–9 sp, (ch 5, sc in ch–5 sp) 3 times**, ch 5, 2 dc in sh; repeat from * around, end at ** on last repeat; ch 2, dc in 3rd ch of ch–3.

RND 37 (DEE): Ch 1, sc in join; (ch 5, sc in next ch sp) 5 times, ch 5; *(sh in sh, ch 5, sc in ch–3 sp, ch 3, sc in next

ch-3 sp, ch 5, sh in sh, (ch 5, sc in next ch sp) 9 times, ch 5, sh in ch-5 sp, ch 3, sc in sc, ch 3, sh in ch-5 sp, ch 5, sc in ch-7 sp, ch 5, sh in ch-5 sp, ch 3, sc in sc, ch 3, sh in ch-5 sp**; (ch 5, sc in next ch sp) 9 times, ch 5); repeat from * around, end at ** on last repeat, (ch 5, sc in next ch sp) 3 times; ch 2, dc in first sc.

RND 38 (EEE): Ch 1, sc in join; (ch 5, sc in next ch sp) 6 times, ch 5; *(sh in sh, ch 5, sc in ch-3 sp, ch 5, sh in sh, (ch 5, sc in next ch sp) 10 times, ch 9, jdc in next two sh, ch 9, sc in next ch sp, ch 5, sc in next ch sp, ch 9, jdc in next two sh, ch 9**, (sc in next ch sp, ch 5) 10 times; repeat from * around, end at ** on last repeat; (sc in next ch sp, ch 5) twice; ch 2, dc in first sc (do not fasten off).

NOTE: Above each pair of heart-shaped motifs (lying between the 3-pineapple groups) there are 2 pairs of ch-9 sps on Rnd 38. You will be joining a rose to each pair of sps, following directions below.

Add 12 roses to Doily as follows:

With right side of rose facing you, attach ggg threads with a sl st to ch-8 sp of any unfinished rose, ch 1; in ch-8 sp work (sc, hdc, 13 dc, hdc, sc) 4 times, in next ch-8 sp work (sc, hdc, 7 dc), sc in 2nd ch-9 sp on Doily, finish petal with (6 dc, hdc, sc); in next ch-8 sp work (sc, hdc, 7 dc), sc in next ch-9 sp of Doily, finish petal with (6 dc, hdc, sc); sl st in first sc. Fasten off. The 5th and 6th petals are joined to Centerpiece. Mark first petal with a safety pin.

Join 11 more roses in same manner to rem ch-9 sps on Centerpiece.

RND 39 (EEE): Ch 1, sc in join; (ch 6, sc in next ch sp) 6 times; *ch 6, (sh in sh) twice, (ch 6, sc in next ch sp) 9 times, ch 9, sk 1 ch-5 sp, sc between first and last petals of rose, ch 15, sk next sp between petals to sc between 2nd and 3rd petals, ch 15, sk next sp between petals, sc between 4th and 5th petals, (ch 15 will lie behind roses), ch 9; back on Centerpiece, sc in ch-5 between roses, ch 9; on next rose, sc between first and last petals, ch 15, sc between 2nd and 3rd petals, ch 15, sc between 4th and 5th petals, ch 9; on Centerpiece, sk next ch-5 sp, sc in next ch-5 sp**, (ch 6, sc in next ch-sp) 8 times; repeat from * around, end at ** on last repeat; ch 3, dc in first sc.

RND 40 (EEE): Ch 1, sc in join; (ch 6, sc in next ch sp) 7 times, ch 6; *(2 dc in sh) twice, (ch 6, sc in next ch sp) 8

times, ch 6, jdc in ch-6 and ch-9 sps, ch 9 ,** sc between 1st and 2nd petal of next rose, ch 9, fpsc in next joining sc, ch 9, sc between 3rd and 4th petals of rose,** ch 5, repeat from ** to ** once more, ch 9***, jdc in ch-9 and ch-6 sp, (ch 6, sc in next ch sp) 8 times, ch 6; repeat from * around, end at *** on last repeat; jdc in ch-9 sp and first sc. Fasten off.

RND 41 (EEF): Attach threads with a sl st to first ch-9 sp just to the right of any pair of roses, beg sh, ch 5, sh in same ch-9 sp; *ch 5, V-st in next ch-9 sp, ch 5, sh in next ch-9 sp, ch 3, V-st in ch-5 sp, ch 3, sh in next ch-9 sp, ch 5, V-st in next ch-9 sp, ch 5; in next ch-9 sp work (sh, ch 5, sh), (sc in next ch-6 sp, ch 6) 17 times, sc in next ch-6 sp**, in ch-9 sp work (sh, ch 5, sh); repeat from * around, end at ** on last repeat; sl st in 3rd ch of ch-3.

RND 42 (EEF): Sl st in dc and ch-2 sp, beg sh; *ch 3, sc in ch-5 sp, ch 3, sh in sh, ch 3, 8 dc in V-st, ch 3, sh in sh, ch 3, sh in V-st, ch 3, sh in sh, ch 3, 8 dc in V-st, ch 3, sh in sh, ch 3, sc in ch-5 sp, ch 3, sh in sh, (sc in ch-6 sp, ch 6) 16 times, sc in next ch-6 sp**; sh in sh; repeat from * around, end at ** on last repeat; sl st in 3rd ch of ch-3.

RND 43 (EEF): Sl st in dc and ch-2 sp, beg sh; *ch 7, sh in sh, ch 2, (dc in dc, ch 1) 7 times, dc in next dc, ch 2, sh in sh, ch 3, dsh in sh, ch 3, sh in sh, ch 2, (dc in dc, ch 1) 7 times, dc in next dc, ch 2, sh in sh, ch 7, sh in sh, (sc in ch 6 sp, ch 6) 15 times, sc in next ch-6 sp**, sh in sh; repeat from * around, end at ** on last repeat; sl st in 3rd ch of ch-3.

RND 44 (EFF): Sl st in dc and ch-2 sp, beg sh; *ch 4, sc in ch-7 sp, ch 4, sh in sh, ch 5, (sc in ch-1 sp, ch 3) 6 times, sc in next ch-1 sp, ch 5, sh in sh, ch 3, sh in ch-2 sp, ch 3, sh in next ch-2 sp, ch 3, sh in sh, ch 5, (sc in ch-1 sp, ch 3) 6 times, sc in next ch-1 sp, ch 5, sh in sh, ch 4, sc in ch-7 sp, ch 4, sh in sh, (sc in ch-6 sp, ch 6) 14 times, sc in next ch-6 sp**, sh in sh; repeat from * around, end at ** on last repeat; sl st in 3rd ch of ch-3.

RND 45 (EFF): Sl st in dc and ch-2 sp, beg sh; *ch 7, sh in sh, ch 5, (sc in ch-3 sp, ch 3) 5 times, sc in next ch-3 sp, ch 5, sh in sh, ch 3, sh in sh, ch 3, sc in ch-3 sp, (ch 3, sh in sh) twice, ch 5, (sc in ch-3 sp, ch 3) 5 times, sc in next ch-3 sp, ch 5, sh in sh, ch 7, sh in sh, (sc in ch-6 sp, ch 6) 13 times, sc in next ch-6 sp**, sh in sh; repeat from * around, end at ** on last repeat; sl st in 3rd of ch-3.

RND 46 (EFF): Sl st in dc and ch–2 sp, beg sh; *ch 4, work (sc, p, sc) in ch–7 sp, ch 4, sh in sh, ch 5, (sc in ch–3 sp, ch 3) 4 times, sc in next ch–3 sp, ch 5, sh in sh, ch 3, sh in sh, (ch 3, sc in ch–3 sp) twice, (ch 3, sh in sh) twice, ch 5, (sc in ch–3 sp, ch 3) 4 times, sc in next ch–3 sp, ch 5, sh in sh, ch 4, work (sc, p, sc) in ch–7 sp, ch 4, sh in sh, (sc in ch–6 sp, ch 6) 12 times, sc in next ch–6 sp** sh in sh; repeat from * around, end at ** on last repeat; sl st in 3rd ch of ch–3.

RND 47 (FFF): Sl st in dc and ch–2 sp, beg sh; *ch 7, sh in sh, ch 5, (sc in ch–3 sp, ch 3) 3 times, sc in next ch–3 sp, ch 5, (sh in sh, ch 3) twice, sk 1 ch–3 sp, V–st in next ch–3 sp, (ch 3, sh in sh) twice, ch 5, (sc in ch–3 sp, ch 3) 3 times, sc in next ch–3 sp, ch 5, sh in sh, ch 7, sh in sh, (sc in ch–6 sp, ch 6) 11 times, sc in next ch–6 sp**, sh in sh; repeat from * around, end at ** on last repeat; sl st in 3rd ch of ch–3.

RND 48 (FFF): Sl st in dc and ch–2 sp, beg sh; *ch 4, work (sc, p, sc) in ch–7 sp, ch 4, sh in sh, ch 5, (sc in ch–3 sp, ch 3) twice, sc in next ch–3 sp, ch 5, sh in sh, ch 3, dsh in sh, ch 3, 8 dc in V–st, ch 3, dsh in sh, ch 3, sh in sh, ch 5, (sc in ch–3 sp, ch 3) twice, sc in next ch–3 sp, ch 5, sh in sh, ch 4, work (sc, p, sc) in ch–7 sp, ch 4, sh in sh, (sc in ch–6 sp, ch 6) 10 times, sc in next h–6 sp** sh in sh; repeat from * around, end at ** on last repeat; sl st in 3rd ch of ch–3.

RND 49 (FFF): Sl st in dc and ch–2 sp, beg sh; *ch 9, sh in sh, ch 5, sc in ch–3 sp, ch 3, sc in next ch–3 sp, ch 5, sh in sh, (ch 3, sh in ch–2 sp) twice, ch 2, (dc in next dc, ch 1) 7 times, dc in next dc, ch 2, (sh in ch–2 sp, ch 3) twice, sh in sh, ch 5, sc in ch–3 sp, ch 3, sc in ch–3 sp, ch 5, sh in sh, ch 9, sh in sh, (sc in ch–6 sp, ch 6) 9 times, sc in next ch–6 sp**, sh in sh; repeat from * around, end at ** on last repeat; sl st in 3rd of ch–3.

RND 50 (FFG): Sl st in dc and ch–2 sp, beg sh; *ch 5, work (sc, p, sc) in ch–9 sp, ch 5, dsh in sh, ch 5, sc in ch–3 sp, ch 5, sh in sh, ch 3, dsh in sh, ch 3, sh in sh, ch 5, (sc in ch–1 sp, ch 3) 6 times, sc in next ch–1 sp, ch 5, sh in sh, ch 3, dsh in sh, ch 3, sh in sh, ch 5, sc in ch–3 sp, ch 5, dsh in sh, ch 5, work (sc, p, sc) in ch–9 sp, ch 5, sh in sh, (sc in ch–6 sp, ch 6) 8 times, sc in next ch–6 sp**, sh in sh; repeat from * around, end at ** on last repeat; sl st in 3rd ch of ch–3.

RND 51 (FFG): Sl st in dc and ch–2 sp, beg sh; *ch 11, sh in ch–2 sp, ch 3, sh in next ch–2 sp, sh in sh, (ch 3, sh in ch–2 sp) twice, ch 3, sh in sh, ch 5, (sc in ch–3 sp, ch 3) 5 times, sc in next ch–3 sp, ch 5, sh in sh, (ch 3, sh in next ch–2 sp) twice, ch 3, sh in sh, sh in next ch–2 sp, ch 3, sh in next ch–2 sp, ch 11, sh in sh, (sc in ch–6 sp, ch 7) 7 times, sc in next ch–6 sp**, sh in sh; repeat from * around, end at ** on last repeat; sl st in 3rd ch of ch–3.

RND 52 (FFG): Sl st in dc and ch–2 sp, beg sh; *ch 6, work (sc, p, sc) in ch–11 sp, ch 6, sh in sh, ch 5, (2 dc in sh) twice, ch 5, sh in sh, ch 3, sc in ch–3 sp, (ch 3, sh in sh) twice, ch 5, (sc in ch–3 sp, ch 3) 4 times, sc in next ch–3 sp, ch 5, sh in sh, ch 3, sh in sh, ch 3, sc in ch–3 sp, ch 3, sh in sh, ch 5, (2 dc in sh) twice, ch 5, sh in sh, ch 6, work (sc, p, sc) in ch–11 sp, ch 6, sh in sh, (sc in ch–7 sp, ch 7) 6 times, sc in next ch–7 sp**, sh in sh; repeat from * around, end at ** on last repeat; sl st in 3rd ch of ch–3.

RND 53 (FGG): Sl st in dc and ch–2 sp, beg sh; *(ch 13, sh in sh) twice, ch 5, sc in sc, ch 5, sh in sh, ch 3, sh in sh, ch 5, (sc in ch–3 sp, ch 3) 3 times, sc in next ch–3 sp, ch 5, sh in sh, ch 3, sh in sh, ch 5, sc in sc, ch 5, (sh in sh, ch 13) twice, sh in sh, (sc in ch–7 sp, ch 7) 5 times, sc in next ch–7 sp**, sh in sh; repeat from * around, end at ** on last repeat; sl st in 3rd ch of ch–3.

RND 54 (FGG): Sl st in dc and ch–2 sp, beg sh; *[ch 7, work (sc, p, sc) in ch–13 sp, ch 7, sh in sh] twice, ch 7, sc in sc, ch 7, (sh in sh, ch 5) twice, (sc in ch–3 sp, ch 3) twice, sc in next ch–3 sp, (ch 5, sh in sh) twice, ch 7, sc in sc, ch 7, [sh in sh, ch 7, work (sc, p, sc) in ch–13 sp, ch 7] twice, sh in sh, (sc in ch–7 sp, ch 8) 4 times, sc in next ch–7 sp**, sh in sh; repeat from * around, end at ** on last repeat; sl st in 3rd ch of ch–3.

RND 55 (FGG): Sl st in dc and ch–2 sp, beg sh; *(ch 15, sh in sh) twice, ch 9 sc in sc, ch 9, sh in sh, ch 7, sh in sh, ch 5, sc in ch–3 sp, ch 3, sc in next ch–3 sp, ch 5, sh in sh, ch 7, sh in sh, ch 9, sc in sc, ch 9, (sh in sh, ch 15) twice, sh in sh, (sc in ch–8 sp, ch 8) 3 times, sc in next ch–8 sp**, sh in sh; repeat from * around, end at ** on last repeat; sl st in 3rd ch of ch–3.

RND 56 (GGG): Sl st in dc and ch–2 sp, beg sh; *(ch 8, dc in ch–15 sp) twice, ch 8, sh in sh, (ch 8, dc in ch–15 sp) twice, ch 8, sh in ch–9 sp, ch 5, sc in sc, ch 5, sh in ch–9 sp, ch 8, dc in ch–7 sp, ch 8, sh in sh, ch 5, sc in ch–3 sp, ch 5, sh in sh, ch 8, dc in ch–7 sp, ch 8, sh in ch–9 sp, ch 5, sc in sc, ch 5, sh in ch–9 sp, [(ch 8, dc in ch 15 sp) twice, ch 8, sh in sh] twice, (sc in ch–8 sp, ch 8) twice, sc in next ch 8 sp** sh in sh; repeat from * around, end at ** on last repeat; sl st in 3rd of ch–3.

RND 57 (GGG): Sl st in dc and ch–2 sp, beg sh; *ch 5, [work (sc, p, sc) in ch–8 sp, ch 3, dc in dc, ch 3] twice, work (sc, p, sc) in ch–8 sp, ch 5, sh in sh, ch 5, [work (sc, p, sc) in ch–8 sp, ch 3, dc in dc, ch 3] twice, work (sc, p, sc) in ch–8 sp, ch 5, sh in ch–5 sp, ch 3, sc in sc, ch 3, sh in ch–5 sp, ch 5, work (sc, p, sc) in ch–8 sp, ch 3, dc in dc, ch 3, work (sc, p, sc) in ch–8 sp, ch 5, (sh in sh) twice, ch 5, work (sc, p, sc) in ch–8 sp, ch 3, dc in dc, ch 3, work (sc, p, sc) in ch–8 sp, ch 5, sh in ch–5 sp, ch 3, sc in sc, ch 3, sh in ch–5 sp, ch 5, [work (sc, p, sc) in ch–8 sp, ch 3, dc in dc, ch 3] twice, work (sc, p, sc) in ch–8 sp, ch 5, sh in sh, ch 5, [work (sc, p, sc) in ch–8 sp, ch 3, dc in dc, ch 3] twice, work (sc, p, sc) in ch–8 sp, ch 5, sh in sh, sc in ch–8 sp, ch 10, sc in ch–8 sp**, sh in sh; repeat from * around, end at ** on last repeat; sl st in 3rd of ch–3.

RND 58 (GGG): Ch 1, sc in join, sc in dc, work (sc, p, sc) in ch–2 sp, sc in next 2 dc; work remainder of row in steps.

STEP 1: (Fan st, sc in dc) 3 times.

NOTE: Mark the center picot of the first fan st worked with a small safety pin; this is where you will join the final roses.

STEP 2: Sc in next 2 dc, work (sc, p, sc) in ch–2 sp, sc in next 2 dc.

STEP 3: Repeat Steps 1 and 2 once.

STEP 4: Sc in 2 dc, work (sc, p, sc) in ch–2 sp, sc in next 2 dc.

STEP 5: (Fan st, sc in dc) twice.

STEP 6: Repeat Steps 2, 4, 5, 2, and 4 in that order.

STEP 7: Repeat Steps 1 and 2 twice.

STEP 8: Sc in next sc, work (6 sc, p, 5 sc) in ch–10 sp, sc in sc.

STEP 9: Repeat Step 4.

Repeat Steps 1–9 around, ending at Step 8 on last repeat; sl st in first sc. Fasten off.

Complete and join rem 6 roses to Rnd 58 as follows:

ROSE RND 13: Attach (GGG) threads with a sl st to any ch–8 sp of an unfinished rose, ch 1; *in ch–8 sp work (sc, hdc, 13 dc, hdc, sc) 3 times, in next ch–8 sp work (sc, hdc, 7 dc), sc in 3rd p of marked fan st on Step 1 of Rnd 58, finish petal with (7 dc, hdc, sc); in next ch–8 sp work (sc, hdc, 7 dc), sc in p of Step 8, finish petal with (7 dc, hdc, sc), in next ch–8 sp work (sc, hdc, 7 dc), sc in 3rd p of next fan st, finish petal with (7 dc, hdc, sc); sl st in first sc. Fasten off.

Join 5 more roses in same manner.

FINISHING

Block Centerpiece with right side of roses facing up.

FREE-FORM CROCHET

with
Prudence Mapstone

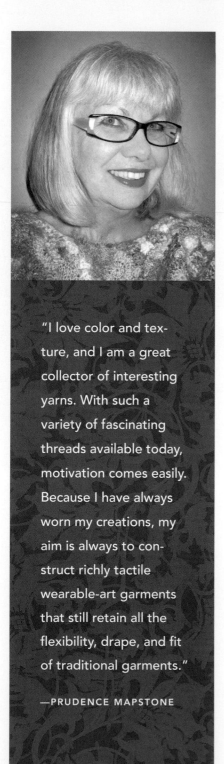

Before she entered school in her home city of Sydney, Australia, Prudence had learned to knit. In fact, she was so proficient that while the rest of the class pored over their garter stitch squares, Prudence was knitting a V-neck pullover with a blackberry stitch up the front, taken from her own pattern.

Years later while living in subtropical Queensland, Australia, Prudence became hooked on intarsia knitting, spending hours graphing out complex designs that she would follow to create one-of-a-kind pieces. During this period, she started to experiment with her own style of free-form knitting, either creating random cloudlike effects across long rows, or working outward in all directions from a central point to build up a piece of fabric.

She did so much knitting that she ended up suffering with strain from overuse, which led her to seek other, less repetitive, ways of working. She had learned to crochet earlier, but she never followed crochet patterns. In fact, she didn't even know the correct names for most of the crochet stitches until she was forced to learn them when she wrote her first book. Because crochet required a different motion, she found relief, and she was soon adding crochet to her accomplishments.

The real turning point in her life came when she learned that the crochet artists James Walters and Sylvia Cosh, who were the early masters of free-form work, were coming to Australia. Prudence flew to Sydney and took a two-day crochet workshop with them. Seeing their wonderful free-form crochet pieces up close inspired Prudence to add even more crochet to her free-forming. Their "scrumbling" methods mitigated the strain from her fatigued fingers and wrists, and free-form work became her focus.

After demonstrating at a major needlework and craft fair in 1998, Prudence's work generated so much interest that she was invited to give workshops. Posting photos of her work on her website soon led to numerous inquiries, especially from

crocheters in the United States. In 2002, Prudence published the first of several books explaining free-form and showing her work.

Today Prudence travels throughout the world conducting workshops and tutorials in places as far apart as Bermuda and Tasmania. Twice she has been invited to teach her techniques in Denmark, where her books have been translated into Danish. Her work has been exhibited widely across Australia and at various shows and events in the United States, the United Kingdom, New Zealand, Israel, and Denmark. Many examples of her free-form creations can be found on her website, www.knotjustknitting.com.

Prudence's fashion garments are truly wearable art, and passersby often stop to examine the piece she's wearing and ask about the free-form technique. The tactile nature of her designs, and her ability to blend interesting yarns and colors, make for showstopping jackets, hats, vests and coats.

HOW TO DO **FREE-FORM** CROCHET

Free-form crochet is the term used to describe a type of crochet that is worked without a pattern, created in the designer's mind as it is worked. Free-formers like to think of it like painting, where, as they explain it, "The hook is a brush and the yarn is paint."

British crochet designers and teachers James Walters and Sylvia Cosh are credited with introducing the art of free-form to the crochet world. For more than twenty-three years until Sylvia died in 2000, the duo conducted crochet workshops all over the world, explaining their theories and concepts.

They used the term *scrumbling*, which meant making things up as you go along, to explain their concept of free-form crochet. As different artists have developed different techniques and philosophies over the years, the one factor that has remained is that there are no rules. The crocheter needs no pattern but merely starts with a hook and some thread and creates her own "scrumbles" and her own fabric.

CHOOSING THE YARN

One of the best things about free-form is that you can use just about any yarn—if you can crochet with it, you can use it in free-form! Fine yarn, thick yarn, fuzzy yarn, or metallics will all work well in the mixture that makes up a free-form fabric. And you can use just small amounts of especially interesting, expensive yarns to spice up the project. A few yards of a leftover yarn you may have on hand from a previous project can go a long way in making a few free-form motifs. Unlike most projects, you don't have to use just one weight of yarn in a project. Mixing up weights will make the project more interesting.

CHOOSING THE HOOK

Use a hook that works well with the yarn. You may use many different hook sizes in one project. Use a smaller hook than usual for a specific yarn to get a tighter, firm texture; use a larger one for a more lacy, open effect.

COLOR PLANNING

Free-form projects look exciting when they are made up of many colors, and even ombre or variegated yarn can be included. A monotone colorway also works well. If going with monotone, you can either select a wide range of shades within the color, or use just one shade.

If you are working entirely in pastel shades, choose one fairly deep pastel to serve as an anchor for the lighter colors. Garments especially, when made entirely in pastels, seem to need the "punch" of a deeper tone.

DIMENSION AND TEXTURE

In the Spring or Fall Free-Form Shawl (see page 165), all of the motifs are worked flat because this improves the drape of the fabric. But in most free-form projects, you'll want to add dimension and texture by using post stitches, clusters, popcorns, bullion stitches, shells, and many other interesting ones. Little dome-shaped patches or ones that are cone shaped are nice for filling in spots. Dimensional flowers spaced here and there also add to the look.

The more interesting stitches and textures you use, the more attractive the finished piece will be.

TEMPLATES

A template of some sort, often just cut from paper, will be needed so you can plan out the placement and joining of the individual motifs and scrumbles. Following the shawl pattern, you can make a paper template to your own body measurements. For other garments, you can use something you own that fits well and draw around it for the template. If you are making a cover for a handbag, a belt, or anything else, create a template before starting to join the free-form pieces. Remember, you will be joining the pieces to each other, not to the template!

PLANNING PLACEMENT

Once you have made a significant number of motifs, you can start laying them out on the template. Move the pieces around until you are satisfied with the overall balance of the different colors and motifs. You may find that you need to make more motifs, or you might decide to take out one that doesn't please you. Use small safety pins to join the motifs until you are completely happy with the placement, and then start sewing or crocheting them together according to your plan.

JOINING THE PIECES

To join, you can either crochet pieces together or sew them, or use a combination of both. You can crochet or sew through both loops of a stitch, or only the front or back loop, depending on the look you want. The mattress stitch works well for sewing, but use any stitch method that works for you. Either contrasting or matching yarn or thread can be used, depending on the effect you want. Sew the motifs in groups of four or five, then place them back on the template and see how they look. You may need to rearrange things a bit. If not, join another small group, then join it to the first. Keep going in this way, each time returning the joined pieces to the template to see the overall effect. Don't be afraid to make adjustments as you go along.

You will probably find it easiest to strike a happy medium when free-forming—one that fits somewhere between creating a garment all in one piece and having to stitch a million little pieces together toward the end of the project. I encourage you to join things to each other only until you don't quite know what to do next! Then you should just stop working on that piece and start on another. That way you are much less likely to try to fit the 'wrong' number of stitches into a space just because you have your hook in hand and are on a roll.

For the Spring and Fall examples given here, I initially joined just three or four motifs to each other as I worked. Gauge was not important because I knew that I was going to eventually arrange all of the pieces over the top of a paper template that would act as a guideline for the garment shape. By working with small 'scrumbles' in this manner, you will find that it is easy to move the pieces around until you are happy with the overall balance of the different colors and motifs. Once you start to add the random filling stitches, keep checking, by putting the patch back in position on the template, to see that the piece will still fit well into the space you had allocated to it.

Although there is sometimes a temptation to start stitching patches to each other early in the process, try to avoid doing so. With just a few large pieces to work with you will often find that there is just no way that you can get them to fit together into the desired shape. Pin a few together if you wish, but leave the actual stitching until you can see the whole garment laid out before you.

I usually like to stitch the pieces together using mattress stitch, although sometimes you will come to an intersection where another stitch seems more appropriate. Listen to that inner voice, and use whatever stitch you feel is going to work best at any point, even if you have to change stitch techniques part of the way along a seam. When creating garments such as these, where there are areas of open work, you can still continue to stitch across the edge of a 'space' by working a backstitch or two at the end of one section before moving on. Once you have made the backstitch, take the needle behind the loops at the back of the work until you come to the next part to be joined, and then start the new join with a backstitch or two as well.

SPRING OR FALL **FREE-FORM SHAWL**

Designed by Prudence Mapstone

SKILL LEVEL

■■■□ Intermediate

SIZE
Shawl is customized to fit any body size

MATERIALS
For Spring version:
- Habu Textiles *A-60 Shosenshi Paper* (100% linen, each approximately 2 oz [28g] and 280 yd [250m], **②** fine/sport weight)
  - 280 yd (250m) / 1 hank in color 121 Orange
  - 280 yd (250m) / 1 hank in color 115 Gray
  - 280 yd (250m) / 1 hank in color 114 Green

Note: This interesting and unusual linen yarn may feel a little "crunchy" at first, but you will find that it relaxes considerably as you work with it, and it softens even more with wear.

For Fall version:
- Frog Tree *Sport* (100% alpaca, each approximately 1¾ oz [50g] and 130 yd [119m], **②** fine/sport weight)
  - 130 yd (119m) / 1 ball in color 26 Red
  - 130 yd (119m) / 1 ball in color 309 Blue
  - 130 yd (119m) / 1 ball in color 55 Dark Purple

CONTINUED ON PAGE 162

Because every free-form garment is an original work of art, these instructions are not an exact pattern in the traditional sense. Begin by choosing your materials for either the Spring or Fall version.

The simple shape of this shawl offers a chance to play with color and texture to create a striking one-of-a-kind garment with front lappets and a flowing back. It is easy to adjust to any size, and can be made to any desired length. Change the color palette to match the season.

CONTINUED FROM PAGE 160

130 yd (119m) / 1 ball in color
511 Light Purple
390 yd (357m) / 3 balls in color
41 Green
- One size 7 (4.5mm) crochet
  hook, or size needed to give
  your work a suitable drape
- Tape measure
- Pencil
- Roll of paper or newspaper (for
  pattern templates)
- Scissors
- Small safety pins (for pinning
  motifs together prior to
  stitching)
- Yarn needle or large-eye
  tapestry needle

GAUGE
Gauge is not important.

SHAWL

The shawl is made in four steps:

STEP 1: Make a variety of motifs and small patches in colors and yarns of your choice from the two suggested colorways, and then join them in small groups, called scrumbles.

STEP 2: Measure your body and make a custom paper pattern or template.

STEP 3: Arrange the scrumbles on the paper template.

STEP 4: Join the motifs with filler stitches.

When creating free-form garments, keeping to an exact gauge is not important. You only need to work to a tension that will eventually produce a fabric that is neither too stiff nor too stretchy. The size and shaping of the garment will only be determined once the motifs and patches are fitted together over the paper pattern.

Each of the motifs should lie flat. When working the filler stitches, keep a careful eye on your work so that you do not add either too many or too few in any one position. Use your discretion. If at any point you find that the work is cupping up (or ruffling out), it means that you actually require more (or fewer) stitches in that area. Lay your work flat often, even after just a new few stitches, to check how things are progressing. If you sometimes feel the need for a stitch or two more (or fewer) than you originally envisioned, make the necessary adjustment immediately.

PLANNING THE MOTIFS
To make the final stitching together a little easier, join a few of the motifs in small groupings (scrumbles) as they are completed. The work is less likely to go out of shape if you join only a few at a time, so small groups of just 2, 3, or 4 motifs are best.

To join 2 motifs, hold the right sides of the pieces together (before you cut the yarn on the 2nd motif), and crochet together with 2 or 3 slipstitches. Do not work the slipstitches too tightly.

Add a chain between the slipstitches if you feel the need for more ease. Or if you prefer, you can sew the pieces together.

To achieve a final overall balance of stitches and colors, do not join the same shapes or colors to each other in any one group. The more motifs and patches you initially make, the less random filling stitches your design will require.

MOTIF COLORS

For Spring version:

Work all 5- and 6-petal flowers in orange.

Work all wheel motifs in gray.

Work small crochet circle motifs in all 3 colors.

Work all random filling stitches in green.

For Fall version:

Work all 5-petal flowers in dark purple.

Work all 6-petal flowers in red.

Work all wheel motifs in blue.

Work all small circle motifs in light purple.

Work all random filling stitches in green.

MOTIF INSTRUCTIONS

5-PETAL FLOWER (MAKE 15 TO 20)

Ch 3; join with a sl st to form a ring.

RND 1: Ch 4 (counts as a dc and ch–1 sp); (dc in ring, ch 1) 9 times; join with a sl st into 3rd ch of beg ch–4—10 ch–1 sps.

RND 2: In first ch–1 sp work (sc, ch 6, sc); *3 sc in next ch–1 sp, in next ch–1 sp work (sc, ch 6, sc); repeat from * 3 times more, 3 sc in the last ch–1 sp; join with a sl st in beg sc—5 petal lps made.

RND 3: Work 10 hdc in the first ch–6 petal lp; *sk next sc, sl st in next sc, sk next sc, work 10 hdc in next petal lp; repeat from *3 times more; sk next sc, sl st in next sc, sk next sc, join with a sl st in top of beg hdc. Fasten off.

6-PETAL FLOWER (MAKE 10 TO 14)

Ch 7; join with a sl st to form a ring.

RND 1: Ch 3 (counts as a dc), work 18 dc in ring; join with a sl st in top of beg ch–3—19 dc.

RND 2: *Ch 7, sc in each of the next 3 dc; repeat from * 5 times more—6 petal lps made.

RND 3: Ch 1, work 14 hdc into 1st petal lp; *sk next sc, sl st in next sc, sk next sc, work 14 hdc in next petal lp; repeat from * 4 times more, join with a sl st in top of beg hdc. Fasten off.

WHEEL MOTIF (MAKE 16 TO 24)

Ch 3; join with a sl st to form a ring.

RND 1: Ch 7 (counts as a tr and ch–3 sp); (tr in ring, ch 3) 9 times, join with a sl st in 4th ch of beg ch–7.

RND 2: Sl st into first ch–3 sp, ch 2, work 4 hdc in same sp; (work 5 hdc in next ch–3 sp) 9 times, join with a sl st in top of beg hdc. Fasten off.

SMALL CIRCLE MOTIF (MAKE 25 TO 35)

Ch 6; join with a sl st to form a ring.

RND 1: Ch 3 (counts as a dc), work 18 dc in ring; join with a sl st in top of beg ch–3. Fasten off.

PATTERN TEMPLATE

Place a tape measure straight across your upper chest at a point just below the base of your neck. Take a measurement from the midpoint on the outside of one arm (just below the shoulder) to the midpoint on the other. This will be the width of your paper pattern.

Cut two rectangles from a large roll of paper (or a couple of pages from a broadsheet newspaper). Both rectangles should be the width that you just measured and about 28" (71cm) long. One piece will be the basic rectangle pattern shape for the back.

For the fronts [**FIG 1**], measure and mark the midpoint on both short sides of the other piece (Points A and B). Draw a line to divide the rectangle in two lengthwise (i.e., from Point A to Point B). Mark a point 3" (7.5cm) out in each direction from Point A (Points C and D). Mark a point 8" (20.5cm) down on the centerline from Point A (this is Point E). Draw lines from Point C and Point D to Point E. Write "left front (right side facing)" and "right front (right side facing)" as shown on the diagram. Cut along the lines that have been drawn. Discard the triangular

piece between Points C, D, and E. To give your design a more "organic" look, sketch a gently curving line around the bottom of each of the front pattern pieces, as shown. When you are happy with the flow of the lower edge, cut the pieces to their final shape. Draw and cut a similar organic lower edge for the back. [FIG 1]

Arrange all motifs and small patches on the 3 paper pattern pieces. Move them around and space them so that they look balanced, taking care with color placement, and make additional motifs if needed. Fill in the gaps with random areas of crochet. Don't even up the side edges of the pieces too much. As with the lower edges, a gentle flow to the design generally looks best.

Random Filling Stitches

Since these will be done in a totally free-form manner, it will be up to you to decide where you will put these stitches, how tall you will make them, and how many you will use. Pick up each motif or patch from the pattern and work an area of random crochet onto its edge. Keep in mind where you are going to fit the piece back onto the pattern, and aim to make your stitches fit back into that space. Put the patch back in position once it is done, and begin working on another. Once a few pieces have been completed to fit together well, pin and stitch them together neatly, then again place them back on the pattern. It is rather like putting together a jigsaw puzzle, but you are creating the design as you work.

Continue to gradually fill all of the spaces in this manner, until the fabric is completed to the size and shape of the paper patterns. Finally, pin and stitch the shoulder seams.

If desired you can work a row of stitches around the outside edge of the garment (this has been done for the Fall example, but not for Spring). Again, be sure that you do not add too many or too few stitches in any one area. Placing the piece flat after every few stitches, especially when working around humps and dips, is the best way to keep an eye on how things are progressing and will save you having to rip the edging back too far if things go slightly askew.

Wear your free-form garment with flair, knowing that it is truly the only one of its kind in the world!

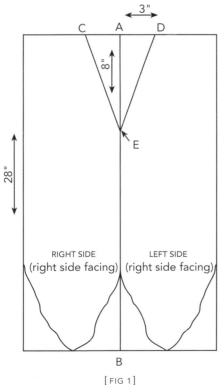

RIGHT SIDE (right side facing)   LEFT SIDE (right side facing)

[FIG 1]

IRISH CROCHET

with

Máire Treanor

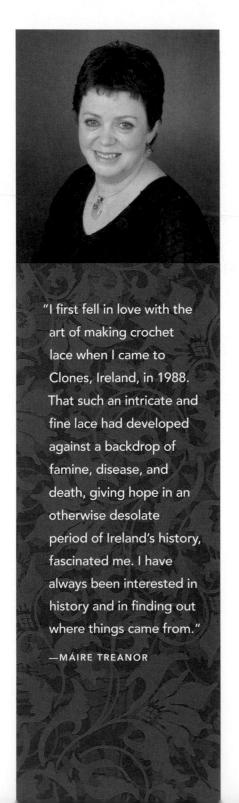

"I first fell in love with the art of making crochet lace when I came to Clones, Ireland, in 1988. That such an intricate and fine lace had developed against a backdrop of famine, disease, and death, giving hope in an otherwise desolate period of Ireland's history, fascinated me. I have always been interested in history and in finding out where things came from."

—MÁIRE TREANOR

M áire Treanor was born and educated in Armagh, Northern Ireland, and completed a degree in Irish studies at the University of Ulster in Coleraine. As a child, she hated sports because she was left-handed and had a hard time using the equipment.

Being left-handed, however, did not deter Máire from becoming an expert crocheter by the time she was thirteen. In school, Máire loved history, especially Irish history, which might explain her interest in helping to rediscover this fabulous form of crochet.

In 1988, Máire married and moved with her new husband to Clones, a small town in western County Monaghan in the border area of Ireland. More than one hundred years before Máire arrived, a particular form of Irish crochet lace had been introduced to this town as a remedy for famine relief. Within a very short time, nearly every family in town was producing Clones lace—as this form of Irish crochet lace became known—to supply markets in the fashion capitals of the world, including New York, London, and Paris.

By the time Máire arrived in Clones, only a few elderly lacemakers were left in the area. Máire's job in Clones included setting up a heritage project in the town, and she became fascinated with the history of the local traditional craft, the special Clones crochet lace.

She soon realized that this beautiful craft would become extinct if she didn't learn it from the older crocheters in the area before they passed away. Along with the famous spokesperson on Irish women's affairs, Mamo MacDonald, she formed the Clones Lace Guild. For several years this group has made and sold Clones lace. In addition, they established the Cassandra Hand Summer School of Clones Lace, where those interested in learning more about this beautiful technique can attend full workshops or single sessions.

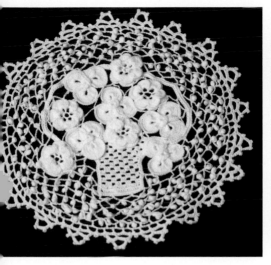

Máire continues to spread the word about Clones lace and has traveled to the United States and France teaching workshops. She authored the definitive book on Clones lace, *Clones Lace: The Story and Patterns of an Irish Crochet*, a best-seller serving people all over the world interested in Irish crochet. The book includes glorious photos of beautiful crochet pieces that were made for Máire's three daughters, Máiread, Áine, and Cáit.

Six examples of Irish Crochet, considered the most delicate and beautiful form of crochet, by Máire Treanor. The work is created with individual motifs—usually with dimension—worked separately, then joined with a lacy ground.

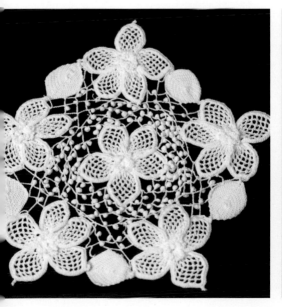
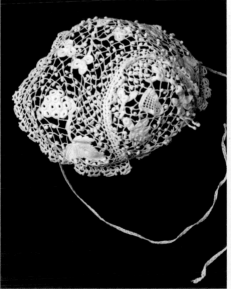

HOW TO DO IRISH CROCHET

Because Irish crochet is made up of many small motifs, the crocheter's individuality is showcased in the way she or he chooses to compose the designs. Unlike ordinary crochet where the work moves along in rows or rounds, one worked upon the other with carefully counted stitches, in Irish crochet, separate motifs are joined either by mesh or crocheted bars. The motifs—sprays, flowers, shamrocks, and vines—are worked over a foundation cord. Usually a corded padding is used. The pieces are finally creatively arranged on a foundation pattern with the spaces between the pieces filled with bars of crochet. The crocheter is free to adjust the number of stitches because the pattern is meant merely as an idea, leaving much to the skill of the crocheter. No two people working the same motif will necessarily turn out the same result.

The technique of Irish crochet is simple, and the rules are few. Here is what was published in 1909 in the famous *Priscilla Irish Crochet Book*. The rules still apply:

"There are two threads, as it were, used in working this lace. One is the working thread, which is used to make the stitches; the other thread, or cord, is only used to work over, which gives this lace the rich effect so different from ordinary crochet work. This cord is sometimes held close to the work and the stitches are made over it into the row of stitches made before (working only in the back loops) or the stitches are worked over it alone, using it as a foundation. In making Irish crochet the stitches should be uniform, close, and compact; loose or ragged crochet makes inferior lace, wanting in crispness, and the padding cord should never show through the work."

Today, Irish crochet is still made in thin cotton threads with a fine crochet hook. The instructions for the bookmark on page 170 specify 80-, 60-, and 20-weight threads; if these are unavailable or if you prefer to work with slightly heavier threads, you can substitute if you wish, resulting in a slightly larger bookmark.

CLONES LACE

Clones lace is a version of Irish crochet named after the town in Ireland where it was marketed. The making of the lace was introduced to Clones by the wife of the local minister in 1847. Clones soon became one of the most important centers of crochet lacemaking and developed its own character after nearly 150 years.

As with most Irish crochet, the motifs are worked using a packing cord rather than a foundation chain. The packing cord needs to be made with a thicker thread, which is cut to a specific length, then folded in half and the doubled thickness worked together as one.

When all of the motifs for the project are made, Clones knots (see page 174) are used to join and fill the space between the motifs.

HISTORY OF IRISH CROCHET

The Irish tradition of producing Irish crochet dates back to the sixteenth century, when it was known as nun's work because the craft was developed in Irish convents in imitation of Venetian Rose Point lace as well as Honiton lace from England and Mechelen, the Flemish lace.

The manufacture of crochet lace, however, did not become a cottage industry in Ireland until the middle of the nineteenth century, when Ireland was in the midst of a terrible famine. A potato blight had almost completely destroyed the agricultural industry that was the main income producer in Ireland. The country was in desperate need of an occupation that could support the population. At that time the fashion in vogue called for an abundance of lace. Even men wore lace in jabots and evening shirts, and some women wore complete lace dresses. Making exquisite lace, however, was extremely time-consuming, and the economy needed something that could be completed quickly.

It is now generally accepted that Mademoiselle Riego de la Branchardiere invented the style referred to today as Irish crochet. Born in England to a Spanish noble father and an Irish mother, Mlle Riego reasoned that Spanish needle lace, which was very similar to the desirable Venetian needlepoint lace, could be created with a crochet hook. In addition, it was at least ten times faster.

Since many of the people who were to work the lace patterns could not read, it was important that the information be passed along with pictures. Mlle Riego published the first book of Irish crochet patterns in 1846. Her book was not only used by the schools of crochet that sprang up but also by the constantly growing cottage industry.

Soon entire families became involved in the making of lace as a way of surviving. All levels of ability could do the work, and everyone in the family, including the men and the children, added to the lace. The involved patterns were made by the most experienced crocheter, and the simple leaves and stems might be worked by young children or those with less experience. One person often made the same piece over and over again.

The making of lace served as a vital cottage industry throughout the famine. In the years following the famine, the interest in Irish crochet lessened. Eventually, the fashion world no longer wanted lace jabots, and the demand for luxuries such as lace declined while the world fought two world wars. Irish crochet had succeeded in reviving a nation. Today it remains as one of the most beautiful of crochet techniques.

CLONES LACE **BOOKMARK**

Designed by Máire Treanor

SKILL LEVEL

■■■■▷ Experienced

SIZE
Approximately 3½" x 9"
(9cm x 23cm)

MATERIALS
- DMC® *Cordonnet Special Size 60 Crochet Thread* (100% mercerized cotton, each approximately .7 oz [20g], 324 yd [296m])
  324 yd (296m) / 1 ball in color Ecru
- DMC® *Cordonnet Special Size 80 Crochet Thread* (100% mercerized cotton, each approximately .7 oz [20g], 398 yd [364m])
  - 398 yd (364m) / 1 ball in color Ecru
- DMC® *Cordonnet Special Size 20 Crochet Thread* (100% mercerized cotton, each approximately .7 oz [20g], 174 yd [159m])
  174 yd (159m) / 1 ball in color Ecru
- One size 14 (.75mm) steel crochet hook
- One size 19 (15mm) knitting needle
- Tapestry needle
- Sewing needle
- Rustproof straight pins
- Ecru and contrasting color sewing threads
- One 3½" x 9" (9cm x 23cm) piece of solid color fabric for template

GAUGE
Gauge is not important.

I designed this bookmark because it is simple yet exquisite. There are basically two motifs: the shamrock and the scroll. I would do the ten shamrocks first. Then I would make the scrolls and place them on the template. I would make the template from a rectangular piece of material as indicated in the pattern. (To determine the center, I fold the template in half and half again, then open it out.) Finally, I would then make the button, which I would place in the center of the folds and attach with chains to the shamrocks.

STITCH GUIDE

PICOT: Ch 4, sl st in first ch. Pull thread gently to tighten picot.

MOTIFS

SHAMROCK MOTIF

For each motif, 3 leaves are made. For each leaf, make a packing cord from a 30" (76cm) length of size 20 thread. Fold piece in half and work over the 2 strands as one for all rounds.

Leaf (Make 3)

RND 1: Using size 60 thread, join yarn with a sl st in fold of packing cord; work (2 sc, 16 dc, 2 sc, sl st) over packing cord.

RND 2: Sl st in first sc; pull lp into circular shape, sc in next sc and in next 2 dc; (2 sc in next dc, sc in each of next 2 dc) 4 times; 2 sc in next dc, sc in next dc and in each of next 2 sc; join with a sl st in first sc and pull packing cord into circular shape, making sure leaf is flat. **[FIG 1]**

SCROLL MOTIF

For each motif, one packing cord is needed. For each packing cord, cut a piece of size 20 thread about 30" (76cm) long, then fold piece in half so that you are working over 2 strands.

RND 1: Using size 60 thread, join thread with a sl st in fold of packing cord; over packing cord work (25 sc, ch 2, 15 sc); join with a sl st around packing cord below ch–2 sp;

[FIG 1]

coming from the underside of lp, pull packing cord into a circle; drop packing cord; turn—40 sc. [**FIG 2**]

Work remainder of scroll in rows.

ROW 1: Ch 4, sk first sc, sl st in next sc; *ch 4, sk next sc, sl st in next sc; repeat from * around circle to beg of work; turn—20 ch-4 sps.

ROW 2: Sl st in first ch-4 sp, *ch 4, sl st in next ch-4 sp; repeat from * across, ch 4, sl st in ch-2 sp; turn—19 ch-4 sps. [**FIG 3**]

ROW 3: Pick up packing cord and working over it, 3 sc in each of first 9 ch-4 sps; drop packing cord; turn—27 sc.

ROW 4: Ch 6, sk first 3 sc, sl st in next sc, ch 6, sk next 3 sc, sl st in next sc; turn, leaving rem sc unworked—2 ch-6 sps.

ROW 5: In first ch-6 sp work (2 sc, picot, 3 sc), 3 sc in next ch-6 sp, ch 6, turn, sk first 5 sc, sl st in next sc; turn.

ROW 6: In next ch-6 sp work (2 sc, picot, 2 sc, picot, 2 sc), in next sp work (sc, picot, 2 sc); pick up packing cord, 3 sc in each of next 3 ch-4 sps on Row 2; turn. [**FIG 4**]

ROWS 7–9: Repeat Rows 4–6.

ROWS 10 AND 11: Repeat Rows 4 and 5.

ROW 12: In next ch-6 sp work (2 sc, picot, 2 sc, picot, 2 sc), in next sp work (sc, picot, 2 sc); pick up packing cord, working over packing cord, 3 sc in each rem ch-4 sp on Row 2, (sc, sl st) in last ch-4 sp on Row 1. [**FIG 5**]

Fasten off; cut packing cord.

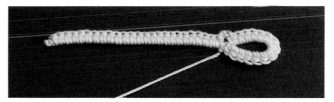

[FIG 2]

[FIG 3]

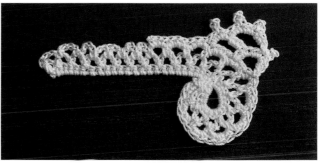

[FIG 4]

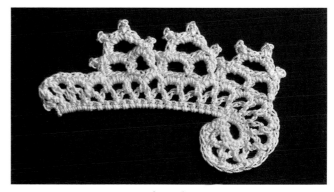

[FIG 5]

BUTTON

A packing cord is not used with this motif. Wrap size 60 thread around knitting needle 13 times, creating a ring; do not cut thread. Remove ring from needle. With crochet hook, work 18 sc in ring; join with a sl st in first sc. Fasten off; weave in thread end.

CLONES KNOT

STEP 1: With size 80 thread, ch 5; make lp about ½" (13mm) from end of hook at wider part to make it easier to pull thread through later. [FIG 6]

STEP 2: Yo; rotate hook to left and backward [FIG 7] then right [FIG 8], catching thread around shaft, 10 times.

STEP 3: Catch thread with hook and pull it smoothly and gently through the loop made. [FIGS 9 , 10]

STEP 4: Make a sl st over top of knot [FIG 11]; ch 2 [FIG 12]; sl st to left of knot [FIGS 13, 14], gently pulling thread tightly.

STEP 5: Ch 5 [FIG 15], join with a sl st to motif as directed in pattern.

BOOKMARK

Following Motif instructions, make 10 Shamrocks, 4 Scrolls, and 1 Button.

Joining Motifs

The fabric template and pins are used to hold the motifs in place while joining. Mark the exact center of the template and pin the button there. Pin one shamrock ½" (13mm) away from button top, bottom, and from each side—4 shamrocks used.

With sewing needle and matching sewing thread, sew shamrocks together at joining points (see photo). As shown in photo, pin one scroll motif on each side of the bottom and top shamrocks, being careful to turn the scrolls in the direction shown in photo.

Pin 3 shamrocks along top and bottom. Join shamrocks to each other as center 4 shamrocks were joined.

With contrasting sewing thread, temporarily tack all motifs to template and remove pins.

With crochet hook, join size 80 thread with a sl st in any sc on button opposite one shamrock joining; ch 10, join with a sl st in shamrock joining. Fasten off. Join button in same manner to remaining 3 shamrock joinings.

Filler Sections

Join size 80 thread with a sl st to one shamrock at top of template.

Work Clones knots to fill section, working toward center 4 shamrocks, as follows: *ch 5 (or more or less chs as needed), work Clones knot; repeat as many times as needed to reach opposite side, sl st to side; repeat randomly across space to be filled. When strands cross each other, sl st them together. Work as many strands of chs and Clones knots to adequately fill center.

Repeat for bottom of piece.

FINISHING

Turn to wrong side, clip tacking threads. and remove template fabric. To block, wash piece in warm water; remove excess water by squeezing gently. Place piece on a smooth surface, such as an ironing board, and using rustproof pins, pin out shamrocks and loops of scrolls evenly. Piece may be pressed on wrong side if needed.

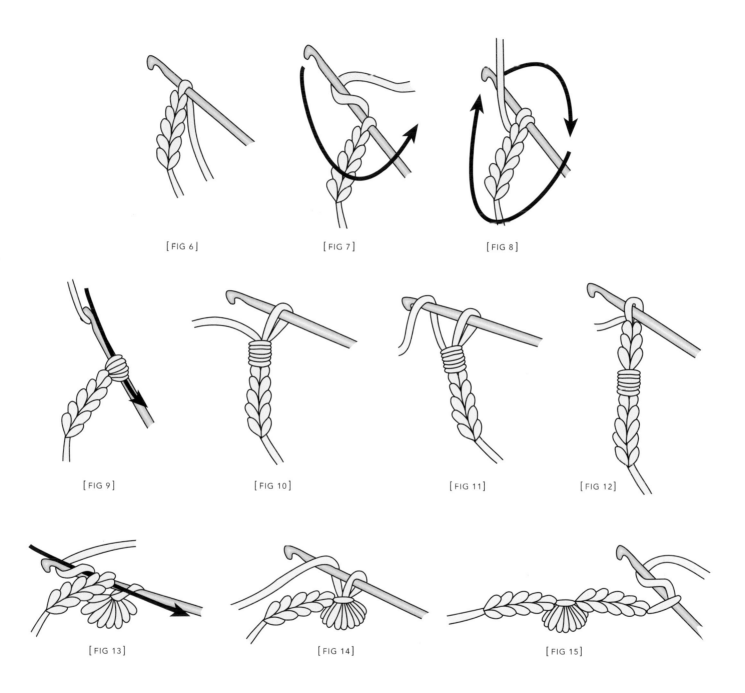

[FIG 6] [FIG 7] [FIG 8]

[FIG 9] [FIG 10] [FIG 11] [FIG 12]

[FIG 13] [FIG 14] [FIG 15]

WIRE CROCHET

with
Nancie Wiseman

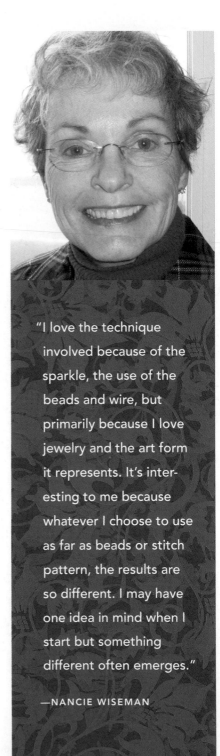

As the youngest child in a family with two older brothers, Nancie, sitting at her mother's side, did whatever her mother—an expert seamstress and needleworker who worked in fabric stores and needlework shops—was doing. So Nancie became an expert at an early age in crochet, knitting, embroidery, sewing, and quilting.

When Nancie grew up, she went to college, studied nursing, and became a critical care nurse in Sacramento, California. She worked long hours, sometimes at two jobs, but she always found time to occupy herself with one of her needlework passions, whether it was crochet or quilting.

Eventually, Nancie opened a yarn store in Sacramento called Nancie Knits. Although still working as a nurse, she ran the store and taught classes. One day a young man came into the store to have a sweater repaired. When he kept returning with more sweaters that needed repairing, one of Nancie's customers pointed out that there was something other than knitting on the young man's mind. Fifteen months later, Nancie married the man with the repair problem, and they moved to Whidbey Island near Seattle.

Eventually, the store closed, but Nancie continues to teach, design, and write knitting and crochet patterns and books. She continues to reach crocheters through her website, www.nancieknits.com, and by all her teaching throughout the United States and Canada.

She designs and writes patterns for several yarn companies as well as articles and designs for all of the major magazines. She has written more than ten books on knitting and crochet, including *Crochet with Wire* and *Crochet Finishing Techniques*, as well as produced seven videos and DVDs.

OPPOSITE: Nancie Wiseman's designs show off a variety of beads, from crystal to glass to gemstones.

HOW TO CROCHET WITH WIRE

If you have never crocheted with wire before, it may feel awkward at first to work with the wire, which is stiffer than the usual yarn or thread. The fine wires, such as 28 and 30 gauge, however, bend easily with just a little stiffness.

Beginning wire crocheters may find that it is a little clunky to crochet with wire and a small crochet hook. The crochet stitches won't be as smooth and tight as you would expect if you were using the thread you normally use on that size hook. You will still place the crochet hook under the 2 loops of wire at the top of the stitch, just as you do in regular crochet.

Beads are strung on the wire before you begin, with the wire acting as its own beading needle. The wire end will get bent and "wimpy" after a while, so straighten it out with your fingernails, or just trim it off with wire cutters to get a fresh end.

The beads help keep the wire straight, but there will be an occasional tangle. Don't overmanipulate the tangle; just use your fingers to straighten it enough so the beads will slip over it. That's all it needs; the beads will take care of the rest.

The purse is made with rows of beaded single crochet with half double crochet rows in between the bead rows. [FIG 1]

When working the half double crochet row above the bead row, the stitches will be distorted a little by the beads, so it is important to look for the correct part of the stitch just a little to the left of the beads.

Work with the strung wire and beads placed on the floor, rather than on a table, as pulling the wire up the distance from the floor will eliminate some tangles and keep the wire moving smoothly off the spool. Pull up the beads as you need them.

You will need to take some precautions: Cut wire is sharp and can easily pierce your fingers if you are not careful. Always use wire cutters designed just for this purpose. Never try to cut the wire with scissors or clippers. The wire cutter has a smooth side and a beveled side for cutting. For a smoother edge, always cut with the smooth side toward the work.

Keep a small plastic bag handy and as you cut, drop all wire ends immediately in the bag to keep them off the floor. Otherwise human or animal feet will be sure to find them!

If crocheting with beads is new to you, you may find it helpful to practice with yarn and bigger beads before you start with the wire. This will help you get the feel of working the crochet stitches around the beads.

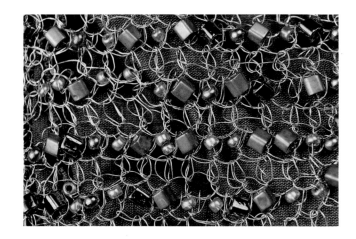

ANTIQUE WIRE CROCHET **PURSE**

Designed by Nancie Wiseman

Once you have completed your purse, you can line it, but this is not necessary. What is necessary is to be able to answer the admirers who will find it hard to believe that you crocheted the purse yourself!

SKILL LEVEL
■■■□ Intermediate

SIZE
Approximately 4½" (11.5cm) wide x 5" (12.5cm) high

MATERIALS
- Artistic Wire *30 Gauge Wire* (each approximately 30 yd [27.5m])
  - 240 yd (220m) / 8 spools in color AW2261 Non-Tarnish Brass
- One size 4 (2.00mm) steel crochet hook, or size needed to obtain gauge
- 4 tubes of assorted size 6/0 antique gold seed beads
- One 5" (12.5cm) wide handbag frame
  Note: Photographed model made with Antique Champagne Gold frame by www.BagLady.com.
- One 12" (30.5cm) gold rope chain
- 2 gold split rings, ⅜" (10mm) diameter
- ¼ yd (23cm) lining fabric (optional)
- Sewing needle and matching thread (optional)
- Wire cutters

GAUGE
10 sts and 9 rows = 2" (5cm)

STITCH GUIDE

BEAD SINGLE CROCHET (BSC): Insert hook in specified st, slide a bead up next to hook, yo and draw up a lp, yo and draw through both lps on hook—bsc made.

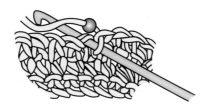

BACK

String half the beads on the wire before crocheting.

Beg at top edge, ch 22. Chain should fit across center straight top of purse frame. If chain is shorter than width of purse frame, work additional chains. If chain is about ½" (13mm) longer, don't rip out chains. Start again with fewer chains to make it fit. The stitch number doesn't matter.

ROW 1 (WRONG SIDE): Sc in 2nd ch from hook and in each rem ch across—21 sc; ch 1, turn.

ROW 2 (RIGHT SIDE): Sc in each st across; ch 1, turn.

ROW 3 (BEAD ROW): Bsc in first st (see stitch guide), bsc in each st across—21 bsc; ch 2 (counts as hdc on next row), turn.

NOTE: Keep checking to make sure piece is fitting the frame. If necessary, increase in the middle of the work on the wrong side (bead row) to keep the purse the correct size. Keep testing it in case the crochet pulls in a little. Make sure both pieces match in stitch number when you get to the end of both pieces.

ROW 4: Hdc in next st and in each st across; ch 1, turn.

ROW 5: Bsc in first st, bsc in each st across, bsc in 2nd ch of turning ch-2—21 bsc; ch 2, turn.

Repeat Rows 4 and 5 until piece measures approximately 5" (12.5cm), ending by working a Row 4. Fasten off.

FRONT

Work as Back.

FINISHING

If you are going to line the purse, see Lining instructions, below, before proceeding.

Place crochet pieces in frame and measure down the sides of the frame to determine where to begin and end the crocheting to put the purse together. Our model was made with the foundation chain and the edges of the first 8 rows sewn to the frame. Before sewing purse pieces to frame, side and bottom edges of purse pieces must be crocheted together. Hold pieces with the wrong sides together and the piece you have determined to be the front toward you (beads should be facing outside). With beads strung on wire, bsc sides and bottom edges together through both thicknesses (front and back), beginning and ending as indicated by the frame size (approximately 7–8 rows below top of pieces).

Attach the crochet pieces to the bottom holes on the frame using the wire without beads, starting in the middle of the frame and working toward the sides. Sew the crochet pieces to the purse frame with an overhand stitch, coming up through the crochet from the wrong side and down on the right side through the hole of the frame. Pull tightly. Repeat across, stretching the crochet, if necessary, to keep the crochet piece fitting the frame. If you have a little more purse than frame, use a hole in the purse frame twice. Sew the other half of the piece to the frame, starting in the middle of the frame and working toward the sides. Repeat for the other side of the purse.

Sew in the ends of wire (you can't really weave in the ends, because there is no place or "fabric" to hide them well). Try to wiggle the wire ends through the crochet wire pieces and finish them off by going through a bead before cutting.

Sew beads to length of chain by taking 24" (61cm) of wire and sewing beads around the chain. Use the same beads you used on the purse. Sew into the chain, place one or two beads onto the wire, turn the chain a quarter turn, and sew into chain again. Repeat this process until the chain is covered with beads. Weave in wire ends. Attach ends of chain to top of purse frame with split rings.

Lining (optional)

Use the crochet purse pieces as a pattern for lining. Fold lining fabric in half and place bottom of purse on top of fold. Draw around the top and sides of purse, adding ¼" (6mm) seam allowance around all edges and mimicking curve along top edge. Cut along the remaining three sides. Unfold lining. Zigzag (by machine) or blanket stitch (by hand) the raw edges around the entire piece. Fold lining in half. Mark the side opening of the purse below the handles on the lining. Sew the side seams with ¼" (6mm) seam allowance. Place the lining in the purse with the fold at the bottom and the seams facing toward the crochet pieces. Fold the top edges of the lining over toward the crochet pieces and hand stitch the lining through the bottom holes on the handle.

APPENDIX

A **REFRESHER COURSE** IN CROCHET

Slip Knot

To begin, make a slip knot (sometimes called a slip loop) on the hook, leaving a 6" (15cm) tail of yarn. **[FIG 1]**

Insert the crochet hook and draw the loop onto the hook by pulling on the end marked A. **[FIG 2]**

The knot should be snug on the hook but should slide easily. **[FIG 3]**

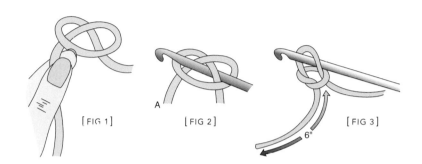

[FIG 1]   A   [FIG 2]   6"   [FIG 3]

Chain (ch)

The chain is the foundation on which all crochet is built. It is rather like the bottom row of a brick wall.

Hold the hook in your dominant hand and the yarn in the other hand. Take the yarn from back to front over the hook and catch it with the hook head and draw it through the slip knot on the hook. **[FIG 4]**

You have now made 1 chain stitch. Repeat this step for each additional chain required, moving your thumb and index finger up close to the hook after each stitch or two. **[FIG 5]**

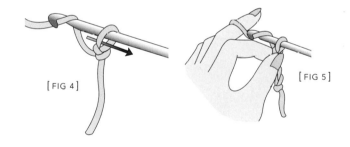

[FIG 4]   [FIG 5]

Single Crochet (sc)

First make a chain to the desired length.

STEP 1: Insert the hook under the top loop of the 2nd chain from the hook. **[FIG 6]**

STEP 2: Hook the yarn, bringing the yarn over the hook from the back to the front, and draw through. **[FIG 7]**

STEP 3: There are now 2 loops on the hook. **[FIG 8]** Take the yarn over the hook again from back to front, hook it, and draw through both loops on the hook: 1 loop now remains on the hook and you have made one single crochet stitch. To make the next stitch, continue to work in this manner.

To work additional rows, chain 1 (the turning chain), and turn work counterclockwise.

Skip the turning chain and work one single crochet in the single crochet nearest your hook, inserting the hook under the top 2 loops of the stitch. **[FIG 9]**

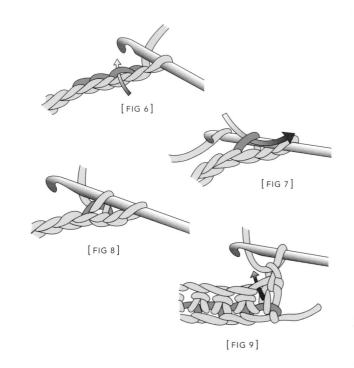

[FIG 6]

[FIG 7]

[FIG 8]

[FIG 9]

Half Double Crochet (hdc)

Make a chain to the desired length.

STEP 1: Yarn over the hook. Insert the hook into the back loop of the 3rd chain from the hook; yarn over and draw up a loop: 3 loops are now on the hook.

STEP 2: Yarn over again and draw the yarn through all 3 loops on the hook at one time. You have made 1 half double crochet stitch **[FIG 10]**. To work the next half double crochet stitch, repeat Step 1 but insert the hook into the back loop of the next chain rather than the 3rd chain from the hook. Repeat Step 2, continuing in this manner across the row.

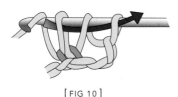

[FIG 10]

To work additional rows, make 2 chains and turn work counterclockwise. Beginning in 2nd stitch (2 chains count as first half double crochet), work a half double crochet in each stitch across. Work the last stitch into the top chain.

Double Crochet (dc)

Make a chain to the desired length.

STEP 1: Yarn over the hook. Insert the hook into the back loop of the 4th chain from the hook. **[FIG 11]**

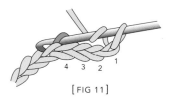

[FIG 11]

STEP 2: Hook the yarn and draw it through. There are now 3 loops on the hook. **[FIG 12]**

[FIG 12]

STEP 3: Hook the yarn again and draw it through the first 2 loops on the hook. There are now 2 loops on the hook. **[FIG 13]**

[FIG 13]

STEP 4: Hook the yarn again and draw it through the remaining 2 loops. You have made 1 double crochet stitch. To work the next double crochet stitch, repeat Step 1 but insert the hook into the back loop of the next chain rather than the 4th chain from the hook. Repeat Steps 2 through 4 again and continue in this manner across the row.

To work additional rows, make 3 chains and turn the work counterclockwise. **[FIG 14]**

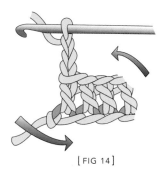

[FIG 14]

Beginning in 2nd stitch of the previous row (3 chains count as first double crochet), work a double crochet in each stitch. **[FIG 15]**

[FIG 15]

At the end of the row, work the last double crochet into the top chain of the turning chain of the previous row. **[FIG 16]**

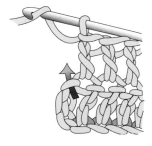

[FIG 16]

Triple Crochet (tr)

Make a chain the desired length.

STEP 1: Bring the yarn over the hook twice. Insert the hook into the back loop of the 5th chain from the hook. [**FIG 17**]

STEP 2: Hook the yarn and draw through the chain. There are now 4 loops on the hook. [**FIG 18**]

STEP 3: Hook the yarn over again and draw through the first 2 loops on the hook. There are now 3 loops on the hook.

STEP 4: Hook the yarn over again and draw through the first two loops on the hook. There are now 2 loops on the hook.

STEP 5: Hook the yarn over and draw through the remaining 2 loops. You have now made one triple crochet stitch. [**FIG 19**]

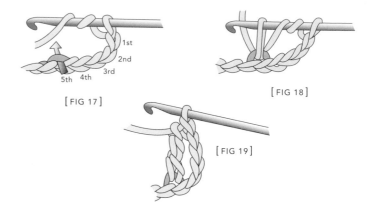

[FIG 17]

[FIG 18]

[FIG 19]

To work the next stitches in triple crochet, repeat steps 1 through 5 in the back loop of each chain, working Step 1 in the next chain rather than the 4th chain from the hook.

Slip Stitch (sl st)

STEP 1: Insert hook in indicated stitch. Hook yarn and draw through both stitch and loop in one motion.

Working in a Circle

Begin by making a chain the desired length.

STEP 1: Join the stitches with a slip stitch to form a ring. [**FIG 20**]

STEP 2: Chain the required stitches and work into ring or into the next stitch as directed. [**FIG 21**]

[FIG 20]

[FIG 21]

ABBREVIATIONS, SYMBOLS, AND TERMINOLOGY

Abbreviations

Crochet patterns are written in a special shorthand that is used so instructions don't take up too much space. They sometimes seem confusing, but once you learn them, you'll have no trouble following them.

BB	bobble
beg	begin(ning)
BL	back loop
BPdc	back post double crochet
BPsc	back post single crochet
Bst	bullion stitch
Cl(s)	cluster(s)
ch(s)	chain(s)
cm	centimeter
cont	continue
dc	double crochet
Dc Cl	double crochet cluster
Dc dec	double crochet decrease
Dc inc	double crochet increase
dec	decreas(e)(ing)
dtr	double triple crochet
Dtr Cl	double triple crochet cluster
fig	figure
FL	front loop
FPdc	front post double crochet
FPsc	front post single crochet
FPtr	front post triple crochet
hdc	half double crochet
hdc dec	half double crochet decrease
inc	increas(e)(ing)
Long dc	long double crochet
Long sc	long single crochet
lp(s)	loop(s)
Lp St	loop stitch
mm	millimeter(s)
oz	ounce(s)
patt	pattern
PB	puff stitch bobble
PC	popcorn
Prev	previous
PS	puff stitch
rem	remain(s)(ing)
rnd(s)	round(s)
sc	single crochet
sc dec	single crochet decrease
sc2tog	single crochet 2 stitches together decrease
sk	skip
sl st	slip stitch
sp(s)	space(s)
st(s)	stitch(es)
tr	triple crochet
trtr	triple triple crochet
V-st	V-stitch
wrsc	wrapped single crochet
yo	yarn over hook

Standard Symbols

* An asterisk (or double asterisks**) in a pattern row or round, indicates a portion of instructions to be used more than once. For instance, "repeat from * three times" means that after working the instructions once, you must work them again three times for a total of 4 times in all.

— The number of stitches after a long dash tells you the number of stitches you will have when you have completed a row or round.

( ) Parentheses enclose instructions that are to be worked the number of times following the parentheses. For instance, "(ch 1, sc, ch 1) 3 times" means that you will chain one, work one sc, and then chain again three times for a total of six chains and three scs.

Parentheses often set off or clarify a group of stitches to be worked into the same space of stitch. For instance, "(dc, ch2, dc) in corner sp."

[ ] Brackets and ( ) parentheses are also used to give you additional information.

Terminology

FRONT LOOP: This is the loop toward you at the top of the crochet stitch.

BACK LOOP: This is the loop away from you at the top of the crochet stitch.

POST: This is the vertical part of the crochet stitch.

JOIN: This means to join with a sl st unless another stitch is specified.

FASTEN OFF: This means to end your piece by pulling the cut yarn end through the last loop remaining on the hook. This will prevent the work from unraveling.

CONTINUE IN PATTERN AS ESTABLISHED: This means to follow the pattern stitch as it has been set up, working any increases or decreases in such a way that the pattern remains the same as it was established.

WORK EVEN: This means that the work is continued in the pattern as established without increasing or decreasing.

RIGHT SIDE: This means the side of the garment that will be seen.

RIGHT-HAND SIDE: This means the side of the garment that is near the right hand when worn.

LEFT-HAND SIDE: This means the side of the garment that is near the left hand when worn.

The patterns in this book have been written using the crochet terminology that is used in the United States. Terms that may have different equivalents in other parts of the world are listed below.

UNITED STATES	INTERNATIONAL
double crochet (dc)	treble crochet (tr)
gauge	tension
half double crochet (hdc)	half treble crochet (htr)
single crochet (sc)	double crochet (dc)
skip (sk)	miss
slip stitch (sl st)	single crochet (sc)
triple crochet (tr)	double treble crochet (dtr)
yarn over (yo)	yarn forward (yfwd)
yarn over (yo)	yarn around needle (yrn)

Gauge

This is probably the most important aspect of crocheting!

Gauge simply means the number of stitches per inch, and the number of rows per inch that result from a specified yarn worked with a hook in a specified size. But since everyone crochets differently—some loosely, some tightly, some in between—the measurements of individual work can vary greatly, even when crocheters use the same pattern and the same size yarn and hook.

If you don't work to the gauge specified in the pattern, your garment will never be the correct size, and you may not have enough yarn to finish your project. The hook size given in the instructions is merely a guide and should never be used without a gauge swatch.

To make a gauge swatch, crochet a piece that is about 4" (10cm) square, using the suggested hook and the number of stitches given in the pattern. Measure your swatch. If the number of stitches is fewer than those listed in the pattern, try making another swatch with a smaller hook. If the number of stitches is more than is called for in the pattern, try making another swatch with a larger hook. It is your responsibility to make sure you achieve the gauge specified in the pattern.

Steel Crochet Hook Conversion Chart

U.S.	METRIC
00	3.50mm
0	3.25mm
1	2.75mm
2	2.25mm
3	2.10mm
4	2.00mm
5	1.90mm
6	1.80mm
7	1.65mm
8	1.50mm
9	1.40mm
10	1.30mm
11	1.10mm
12	1.00mm
13	.85mm
14	.75mm

Yarn Crochet Hook Conversion Chart

U.S.	METRIC
B-1	2.25mm
C-2	2.75mm
D-3	3.25mm
E-4	3.50mm
F-5	3.75mm
G-6	4.00mm
7	4.50 mm
H-8	5.00mm
I-9	5.50mm
J-10	6.00
K-10½	6.50mm
L-11	8.00mm
M-13	9.00mm
N-15	10.00mm
P-16	12.00mm

Skill Levels

Yarn manufacturers, publishers, and needle and hook manufacturers have worked together to set up a series of guidelines and symbols to bring uniformity to patterns. Before beginning a project, check to see if your skill level is equal to the one listed for the project.

BEGINNER — Projects for first-time crocheters using basic stitches and minimal shaping.

EASY — Projects using yarn with basic stitches, repetitive stitch patterns, simple color changes, and simple shaping and finishing.

INTERMEDIATE — Projects using a variety of techniques, such as basic lace patterns or color patterns, midlevel shaping, and finishing.

EXPERIENCED — Projects with intricate stitch patterns, techniques and dimension, such as nonrepeating patterns, multicolor techniques, fine threads, small hooks, detailed shaping, and refined finishing.

Standard Yarn Weights

To make it easier for yarn manufacturers, publishers, and designers to prepare consumer-friendly products and for consumers to select the right materials for a project, the following standard yarn weight system has been adopted.

Categories of yarn, gauge, ranges, and recommended needle and hook sizes

Yarn Weight Symbol & Category Names	(0) LACE	(1) SUPER FINE	(2) FINE	(3) LIGHT	(4) MEDIUM	(5) BULKY	(6) SUPER BULKY
Type of Yarns in Category	Fingering 10 count crochet	Sock, Fingering, Baby	Sport, Baby	DK, Light, Worsted	Worsted, Afghan, Aran	Chunky, Craft Rug	Bulky, Roving
Crochet Gauge* Ranges in Single Crochet to 4 inch	32-42 sts*	21-32 sts	16-20 sts	12-17 sts	11-14 sts	8-11 sts	5-9 sts
Recommended Hook in Metric Size Range	Steel** 1.6-1.4mm Regular Hook 2.25mm	2.25-3.5mm	3.5-4.5mm	4.5-5.5mm	5.5-6.5mm	6.5-9mm	9mm and larger
Recommended Hook U.S. Size Range	Steel** 6, 7 , 8	B-1 to E-4	E-4 to 7	7 to I-9	I-9 to K-10.5	K-10.5 to M-13	M-13 and larger

* Laceweight yarns are usually crocheted on larger hooks to create lacy, openwork patterns. Accordingly, a gauge range is difficult to determine. Always follow the gauge stated in your pattern.

** Steel crochet hooks are sized differently from regular hooks—the higher the number, the smaller the hook, which is the reverse of regular hook sizing.

INDEX